THE ROOTS OF RELIGION

An outstanding set of authoritative essays, essential reading for all who are interested in the nature of religion.

Keith Ward, Christ Church, Oxford, UK

The cognitive science of religion is a new discipline that looks at the roots of religious belief in the cognitive architecture of the human mind. *The Roots of Religion* deals with the philosophical and theological implications of the cognitive science of religion which grounds religious belief in human cognitive structures: religious belief is 'natural', in a way that even scientific thought is not. Does this new discipline support religious belief, undermine it, or is it, despite many claims, perhaps eventually neutral? This subject is of immense importance, particularly given the rise of the 'new atheism'.

Philosophers and theologians from North America, UK and Australia, explore the alleged conflict between truth claims and examine the roots of religion in human nature. Is it less 'natural' to be an atheist than to believe in God, or gods? On the other hand, if we can explain theism psychologically, have we explained it away. Can it still claim any truth? This book debates these and related issues.

Ashgate Science and Religion Series

Series Editors:

Roger Trigg, *Emeritus Professor, University of Warwick, and Academic Director of the Centre for the Study of Religion in Public Life, Kellogg College, Oxford*

J. Wentzel van Huyssteen, *Princeton Theological Seminary, USA*

Science and religion have often been thought to be at loggerheads but much contemporary work in this flourishing interdisciplinary field suggests this is far from the case. The *Ashgate Science and Religion Series* presents exciting new work to advance interdisciplinary study, research and debate across key themes in science and religion, exploring the philosophical relations between the physical and social sciences on the one hand and religious belief on the other. Contemporary issues in philosophy and theology are debated, as are prevailing cultural assumptions arising from the 'postmodernist' distaste for many forms of reasoning. The series enables leading international authors from a range of different disciplinary perspectives to apply the insights of the various sciences, theology and philosophy and look at the relations between the different disciplines and the rational connections that can be made between them. These accessible, stimulating new contributions to key topics across science and religion will appeal particularly to individual academics and researchers, graduates, postgraduates and upper-undergraduate students.

Other titles in the series:

Being as Communion
A Metaphysics of Information
William A. Dembski
978-0-7546-3857-5 (hbk)

Christian Moral Theology in the Emerging Technoculture
From Posthuman Back to Human
Brent Waters
978-0-7546-6691-2 (hbk)

God and the Scientist
Exploring the Work of John Polkinghorne
Edited by Fraser Watts and Christopher C. Knight
978-1-4094-4569-2 (hbk)

The Roots of Religion
Exploring the Cognitive Science of Religion

Edited by

ROGER TRIGG
University of Warwick and Ian Ramsey Centre, University of Oxford, UK

and

JUSTIN L. BARRETT
Fuller Graduate School of Psychology, USA

LONDON AND NEW YORK

First published 2014 by Ashgate Publishing

Published 2016 by Routledge
2 Park Square, Milton Park, Abingdon, Oxon OX14 4RN
711 Third Avenue, New York, NY 10017, USA

Routledge is an imprint of the Taylor & Francis Group, an informa business

Copyright © 2014 Roger Trigg and Justin L. Barrett

Roger Trigg and Justin L. Barrett have asserted their right under the Copyright, Designs and Patents Act, 1988, to be identified as the editors of this work.

All rights reserved. No part of this book may be reprinted or reproduced or utilised in any form or by any electronic, mechanical, or other means, now known or hereafter invented, including photocopying and recording, or in any information storage or retrieval system, without permission in writing from the publishers.

Notice:
Product or corporate names may be trademarks or registered trademarks, and are used only for identification and explanation without intent to infringe.

British Library Cataloguing in Publication Data
A catalogue record for this book is available from the British Library

The Library of Congress has cataloged the printed edition as follows:
The roots of religion : exploring the cognitive science of religion / edited by Roger Trigg and Justin L. Barrett.
   pages cm. – (Ashgate science and religion series)
 Includes bibliographical references and index.
 ISBN 978-1-4724-2731-1 (hardcover)
 1. Psychology, Religious. 2. Cognitive science.
 I. Trigg, Roger, editor. II. Barrett, Justin L., 1971–editor.
 BL53.R585 2014
 200.1'9–dc23

2014013545

ISBN 9781472427311 (hbk)

Contents

Notes on Contributors   *vii*
Acknowledgements   *ix*

1. Cognitive and Evolutionary Studies of Religion   1
   Justin L. Barrett and Roger Trigg

2. Intuition, Agency Detection, and Social Coordination as Analytical and Explanatory Constructs in the Cognitive Science of Religion   17
   Robert Audi

3. Whose Intuitions? Which Dualism?   37
   Steven Horst

4. Explaining Religion at Different Levels: From Fundamentalism to Pluralism   55
   Aku Visala

5. HADD, Determinism and Epicureanism: An Interdisciplinary Investigation   75
   Robin Attfield

6. Understanding 'Person' Talk: When is it Appropriate to Think in Terms of Persons?   91
   Graham Wood

7. Knowledge and the Objection to Religious Belief from Cognitive Science   113
   Kelly James Clark and Dani Rabinowitz

| 8 | Assessing the Third Way
Jason Marsh | 127 |
| 9 | Cognitive Science of Religion and the Rationality of Classical Theism
T.J. Mawson | 149 |
| 10 | Cognitive Science and the Limits of Theology
John Teehan | 167 |
| 11 | Some Reflections on Cognitive Science, Doubt, and Religious Belief
Joshua C. Thurow | 189 |
| 12 | Human Nature and Religious Freedom
Roger Trigg | 209 |

Index — 225

Notes on Contributors

Editors

Justin L. Barrett: Thrive Professor of Developmental Science, Fuller Theological Seminary, California

Roger Trigg: Emeritus Professor of Philosophy, University of Warwick, and Senior Research Fellow, Ian Ramsey Centre, University of Oxford

Contributors

Robin Attfield: Emeritus Professor of Philosophy, Cardiff University

Robert Audi: John A. O'Brien Professor of Philosophy, University of Notre Dame, Indiana

Kelly James Clark: Senior Research Fellow at the Kaufman Institute and Professor of Liberal Studies, Grand Valley State University, Michigan

Steven Horst: Professor of Philosophy, Wesleyan University, Middletown, Connecticut

Jason Marsh: Assistant Professor of Philosophy, St Olaf College, Minnesota

T.J. Mawson: Fellow and Tutor in Philosophy, St Peter's College, University of Oxford

Dani Rabinowitz: Junior Research Fellow, Somerville College, University of Oxford

John Teehan: Professor of Religion, Hofstra University, New York

Joshua C. Thurow: Assistant Professor of Philosophy, University of Texas at San Antonio, Texas

Aku Visala: Postdoctoral Researcher, Department of Anthropology, University of Notre Dame, Indiana, and Faculty of Theology, University of Helsinki

Graham Wood: Lecturer in Philosophy, University of Tasmania

Acknowledgements

This volume arose from a joint venture of the University of Oxford's Centre for Anthropology and Mind and the Ian Ramsey Centre. The project was the Cognition, Religion, and Theology Project and was funded by a grant from the John Templeton Foundation to Justin Barrett and Roger Trigg, for which we are grateful. This grant provided support for the chapters in this volume among other activities. A subsequent grant from the Templeton World Charity Foundation (to Barrett), concerning how the 'naturalness thesis' of the cognitive science of religion stands up to new research conducted with Chinese populations (past and present), has provided support that allowed for this volume's completion. Many of the authors in this volume make reference to how religious beliefs and practices arise in large part as a normal, natural function of human cognitive systems. Fortunately for this volume, the new data from the China project do not threaten this thesis.

We also thank Tyler Greenway, Matthew Jarvinen, and Thomas Paulus for editorial assistance for the entire volume.

Chapter 1
Cognitive and Evolutionary Studies of Religion

Justin L. Barrett and Roger Trigg

Does the Cognitive Science of Religion (CSR) and allied evolutionary approaches to the study of religion (ESR) present epistemic challenges to religious belief, or support? This central question unifies this volume, recurring in one form or another repeatedly. Popular treatments of the area and even comments by scientists working in the area often suggest that the answer to this question is trivial. In this initial chapter we introduce CSR to argue that simple epistemic conclusions cannot readily be drawn either in support of or against religious beliefs. That is, by itself the science appears neutral with regard to whether or not religious (or non-religious) knowers are warranted in their beliefs. It appears to us that to either challenge or support religious beliefs by use of CSR, scholars must combine its insights with other philosophical commitments, and also restrict their arguments to particular religious beliefs and not attempt to paint them all with the same broad brush. Those arguments offered subsequently in this volume illustrate and support this contention. Insofar as they are successful, their success lies in their appropriation of extra-scientific considerations to frame the findings of CSR in a philosophically potent way and also their restriction to particular religious concepts, such as the existence of a supreme creator God.

Some Historical Observations Concerning CSR

Ryan Hornbeck went to Wuhan, China to study the online gaming activities of late adolescents and emerging adults. He discovered that at least a sizable minority of his informants regarded playing Chinese World of Warcraft as an opportunity for moral development and many regarded it as rich in "spiritual" experiences (Hornbeck, 2012). Why would young people find spiritual and moral meaning in a virtual world, sometimes more frequently than in the real world?

Emma Cohen (2007) conducted ethnographic field research in the northern Brazilian city of Belém, investigating the religious practices of Afro-Brazilian spiritualists. Through her extensive observations and interviews over many months she discovered something peculiar: the way spirit-possession was described and taught by the leader of a cult-house (*pai-de-santo*) did not approximate how it was understood by the laity. The reason was not a disregard for the pai-de-santo's expertise; the lay spiritualists affirmed the authority and trustworthiness of the leader's teachings (Cohen, 2007). Nevertheless, what was taught was not the same as what was received, but why?

Fortunately for Hornbeck and Cohen, they could draw upon insights and strategies from the Cognitive Science of Religion (CSR) to address these problems. Humans in all cultures have a number of conceptual tendencies by virtue of being *Homo sapiens*, and these ideas inform and constrain religious and other cultural expression (Barrett, 2000; Boyer, 2003). For instance, in the absence of the uncommon conditions experts enjoy, ideas that deviate too far from cognitively natural thought are subject to confusion and distortion, a phenomenon termed *Theological Incorrectness* (Slone, 2004).[1] The people Cohen observed were suffering from Theological Incorrectness, because the taught conception of spirit possession (a fusing or mixing of two spirits in a host's body) was too unnatural or *counterintuitive* to be easily communicated faithfully. The laity adopted a view of possession closer to the default-settings of human thought: the spirit fully displaces the agency of the host when it enters the body because only one mind can occupy a body at a single moment.

Hornbeck combined insights from evolutionary psychology concerning moral intuitions to argue that his informants were drawn to Chinese World of Warcraft because of the affordances of the game play for expressing basic moral intuitions, affordances frustrated or confused in their day-to-day lives in a strictly controlled, heavily programmed, materially-oriented urban environment. Further, Hornbeck observed how the team-based play objectives and features of the gaming experience seemed to trigger states readily identified as spiritual or as soul-mergers. As with Cohen's work, Hornbeck combined traditional ethnographic techniques with insights from the cognitive and evolutionary sciences to posit causally plausible explanations for the phenomena they observed.

Just two decades ago, the intellectual resources for such projects did not exist. What has come to be called cognitive science of religion (CSR) was in its infancy,

---

[1] Slone chose this term because *Theological Incorrectness* is a corollary of *Theological Correctness*, a demonstrated distinction between stated theological beliefs and conceptually simpler beliefs used in real-time information processing (see Barrett and Keil, 1996).

and most scholars of religion and culture did not know it existed. Harbingers of a cognitive approach to the study of religion appeared decades ago (Sperber, 1975; Guthrie, 1980), but the sustained, collaborative effort to approach religion from cognitive *and* scientific perspectives did not emerge until the 1990s. Four important books taking cognitive approaches appeared in the first half of the 1990s (Lawson and McCauley, 1990; Guthrie, 1993; Boyer, 1994; Whitehouse, 1995). Notable was the fact that only Stewart Guthrie's line of research (1980; 1993) had any ambitions to provide anything like a comprehensive explanation of religion. Rather, these cognitive approaches were motivated by the modest goal of providing the scholarly study of religion (as practiced by anthropologists, comparative religionists, and the like) with causal explanations for this or that feature of religions by appealing to relevant psychological sciences. For instance, Whitehouse's work (1995) was standard social anthropology except that he creatively drew upon findings from cognitive psychology concerning memory systems to account for patterns he observed in the field.

In 2000, the general cognitive approach was dubbed "Cognitive Science of Religion" (Barrett, 2000), and in the subsequent years closer ties with evolutionary approaches were forged: early titles being Pascal Boyer's *Religion Explained* (2001) and Scott Atran's *In Gods We Trust* (2002). These books were evolutionary in two respects. First, they justified their appeal to pan-human conceptual systems by appropriating theoretical claims and empirical findings from evolutionary psychology. That is, rather than positing pan-human tendencies or psychological mechanisms merely because of the explanatory work such hypotheticals could provide, they drew upon the scientific research of evolutionary and developmental psychologists who had been showing that humans infants and young children seem to solve certain conceptual problems around them in very predictable ways, perhaps to solve important survival problems in our ancestry. Boyer's and Atran's works were also evolutionary in the sense that they proposed that psychological mechanisms place selective pressure on ideas and behaviours, and so, identifying how human minds tend to favour some ideas over others goes a long way to explaining why some types of ideas (and related behaviours) become recurrent within and across cultures. Persuasive leaders and external peculiarities are not the whole story; if an idea is more readily entertained by human minds, it is more likely to be communicated effectively, and spread from person to person and generation to generation.

Atran's book also foreshadowed new connections between CSR and the emerging area now known as evolutionary studies of religion (ESR; e.g., see Wilson, 2002; Johnson and Kruger, 2004; Bulbulia, 2009; and Sosis, 2009). The emphasis of this approach to the study of religion has been on whether certain religious practices and social arrangements may have been (and perhaps still are) adaptive to humans. For instance, does the performance of collective religious rituals serve to make groups more cooperative, thereby accruing fitness benefits, and if so, why? These evolutionary approaches have not always been cognitive (i.e., explicitly concerning themselves with cognitive/psychological mechanisms), but attempts to fuse ESR with CSR are beginning to take shape (e.g., Bering, 2011).

We begin with these historical points about CSR to clarify a few common confusions concerning the area that may be important to philosophers and theologians concerned about implications of this scholarship. First, CSR is not a conspiracy of scientists to take over the study of religion or to "explain away" religious entities, but the chief impetus for the area was (and is) from religion scholars wanting to "science-up" the study of religion, and seeing the cognitive sciences (and evolutionary psychology) as particularly promising resources. Nevertheless, some promoters of CSR regard it as a wholly secular, naturalistic approach to the study of religion, which may entail epistemic problems for religious beliefs.

Second, though there is increasing crossover between the two areas, CSR is not the same as ESR even though both use the language of selection and insights from evolutionary sciences. The level of explanation on which the two areas typically work is different. CSR primarily focuses on cognitive mechanisms exerting causal influences on cultural expression. ESR primarily focuses on how considerations of biological fitness may account for the persistence of certain genetic, cultural, or gene-culture complexes. Exactly what is being explained and how it is being explained may have consequences for drawing philosophical implications. For instance, many cognitive accounts regard religious ideas (such as belief in gods) as evolutionary by-products—non-adaptations that piggyback on adaptations that solve problems unrelated to these religious thoughts. As by-products, these ideas, then, have not necessarily been winnowed via natural selection, and so what are the implications for whether they are warranted? The answer could be very different—or at least the argument would be different—if the guiding science suggests that the religious belief in question is an adaptation that has been encouraged by natural selection, as many ESR approaches suggest.

Foundational Commitments of Cognitive Science of Religion

Primarily CSR draws upon the cognitive sciences to explain how pan-cultural features of human minds, interacting with their natural and social environments, inform and constrain religious thought and action. For instance, how might belief in some kind of afterlife or in superhuman intentional beings (gods) be explained in terms of underlying cognitive structures? CSR research may also consider how particular religious, cultural, and environmental factors stretch or modify natural cognitive tendencies, but such a possibility is largely undeveloped at this point.

A number of foundational convictions, derived from the cognitive sciences, frame the CSR approach. Importantly, CSR scholars reject full-bodied cultural relativism and the idea that minds are blank slates or passive sponges, equally able and willing to learn and use any type of information equally well. Humans naturally have numerous cognitive biases and predilections by virtue of their species-specific biological endowment plus pan-cultural regularities of the environments in which they grow up (e.g., babies have mothers, humans live in groups, etc.). A second presumption, then, is that at least some important and content-rich aspects of human cognition are pre- or extra-cultural. Uncontroversial examples include preferential attention to and processing of human faces (Meltzoff and Moore, 1983), reasoning about the properties and movement of bounded physical objects, and the distinction between ordinary physical objects and *agents,* those objects that can move themselves in a goal-directed manner (Spelke and Kinzler, 2007). Other well-supported domain-specific cognitive subsystems that appear to be largely invariant in terms of their basic parameters and developmental courses include language, folk psychology (or Theory of Mind), folk biology, and some aspects of moral thought and social exchange reasoning (Hirschfeld and Gelman, 1994). Barrett has referred to these various extra-cultural, content-rich cognitive systems as *mental tools* (Barrett, 2004; 2011). These mental tools inform and constrain the ways people will typically think, but certainly do not determine human cultural expression.

The precise relationship between these mental tools and cultural expression continues to develop, but a common way of framing the relationship between these cognitive system and explicit beliefs is a two-systems approach (Kahneman, 2011; for examples in CSR, see Boyer, 2001; Barrett, 2004; 2011; Gervais and Norenzayan, 2012). In brief, these domain-specific mental tools are components of a fast processing system that operates largely independent of conscious awareness or volitional direction. Given certain input conditions, they generate specific outputs, often registered as intuitions. The slow, reflective system receives intuitions and other outputs of the fast system and then produces syntheses or judgments from those fast system outputs. For instance, Boyer has suggested that religious ideas that resonate with intuitions (delivered by the domain-specific components of the fast system) are more likely to be regarded as true by the slow, reflective system. Following Boyer, Barrett (2004; 2011) redescribed the outputs of these two systems in terms of non-reflective and reflective beliefs,[2] with non-reflective beliefs serving as the default assumptions for the reflective system.[3] That is, rather than beliefs being formed through the weighing of various pieces of evidence including intuitions, intuitions will generate explicit beliefs *unless* sufficient contrary evidence becomes salient. Indeed, based on numerous experimental studies, Daniel Kahneman argues that ideas that merely come to mind easily (even if not natural deliverances of these mental tools) are given the benefit of the doubt in terms of their truth and goodness, a dynamic he calls the accessibility bias (2003).

The relationship between these two different systems—particularly the ability of the fast system to influence the outputs of the slow system—generates a third commitment of CSR: mental tools inform and constrain religious thought, experience, and expression. For those scholars interested in the variability more than the recurrent patterns, CSR is still helpful in helping to identify just which aspects of religious expression are more likely to be explainable in terms of cultural particulars—those that deviate considerably from the natural outputs of mental tools.

A fourth commitment of CSR is a focus on ideas that are distributed across individuals and not on individual religious experience or expression. Drawing upon Sperber's epidemiological approach to explaining cultural expression (Sperber, 1996), an idea that is not shared by a community of individuals is not religious, but is idiosyncratic and CSR has little (or nothing) to say about it. Consequently, CSR has little to say about why one individual holds the religious beliefs they do, but only why people generally tend to hold some kinds of beliefs and engage in some kinds of actions as opposed to others. It follows that the task for CSR is to account for recurrent patterns of religious expression—types of ideas, identifications, experiences, and practices—that are distributed across some population (or even across cultures). "Explaining religion," then, is explaining how mental tools working in particular environments resist or encourage the spread of these ideas and practices we might call "religious."

Finally, in general CSR scholars do not regard *religion* as a coherent natural kind meriting a *sui generis* approach. CSR scholars have typically avoided trying to define *religion* as a whole. Instead of defining *religion* as a whole, they have chosen to approach "religion" in a piecemeal fashion, by identifying human thoughts or practices that are generally considered religious and then try to explain why those

---

    [2]   Earlier, Sperber (1996) dubbed these intuitive versus reflective beliefs.
    [3]   Possible parallels with aliefs versus beliefs (Gendler, 2008) and with Reidian epistemology (Wolterstorff, 2001), may be drawn.

are cross-culturally recurrent. If the explanations turn out to join up in accounting for larger recurrent complexes of cultural expression, all the better.

This final commitment, that religion is not a natural kind, is particularly important for drawing appropriate epistemic conclusions from the findings. An explanation of one sort of religious belief, such as belief in gods, may or may not apply to another class of religious belief, such as belief in an afterlife. Even within categories, it could be that belief in one type of god (e.g., a cosmic creator) has a different causal pathway than belief in another type of god (e.g., an ancestor spirit). It follows, then, that even if an explanation of one religious idea raises epistemic concerns for it, these concerns do not necessarily apply to all religious ideas. Likewise, a defense of a particular religious concept's rational justification may fail to generalize to all religious concepts by virtue of the two diverging causally, a point we expand below.

Topics of Exploration

An enduring thread in CSR has been trying to account for the prevalence of beliefs in superhuman agents (gods) (Guthrie, 1993; Barrett, 2004; 2012; Bering, 2011). But CSR is much broader than that, having made starts on many topics including: afterlife, prelife, and death beliefs (Bering, Hernández-Blasi and Bjorkland, 2005; Astuti and Harris, 2008; Emmons, 2012); magic (Sørensen, 2005); prayer (Barrett, 2001); religion and morality (Boyer, 2001; Hornbeck, 2012); religious development in children (Barrett, 2012); religious ritual and ritualized actions (McCauley and Lawson, 2002; Malley and Barrett, 2003; Liénard and Boyer, 2006); religious social morphology (Whitehouse, 2004); scripturalism (Malley, 2004); the relationship among souls, minds, and bodies (Bloom, 2004; Cohen and Barrett, 2011); spirit possession (Cohen and Barrett, 2008a, b); teleofunctional reasoning and origin of the natural world (Evans, 2001; Kelemen, 2004); transmission of religious ideas (Boyer and Ramble, 2001; Gregory and Barrett, 2009); and various superhuman agent concepts (Barrett, 2008).

Depending upon the particular topic, different causal accounts may apply. Thus, the temptation to treat all religious beliefs (or the motivations for religious practices) as relevantly comparable in terms of epistemic considerations borne of the causal accounts should be avoided. For instance, it may be that belief in ghosts and ancestors is a function of strong natural intuitions that support mind-body separation (Bloom, 2004), the relative difficulty of simulating complete mental state cessation (Bering, 2006), the adaptiveness of assuming that one may be being watched (Bering, 2011), and a hypersensitive agency detection system that registers strange events as the product of unseen intentional agents (Barrett, 2004). Whereas, belief in a cosmic creator deity may be encouraged through entirely different pathways such as a natural tendency toward attributing design and purpose to features of the natural world (Kelemen, 2004), a hypertrophied sense of morally-loaded meaning in life events (Bering, 2011), and the ability of a morally-interested high-god to draw large groups of unrelated individuals into adaptive social arrangements (Norenzayan, 2012). Assuming that causal accounts for why people believe in ghosts and God diverge in important ways, an argument that serves as a defeater for belief in ghosts may not apply to God and vice versa. The same moral applies to CSR or ESR-derived defences.

Implications

It may seem odd to argue, as has already been suggested, that the scientific study of religious beliefs may be neutral as to whether religious beliefs are warranted or not. Some may immediately want to jump to the conclusion that if we can explain how we hold certain beliefs, and how they are interrelated with other features of human cognitive architecture, we are explaining such beliefs away. That, though, is far too quick. Many beliefs we naturally develop about the world around us are in fact true. They have to be if we are to function successfully in the world around us. For instance, babies very soon come to understand that objects should not be expected to go through solid walls. That they may have natural dispositions toward such beliefs surely does not count against their warrant.

To take an example that is more pertinent to CSR, we are inclined to look for an agent, if we hear an unexpected rustle in a seemingly deserted forest, or even suspect a burglar when there is a sudden bump upstairs. Often we may be mistaken, but that does not mean that there could not be an animal on the prowl, or an intruder in the house. Just because we find it easy to jump to conclusions does not make those conclusions always wrong, let alone irrational or unwarranted.

We may be sometimes primed to look for agents, even if they are immaterial, or to try to see purpose in events. We may find it easy to understand talk about ghosts, or gods, or even God. These tendencies may be because of basic features of the way humans think. Some evolutionary theorists may want to dismiss all that as an interesting, but ultimately irrelevant, by-product of other features of ordinary human cognitive abilities. They come riding piggy-back, as it were, on other aspects of what it is to be human.

Yet as CSR itself stresses, we are primed to see purpose in so many things, and it may seem too dismissive to see religious beliefs as accidental in this way. Such beliefs appear too central to what it is to be human to be explained away in this fashion. Certainly, even if their appearance was a chance affair, their continued persistence across the millennia might suggest that they do in themselves carry with them some evolutionary advantage. Why, otherwise, have they not been winnowed out by now though evolutionary pressure? Holding on to them may be just to our continuing evolutionary advantage, but there could be further explanations.

To those who believe in God, the origin and persistence of such beliefs may not be quite so strange. Theologians, such as Calvin, have often been prone to talk of a natural *sensus divinitatis*, a feeling of divinity, or a sense of the holy, in humans. We are not born with our minds as a *tabula rasa*, a blank slate, as was widely thought even a generation ago. Cognitive science now sees that the human mind is already inclined in certain directions, and the fact that our minds seem to naturally include some of the building blocks of religion may not be surprising from a scientific point of view. It certainly fits in with a theological understanding that God should perhaps want people to be able to have some rudimentary glimmerings of understanding, which would predispose them to religious belief.

CSR certainly does not support any particular doctrinal view, or even any particular religion. It is probably as consistent with polytheism as monotheism. Anthropology shows us that religion, of one kind or another, is present in all human societies. There are many forms of religion, to the extent that it becomes impossible to pick out any one feature common to them all. This fact powerfully suggests that CSR, however good at explaining some of our most basic impulses as the building blocks of religion, certainly underdetermines the form a religion might take in any particular society. Environmental influences will be important, and those of a religious outlook will want to point to the importance of particular forms of revelation. At least, they will say, we are ready to look for apparent revelation because our minds are already inclined to think of an agent, or agents prepared to reveal themselves to us.

This book is intent on examining the philosophical and theological implications of CSR. The idea that the discipline is neutral in a general sense about religion writ large may be disappointing both for atheists who want to seize on it to undermine religion, and to religious people who would like to have some kind of scientific support for any and all of their beliefs. Both are liable to be thwarted. Finding the defeaters or support within CSR for particular metaphysical views will require much more precise work than concluding blanket defeat or support. Yet that does not mean that the discipline is not of immense importance, and raises issues of profound philosophical importance, not least about the limits of the scientific enterprise, and whether so-called "naturalistic" explanations can be the only rational kind.

One of the most important facts that CSR draws attention to is that religion is not a private and idiosyncratic phenomenon with no place on the public stage. It is there at the heart of human activity, and is in fact the default option for humans. Atheism is not our natural state. Small children find it easier to hold religious beliefs than to reject them. Religion reappears, as in Eastern Europe, even after sustained attempts to eradicate it. Yet it comes in many forms, and even the most religious amongst us would have to admit that some of them are far from beneficial, even downright evil by most any standard.

One conclusion must be that religion cannot, and must not, be ignored in public life. Religious thought and practice appear to be natural modes of thought, action, and social organization. The more religion is privatized and thought to be beyond the scope of public, rational discussion, the more it will fester and break out in all kinds of unpredictable and undesirable ways. We have to recognise that religious tendencies are part of what it is to be human, and we dare not pretend they are of little account and unworthy of the attention of "public reason" (Trigg, 2007; 2012). They are as much part of us as other marks of our identity, such as our race, our gender, and sexual orientation.

It may seem surprising to say that religion is natural and atheism is not. One must beware, however, of reading too much into that. It does not give us a reason to prefer religion over atheism. In any case, that would not give us any guidance as to which, of so many religions, one should choose. Robert McCauley has done much philosophical work in analysing the nature of CSR. His somewhat surprising conclusion is that, although he agrees that religion can in a sense be called "natural," science itself most certainly cannot. His reasoning is that scientific thinking is an achievement that not all can master. Although many run together scientific thinking and common sense ideas, very often in opposition to the apparently strange notions of religion, in fact science directly contradicts common sense in many ways. For instance, talk of apparently solid objects being composed of different sub-atomic particles, and in fact not being as solid as they seem, runs against our normal intuitions. Modern physics can come up with notions that are even stranger than that. As McCauley writes (2011, p.223): "Science bears substantial burdens in the marketplace of ideas...selling radically counterintuitive representations whose appreciation requires painstaking cognitive processing that takes years, if not decades, to master."

Scientific thought does not come naturally to us in the way that the ideas that are the building blocks of religion do. In that respect, the comparison should not be between science and religion, but between science and theology. Similarly, atheism is on the same higher, reflective level. We develop in such a way that we can easily acquire some concepts, without having to think reflectively or analytically about them. We can imagine minds apart from bodies, understand the possibility of non-material agency, spontaneously look for purposive explanations, and so on, differently than how we come to understand water as being composed of hydrogen and oxygen.

To take an example from beyond CSR, stories are often told, and well attested in the medical literature, of so-called "near-death" experiences. Patients, having recovered after being at the point of death, may report an experience of floating near the ceiling of the hospital room, looking down on medical staff frantically trying to resuscitate them. The point is not what we make of these stories from a scientific point of view, or what theory we produce to explain their occurrence. It is rather that we all seem to have little difficulty in understanding what it would be like to have such an experience. We can easily envisage being apart from our body, even if rational reflection might caution us to doubt the possibility. In other words, what our cognitive mechanisms allow, and even encourage us to think, comes before reason is allowed to sit in judgment.

McCauley makes much of what he terms "maturationally natural" cognitive operations. Many human thoughts naturally develop so that we acquire them, just as we may not be born walking, but we do naturally come to learn to walk. It is not a matter of particular cultural training. For McCauley (2011, p.59) such operations of our minds and thought are "effortless, automatic, unreflective, and mostly unconscious." They are, he says, usually "up and running before children remember that they are, and although culture frequently tunes these systems, they do not rely on instruction, structured preparations, or anything else that is culturally distinctive." Religion is at first based on these operations. Clearly the form it takes in different cultures will vary, just as the food we eat varies across cultures, or the language we speak does. Yet we are born needing to eat something, with a built-in desire for food, and we naturally develop into speakers of language, imitating the sounds we hear around us. The fact that languages differ does not make the basic cognitive mechanisms in humans any less crucial for our ability to learn to communicate.

Cultural influence, and, above all our ability to reflect rationally, must not be confused with our basic impulses. It is often difficult to separate the two, since our cognitive capacities have to develop in a social environment. Yet there is such a thing as a human nature that we all share across time and geographical space; that is, what enables us to understand what might motivate people in very different cultures, or even people living in the remote past (Trigg, 2001, p.64ff). Our basic religious impulses are very much an element of that.

Religious impulses are a part of normal human reactions comparable to an elemental fear of snakes, or disgust at the sight of blood. There may be good evolutionary reasons why those appear to be widespread as a part of our common nature. At times, though, it may be important that we do not give in to them. No one who wants to be a zookeeper, in the one case, or a surgeon in the other, can afford to give in to their initial impulses. They must learn to override them.

In the same way, the fact that our cognitive architecture inclines us to religious explanations of various kinds is a simple fact about our starting-point as human beings. Just because we have them does not mean these impulses are reliable. It is open to the atheist to dismiss them as "infantile," as something we must try to grow out of. It is open to theologians to show how, perhaps, these initial impulses are a part of being human because of God's providence.

McCauley says bluntly that "it is atheism, not religion, that humans must work to acquire" (2011, p.221). "Popular" religion may not always accord with sophisticated, rational accounts in theology, as ideas of "theological correctness," already mentioned, indicate. Its presence is not an idiosyncratic feature of some, but is a pervasive force across humanity. What is the philosophical and theological significance of this? The validity of the empirical findings of the cognitive science of religion must be kept separate from the philosophical interpretation put upon them. This volume asks in various ways what that interpretation should be, and what the implications of CSR are for our more general understanding of the world in which we live.

References

Astuti, R. and Harris P.L., 2008. Understanding mortality and the life of the ancestors in rural madagascar. *Cognitive Science,* 32, pp. 713–40.

Atran, S., 2002. *In Gods We Trust: The Evolutionary Landscape of Religion.* New York: Oxford University Press.

Barrett, J.L., 2000. Exploring the natural foundations of religion. *Trends in Cognitive Sciences,* 4, pp. 29–34.

———. 2001. How ordinary cognition informs petitionary prayer. *Journal of Cognition and Culture,* 1(3), pp. 259–69.

———. 2004. *Why Would Anyone Believe in God?* Walnut Creek, CA: AltaMira Press.

——. 2008. Why Santa Claus is not a god. *Journal of Cognition and Culture*, 8(1–2), pp. 149–61.

——. 2011. *Cognitive Science, Religion, and Theology: From Human Minds to Divine Minds*. West Conshohoken, PA: Templeton Press.

——. 2012. *Born Believers: The Science of Childhood Religion*. New York: The Free Press.

Barrett, J.L. and Keil, F.C., 1996. Anthropomorphism and god concepts: conceptualizing a non-natural entity. *Cognitive Psychology*, 31, pp. 219–47.

Bering, J.M., 2006. The folk psychology of souls. *Behavioral and Brain Sciences*, 29, pp. 453–62.

——. 2011. *The Belief Instinct: The Psychology of Souls, Destiny, and the Meaning of Life*. New York: W.W. Norton.

Bering, J.M., Hernández-Blasi, C. and Bjorkland, D.F., 2005. The development of 'afterlife' beliefs in secularly and religiously schooled children. *British Journal of Developmental Psychology*, 23, pp. 587–607.

Bloom, P., 2004. *Descartes' Baby: How Child Development Explains What Makes Us Human*. London: William Heinemann.

——. 2009. Religious belief as an evolutionary accident. In: M. Murray and J. Schloss, eds, 2009. *The Believing Primate: Scientific, Philosophical, and Theological Reflections on the Origin of Religion*. New York: Oxford University Press. pp. 118–27.

Boyer, P., 1994. *The Naturalness of Religious Ideas: A Cognitive Theory of Religion*. Berkeley: University of California Press.

——. 2001. *Religion Explained: The Evolutionary Origins of Religious Thought*. New York: Basic Books.

——. 2003. Religious thought and behavior as by-products of brain function. *Trends in Cognitive Sciences*, 7, pp. 119–24.

Boyer, P. and Ramble, C., 2001. Cognitive templates for religious concepts: cross-cultural evidence for recall of counter-intuitive representations. *Cognitive Science*, 25, pp. 535–64.

Cohen, E., 2007. *The Mind Possessed: The Cognition of Spirit Possession in an Afro-Brazilian Religious Tradition*. New York: Oxford University Press.

Cohen, E. and Barrett, J.L., 2008a. Conceptualising possession trance: ethnographic and experimental evidence. *Ethos*, 36(2), pp. 246–67.

——. 2008b. When minds migrate: conceptualising spirit possession. *Journal of Cognition and Culture*, 8(1–2), pp. 23–48.

———. 2011. In search of 'folk anthropology': the cognitive anthropology of the person. In: J.W. van Huyssteen and E.P. Wiebe, eds, *In Search of Self: Interdisciplinary Perspectives on Personhood*. Grand Rapids: Eerdmans. pp. 104–23.

Emmons, N., 2012. *Children's Reasoning About Themselves as Babies, in Utero, and Prior to Conception: A Developmental Approach to Understanding Personal Origins*. Unpublished doctoral dissertation. Queen's University Belfast.

Evans, E.M., 2001. Cognitive and contextual factors in the emergence of diverse belief systems: creation versus evolution. *Cognitive Psychology*, 42, pp. 217–66.

Gendler, T.S., 2008. Alief and belief. *Journal of Philosophy*, 105(10), pp. 634–63.

Gervais, W.M. and Norenzayan A., 2012. Analytic thinking promotes religious disbelief. *Science*, 336, pp. 493–6.

Gregory, J. and Barrett, J.L., 2009. Epistemology and counterintuitiveness: role and relationship in epidemiology of cultural representations. *Journal of Cognition and Culture*, 9, pp. 289–314.

Guthrie, S.E., 1980. A cognitive theory of religion. *Current Anthropology*, 21, pp. 181–94.

———. 1993. *Faces in the Clouds: A New Theory of Religion*. New York: Oxford University Press.

Hirschfeld, L.A. and Gelman, S.A. eds, 1994. *Mapping the Mind: Domain Specificity in Cognition and Culture*. Cambridge: Cambridge University Press.

Hornbeck, R.G., 2012. *A Pure World: Moral Cognition and Spiritual Experiences in Chinese World of Warcraft*. Unpublished doctoral dissertation. University of Oxford.

Johnson, D. and Kruger, O., 2004. The good of wrath: supernatural punishment and the evolution of cooperation. *Political Theology*, 5, pp. 159–76.

Kahneman, D., 2003. A perspective on judgment and choice: mapping bounded rationality. *American Psychologist*, 58(9), pp. 697–720.

———. 2011. *Thinking, Fast and Slow*. Reprint edition. New York: Farrar, Straus and Giroux.

Kelemen, D., 2004. Are children "intuitive theists"? Reasoning about purpose and design in nature. *Psychological Science*, 15, pp. 295–301.

Lawson, E.T. and McCauley, R.N., 1990. *Rethinking Religion: Connecting Cognition and Culture*. Cambridge: Cambridge University Press.

Liénard, P. and Boyer, P., 2006. Whence collective ritual? A cultural selection model of ritualized behavior. *American Anthropologist*, 108, pp. 814–27.

Malley, B., 2004. *How the Bible Works: An Anthropological Study of Evangelical Biblicism*. Walnut Creek, CA: AltaMira Press.

Malley, B. and Barrett, J.L., 2003. Does myth inform ritual? A test of the Lawson-McCauley hypothesis. *Journal of Ritual Studies*, 17(2), pp. 1–14.

McCauley, R.N., 2011, *Why Religion is Natural and Science is Not*. New York: Oxford University Press.

McCauley, R.N. and Lawson, E.T., 2002. *Bringing Ritual to Mind: Psychological Foundations of Cultural Forms*. Cambridge: Cambridge University Press.

Meltzoff, A.N. and Moore, N.K., 1983. Newborn infants imitate adult facial gestures. *Child Development*, 54, pp. 702–9.

Norenzayan, A., 2012. The idea that launched a thousand civilizations. *New Scientist*, 213, pp. 42–4.

Slone, D.J., 2004. *Theological Incorrectness: Why Religious People Believe What They Shouldn't*. New York: Oxford University Press.

Sørensen, J., 2005. *A Cognitive Theory of Magic*. Lanham, MD: Rowman & Littlefield.

Sosis, R. 2009. The adaptationist-byproduct debate on the evolution of religion: five misunderstandings of the adaptationist program. *Journal of Cognition and Culture*, 9, pp. 315–32.

Spelke, E.S. and Kinzler, K.D., 2007. Core knowledge. *Developmental Science*, 11, pp. 89–96.

Sperber, D., 1975. *Rethinking Symbolism*. Cambridge: Cambridge University Press.

——. 1996. *Explaining Culture: A Naturalistic Approach*. Oxford: Blackwell.

Trigg, R., 2001. *Understanding Social Science*, Second edition. Oxford: Blackwell.

——. 2007. *Religion in Public Life: Must Faith be Privatized?* Oxford: Oxford University Press.

——. 2012. *Equality, Freedom and Religion*. Oxford: Oxford University Press.

Whitehouse, H., 1995. *Inside the Cult: Religious Innovation and Transmission in Papua New Guinea*. Oxford: Clarendon Press.

Whitehouse, H., 2004. *Modes of Religiosity: A Cognitive Theory of Religious Transmission*. Walnut Creek, CA: AltaMira Press.

Wolterstorff, N., 2001. *Thomas Reid and the Story of Epistemology*. Cambridge: Cambridge University Press.

Chapter 2

Intuition, Agency Detection, and Social Coordination as Analytical and Explanatory Constructs in the Cognitive Science of Religion

Robert Audi

Cognitive science is a burgeoning interdisciplinary field and it is appropriate that it should focus on religion as a major area of experimental inquiry and theoretical reflection. Enough work has now been done in the field—particularly in the past five to 10 years—to make this a very good time for dialogue between researchers in the cognitive science of religion (CSR) and philosophers interested in human behavior, philosophy of mind and, especially, philosophy of religion. This chapter will contribute to that dialogue by exploring some important concepts that figure prominently in the literature of CSR: intuition, especially as compared with inference; agency and our tendency to ascribe it; and social coordination as related to religious and kindred concepts. The literature does not contain canonical definitions of these concepts, and my procedure will be to consider a variety of passages in which they figure and, on that basis, to raise questions about their content and their role in understanding religion. The aim is both to understand CSR and the claims of some of its practitioners regarding religion, and to raise questions that may be pursued by researchers in CSR, by philosophers examining their work, or by both.

Intuition and Inference

I begin with Pascal Boyer's ambitiously titled book, *Religion Explained* (2001). Boyer devotes several pages to what he calls a "question of *intuition*" (p. 51, italics in the original) but provides scarcely more than a hint of just what an intuition is supposed to be. It is clear in the context, however, that some intuitions are, in their level of confidence, psychologically stronger than others and that their objects are the kinds of things one affirms or denies—propositions, in a familiar terminology. Moreover, it appears that intuitions are at least in some cases a kind of belief (Boyer, 2001, pp. 52–6). Boyer later says, for example: "We intuitively assume that if an agent has full access to all the relevant information about the situation, that agent will immediately have access to the rightness or wrongness of the behavior" (2001, p. 189). This example has special interest on at least two counts: first, it shows how sophisticated the content of an intuition can be; second, it implicitly affirms a widely held and plausible view important in ethical theory—that the moral properties of an action are determined by (non-moral) facts that pertain to this action.

One way to understand intuition as Boyer and other CSR researchers conceive it is to note how it is connected with inference. At one point he says that:

> what is connected with explicit thought—what we usually call a "belief"—is very often an attempt to justify or explain the intuitions we have as a result of implicit processes in the mental basement ... Seeing a two-year-old, we cannot help assuming she has certain limitations. This prompts us to say "yes" when people ask us "Are children less competent than adults?" (Boyer, 2001, p. 305)

A different but compatible conception is suggested by Justin Barrett in reference to early childhood expectations. He maintains that these:

> expectations or assumptions are intuitive in the sense that they are early developing, often tacit, and largely inflexible. A bounded physical object such as a brick is intuitively assumed to have properties such as occupying a single location in space and time, not moving unless launched by contact. (2008, p. 151)

In terminology common in philosophy, we might say that intuitions are commonly non-inferential cognitions, not in the sense that they have no connection with "inference systems" (Boyer, 2001, p. 305), but in the sense that they are not formed by a process of drawing a conclusion from a premise expressed by some other belief that the person has or from a set of premises expressed by one or more beliefs on the subject. This allows intuitions to play various roles, including that of interpretation, as when we intuitively ascribe agency to a shadowy form moving apparently self-directedly in the distance. It is, however, important to stress the word "commonly." Writers in CSR seem to leave open the question of whether intuitive beliefs are sometimes inferential. In the main, however, they seem to treat such beliefs as non-inferential, information-bearing manifestations of the operation of cognitive mechanisms that give rise to them in response to perceptual or other kinds of experience.

Another way to understand intuition as it figures in CSR is to note how it is related to the counterintuitive. For Boyer, "counterintuitive" "does not mean strange, inexplicable, funny, exceptional or extraordinary ... [but] 'including information contradicting some information provided by ontological categories' ... (The neologism *counterontological* might be a better choice)" (2001, p. 65). An example would be ascribing physiological processes to a category that does not intuitively include biology, as where a mountain is said to bleed or to feed on the meat of sacrificed animals (Boyer, 2001, p. 65). Like the intuitive, the counterintuitive admits of degrees on the intuitive-counterintuitive spectrum, and an important issue in CSR is how counterintuitive certain religious tenets are.

If this characterization of the counterintuitive creates the impression that religions are by their nature committed to affirming falsehoods, that impression is certainly confirmed by the characterization of religion given by Scott Atran: "Roughly, religion is (1) a community's costly and hard-to-fake commitment (2) to a counterfactual and counterintuitive world of supernatural agents (3) who master people's existential anxieties, such as death and deception" (2002, p. 4). As it happens, serious work in CSR does not require presupposing the truth or the falsity of propositions entailing the existence of supernatural entities or of claims about the success of a religion in mastering the anxieties mentioned. But there is a kind of counterintuitiveness that is commonly taken by researchers in CSR to be a mark of genuine religion. Atran may be representative in this. Of supernatural beliefs, for instance, he says: "They are just as counterintuitive for the people who think them true as for those who think them false (e.g., wine as the blood of Christ, a wafer as His body)" (2002, p. 84). How, then, do believers manage to sustain such counterintuitive beliefs?:

> People who believe such counterintuitive beliefs to be true do so by ritually proscribing situations of conflict with intuitively mundane beliefs (e.g., devout Catholics aren't routinely cannibals); such people routinely invoke nonconflictual aspects of intuitive belief systems to give mundane content to "impossible worlds" (e.g., God is everywhere but not likely in the trash). (Atran, 2002, p. 84)

The suggestion here is perhaps that religious people tend to minimize the counterintuitiveness of their beliefs about the supernatural by such things as restricting their scope and hence the domain in which they must be affirmed. Consider a later work in CSR by Atran and Norenzayan. In a section said to "unpack the idea of the supernatural as a counterintuitive world that is not merely counterfactual in the sense of physically impossible or nonexistent," they speak of religious myths as "arresting because they are counterintuitive" (2004, p. 720). What justifies the "because" here?:

> Insofar as category violations shake basic notions of ontology, they are attention-arresting hence memorable. But only if the resultant impossible worlds remain bridged to the everyday world can information be stored, evoked, and transmitted. (Atran and Norenzayan, 2004, p. 720)

One might think that the bridge metaphor could be exemplified by Jesus Christ, as man, serving as a bridge between God, as bodiless, and ordinary human beings, but that is not the kind of example given in the context. Instead, they note that "sudden movement of an object stirred by the wind may trigger the agent-detection system that operates over the domain of folk psychology, and a ghost may be invoked to interpret this possibly purposeful event" (Atran and Norenzayan, 2004, p. 720). I take it that the bridge here to the everyday world is in part the invocation of agency to explain an event and the folk physical presupposition that the wind has causal power.

So far, I have not introduced the concept of a minimally counterintuitive (MCI) concept. One might think that this is a threshold concept, but it does not figure as such (at least not in any precise way) in the literature. A core idea underlying the use of the notion of the MCI concept is expressed by Barrett in saying, for instance, that "concepts that are highly *counterintuitive*—in the technical sense of violating mental tools' automatic expectations—tend to be less plausible" (2009, p. 82), where the plausibility of a concept is (I take it) roughly proportional to that of taking instances of it to be real, using them to explain and predict significant phenomena, and finding the presupposition of its reality supported by apparent explanatory and predictive success and by harmony with what one believes on the basis of one's "mental tools," such as one's agency detection device (a notion which will be discussed below). Thus, he also says that "Concepts that balance meeting most non-reflective beliefs, while violating just a small number (e.g., one or two at a time) have been called minimally counterintuitive (MCI)" (p. 84), where "non-reflective beliefs are the primary stuff from which our minds construct reflective beliefs" (p. 80). Mental tools "automatically and non-reflectively construct most of our beliefs about the natural and social world" and are sometimes called "*intuitive inference systems.* [T]hese mental tools operate on specialized domains of information," such as those in which agency detection is naturally operative, as where it "automatically tells us that self-propelled, goal directed objects are intentional agents" (p. 79).

It is no accident that I have used the agency-detection mental tool as an example here. It is important for illustrating both how the intuitive and counterintuitive are understood in CSR and for connecting those notions with that of inference. A recurrent theme in CSR literature seems to be the inferential potential (or power) of a concept, where this is roughly the "ability to inject explanation or meaning into a broad array of human concerns—and connect a large number of mental tools and salient outputs" (Barrett, 2009, p. 85). Concepts of intentional agents, including gods, have a great deal of such power, as is obvious in the concept of an omnipotent divine agent, whose causal potential, and in that way explanatory potential, is incalculably wide. With the idea of inferential potential in mind, we might now fruitfully consider some points about the role of agency detection devices in CSR.

The Concept of Agency Detection as an Element in CSR

Evolutionary considerations, especially as connected with findings in anthropology, are central in CSR. In a passage of revealing generality, Atran maintains that:

> All supernatural agent concepts trigger our naturally selected agency-detection system, which is trip-wired to respond to fragmentary information, inciting perception of figures lurking in the shadows and emotions of dread or awe. Mistaking a nonagent for an agent would do little harm, but failing to detect an agent, especially a human or animal predator, could well prove fatal ... This is one way that the conceptual ridge of our evolutionary landscape connects to the ridge of social interaction schema, in particular with the evolutionary design for avoiding and tracking predators and prey. (2002, p. 267)

One might think that given the familiarity of human agents, a high degree of anthropomorphism would be predicted. But this is not a consequence of any consensus position in CSR. As Boyer puts it, "gods and spirits are not represented as having *human* features in general but as having *minds*, which is much more specific ... the concept of a mind is not exclusively human" (2001, p. 144).

A commentary on Atran and Norenzayan by Timothy Ketelaar nicely brings out the ideas sketched in Atran's passage about attributions of supernatural agency. He says that for them:

> Religion is essentially a by-product of an evolved bias toward over-attributing agency as the source of unexplained events (e.g., what was that noise in the bush?). A key feature ... is the claim that this bias emerges from the simple evolutionary factor that the recurrent challenge of detecting predators and other dangerous agents can be characterized as a signal-detection problem ... in which a *miss* would have been far less costly than a *false alarm*. (Ketelaar, 2004, p. 740)

His own contribution is to suggest how horror stories may connect with this and thereby illustrate the inferential potential of supernatural agent concepts. He suggests that "the evolved inferential machinery underlying beliefs in supernatural agents could give rise to a fertile, culturally constructed imaginary world populated by predatory monsters and supernatural religious instruments that function to protect us from these dangerous agents" (2004, p. 741). An example that he cites is the fabled repelling of vampires by holy crosses (p. 740).

With the protective role of agency detection in mind, Barrett has spoken of our *hypersensitive* agency detection device (HADD) and has noted its context sensitivity. For instance: "A soldier on a battlefield will have a more sensitive HADD than a person strolling through a park" (2009, p. 87). He also notes that it works in concert with other cognitive mechanisms in a way that bears on the extent to which it may result in false positives:

> If HADD worked alone in determining when or where we discovered the existence of agents, we would never be able to tell definitively when it was wrong ... Other cognitive mechanisms, including our abilities to consider evidence reflectively, can override HADD or any other single cognitive mechanism that tries to generate a belief. (Barrett, 2007, p. 68)

A natural question that now arises is why the number of gods people have taken to be real is not even larger than in fact it is. Here it is useful to note why Barrett holds that Santa Claus is *not* a god:

> His information is marginally strategic at best. He does act in the real world, but only once each year. And Santa only minimally motivates behaviors ... He fails to possess rich inferential or explanatory potential ... and he is not easily linked to moral or social concerns. (2008, pp. 158–9)

The implications of this explanation for what CSR implies about the status of major theistic religions are wide. I am particularly interested in the role of such religions in the development and preservation of human societies. This brings us to the next section.

The Role of Religion in Social Coordination

A major theme in the literature of CSR is the role of religion in the preservation of human society and in making social existence possible. I have already quoted Atran's characterization of religion as committed to "supernatural agents" "who master people's existential anxieties, such as death and deception" (2002, p. 4). He also says of religions that: "They all invoke supernatural agents to deal with emotionally eruptive existential anxieties, such as loneliness, calamity, and death" (2002, p. 266). He is not here committing himself to a specific claim of success for religion in these matters, nor should we assume (despite the sweeping character of his generalities) that he sees no differences among religions in these matters. Clearly, however, he sees religion as in general sufficiently successful in these existential matters to have a kind of cultural value.

These passages about the existential function of religion do not specifically mention how it contributes to social coordination, but they are apparently written with that in mind. Here a major point is that:

> Invocation of supernatural agents constitutes an ecologically rational response to the enhanced possibilities of deception inherent in the evolution of human representational skills and social interaction. Religion, or any moral order, could not long endure if it were unable to forestall defection and escape from the Prisoner's Dilemma (i.e., if you don't cheat others before they have a chance to cheat you, you will be left in the lurch; but if all reason this way, then everyone will lose) ... To keep the morally corrosive temptations to deceive or defect under control, *all concerned* ... must truly believe that the gods are always watching. (Atran, 2002, pp. 144–5)

The emphasis here is on how a pattern of thinking of the gods as observers of human behavior contributes to social coordination. Atran is not alone in stressing this. Johnson and Kruger, for instance, hold that:

> Many of our social norms developed because they promoted cooperation towards public goods in the past. These norms are often driven by religion. We suggest that the origins of these social norms may have spontaneously emerged

in evolution as a result of the specific selective advantages of supernatural punishment. (2004, p. 171)

This emphasis on the effect of assumed observation by gods is not the only element that CSR researchers emphasize in explaining the contribution that religion makes to social coordination. Atran also says, for instance, that "religious rituals involve sequential, socially interactive movement and gesture (chant, dance, murmur, etc.) and formulaic utterances (liturgies, canonical texts, etc.) that synchronize affective states among group members in displays of cooperative commitment" (2002, p. 172). These elements are apparently taken to have significant coordinative effects even apart from the influence of the sense of gods watching human conduct. The importance of religion for social coordination, then, does not depend entirely on fear of punishment as a motivator or indeed entirely on theistic elements of religion. The differential effects of these variables are, of course, a matter for pursuit through framing and pursuing testable hypotheses.

Why might religion be effective in promoting social coordination by rituals and other requirements? One hypothesis is proposed and supported by Sosis and Bressler, who "expect communes that impose greater requirements on their member to produce more committed members and thus more effectively manage the challenge of cooperation than less demanding communes" (2003, p. 216). Moreover, they take their data to confirm that: "Increasing the number of costly requirements results in greater longevity on average for religious communes but not for secular communes" (2003, p. 223). As to why meeting greater requirements should enhance commitment, they do not propose an explanation, but one might think that in part the explanation might be that when we are "invested" in a kind of activity, we have an incentive not to waste it by abandoning it. This would go well with two testable (and perhaps to some extent already tested) hypotheses: the idea, prominent in CSR, that the gods are watching and will reward those who live up to their investment in pleasing the gods; and the idea that cognitive dissonance (an aversive condition) would tend to be created by the prospect of defection, since one would then likely have to regard one's current sacrifices, which one has valued, as wasted.

The question of the role of religion in social coordination is connected with the question of whether it is adaptive, in a sense implying that, at least in some ways, its perpetuation might be explainable in terms of evolutionary considerations. Researchers in CSR differ on this, though there seems to be agreement that genetic factors alone do not explain its perpetuation. One prominent view, represented by Sosis and Alcorta, is that:

Far from being an evolutionary by-product, religion constitutes a uniquely human form of ritualized display that not only regulates social interactions, but also promulgates social cohesion and provides the foundation for social transmission of culture. (2004, p. 750)

Given the importance of social coordination, and especially of the kind of altruistic or, at least, broadly other-regarding elements in human beings that seem required for any society that generally observes moral standards, one might think that the contribution of religion to supporting such a society would more often result in positive attitudes on the part of researchers in CSR. I have not, however, systematically surveyed the literature to compare signs of negative attitudes with signs of positive ones. In any case, my main concern in the rest of this chapter is not to explore attitudes toward religion among CSR researchers, but, first, to formulate some questions that may be of interest both to them and to philosophers, and, second, to explore some epistemological assumptions that may be operating in some of the CSR discussions and, in any case, bear on the implications of CSR findings for the rationality of certain kinds of religious positions. The next section will take up the first task; the second task will be addressed in the final section.

Intuition and Inference, Causation and Agency

Intuition has received much attention in philosophy in recent years,[1] and some of the differences concerning it may be of interest for CSR, and indeed seem to be reflected in the CSR works I have cited so far. The largest single difference concerns whether intuitions are beliefs or at least cognitions with a similar content that produce an inclination to believe, but are not themselves beliefs. These are often called *seemings*.

A related notion is that of an *intuitive proposition*, one that (for the relevant population) seems true on considering it, as with "trees are not made of steel" or "an eleven-sided figure is not a square." These need not be believed *before* being considered, and if they never have been so much as thought, we might want to say not that these are objects of existing intuitions, but that they are intuitive propositions that would yield intuitions upon being considered. The

---

[1] For discussion of the notion of intuition and its epistemological status, see Bealer, 1998; Sosa, 1998; Huemer, 2005; and Audi, 2008. The latter citation indicates how intuition is connected with the self-evident and how the latter, as a case of the *a priori*, is related to facts as "truth-makers."

difference—which seems experimentally confirmable—is between, on the one hand, a kind of representational state with propositional content and, on the other hand, a disposition to enter such a state upon being presented, in an appropriate way, with content of a kind that elicits intuition formation (this distinction is developed in detail in Audi, 1994).

On either conception of intuition, it would appear that intuitions are non-inferential in the sense that the cognitions constituting them—whether beliefs or seemings or something similar—are not based on one or more premises, where premises are truth-valued (true or false) objects taken to support the cognition and are themselves either believed or objects of other cognitive attitudes (such as judgments or conjecture) that are true of false. But there is much difficulty in explaining what constitutes an inference, and if the notion is taken to include the cognitive outputs of cognitive mechanisms or mental tools, such as an agency detection device, then what philosophers tend to call non-inferential cognitions may be inferential on this mental-tool conception found in CSR literature. The question is of course not settled by taking an intuition to be simply a cognition with an intuitive *object*, for such an object may certainly be an object of a cognition that, being derived by an elaborate conscious argument from explicit premises, everyone would call inferential.

One might think that the distinction between an intuition and an inferential cognition is unimportant psychologically. I do not see that this is so, in part because they seem to be outputs of different kinds of psychological mechanisms, but I cannot argue the matter in detail. An important question here for CSR and for psychology in general is perhaps this: does it matter whether a cognition arises from another cognition as a basis or, alternatively, from some causal process, such as perception, memory-activation, or direct rational apprehension, that does not have truth-valued inputs? Consider perception: seeing a sheet of paper commonly causes me, in a way that—psychologically as opposed to neurologically—seems direct, to believe that there is one before me. I do not infer that there is one here from, say, believing that only this can explain my visual experience. To be sure, what the brain does may be as complex here as what it does when I draw an inference, perhaps even more so where, as with recognizing an abstract painting, there is a need for pattern recognition. But the two kinds of what might be called information-processing—propositional in the one case and perceptual in the other—seem empirically as well as conceptually quite different, and some of what I find in CSR suggests that the evolutionary roles of the two may be quite different.

The notion of belief is also variously understood in CSR literature, and its explication continues to be a challenge in philosophy. Beliefs are commonly taken to be cognitions with truth-valued objects and there is much overlap in conceptions of what produces them and, to some extent—as with the power of testimony (Bergstrom, Moehlmann and Boyer, 2006) and of ritual—what sustains them. But must such cognitions, if not before the mind, have been formed, as opposed to being innate, and then be stored in memory, or is it enough that, when asked whether the proposition is true, the person will normally sincerely assent without reflection or inference? Consider the proposition that animals have parents of the same species as themselves.[2] I immediately assented to this on reading it, but I do not think that I ever considered it before, and I doubt that I inferred it from one or more premises (though I do not think that inference must always be introspectively prominent if indeed it is always discernible to introspection as such at all). Perhaps I *presupposed* it; I certainly would be surprised to find it denied. But I do not think that, before considering the proposition, I actually had a belief with this object. In my view, I had a disposition to believe it and came to believe it upon considering it because, whether by inference or not, it seemed obvious on the basis of what I already believe (Audi, 1994). Different cases of such spontaneous belief-formation—especially of intuitive beliefs—doubtless have different explanations, and in some cases the differences may be important for CSR.

Agency detection is another area where I want to pose questions that may be significant for CSR. An interesting hypothesis here is that our most psychologically primitive, and perhaps conceptually most basic, understanding of causation is *agential*. Perhaps children acquire the concept by watching adults make things happen and understand it through that experience and their own experience of causing events. I do not know that this is so. Perhaps one can learn the concept by simply watching natural events in causal patterns. In any case, regardless of how the concept of causation is acquired, it is crucial for explaining events, at least in natural languages. This seems to be presupposed in the CSR literature and is surely independently plausible.

If causal explanation is crucial for ordinary understanding of events and for guiding conduct in a way that is conducive to survival, it is perhaps expectable that human beings should ascribe causal producers of familiar phenomena and, indeed, should have some minimal skill in so doing if they are to survive. What is perhaps not expectable from this point alone is the apparent prominence of HADD in human cognition. If, however, we take the most primitive

---

[2] This example is drawn from Barrett, 2009. His contrast between reflective and non-reflective beliefs may be fruitfully compared with mine between dispositional beliefs and dispositions to believe (in Audi, 1994).

understanding of causation to be agential and if we take causal explanation to be the most natural kind to give in understanding events, then it should come as no surprise that people tend to posit agential explanations in a wide variety of cases and especially where no non-agential, say simple mechanical, explanation is at hand when there is a felt need for explanation of some phenomenon. To be sure, HADD is also expectable on the basis of the need to detect predators, which are after all agents. But it is difficult to see why, from an evolutionary point of view, HADD would have survival value if agential explanation were not a genuine kind having predictive power, as causal explanations typically do.

If we add to these points that our apparently most direct, and perhaps most elemental, experience of causation is one of the apparent causation of our own bodily movements by volitional and other mental events that we do not physically perceive, it should not be surprising that agential explanation and—perhaps partly for that reason—causal explanation by appeal to agential action need not be physicalistic. This is not to propose a psychological theory, but it is intended to suggest a possible explanation of why some of the findings in CSR might be expected. Some of the issues surrounding these points may be experimentally clarified. But one point seems to be of an ontological kind that concerns both scientists in various fields and philosophers: that there are mental events having causal power and playing some important role in the concept of causal explanation. This can be agreed even if there remains (as there does) controversy about whether mental events are really physical.

Some Epistemological Implications

To set the stage for this discussion, I begin with what Boyer maintains in a section entitled "Accommodating Airy Nothing: A Matter of Undue Laxity" (2001, p. 299). He suggests that religious beliefs would:

> vanish if people were more consistent in applying common sense principles of mental management like the following:
> Only allow clear and precise thoughts to enter your mind.
> Only allow consistent thoughts.
> Consider the evidence of a claim before accepting it.
> Only consider refutable claims. (2001, p. 199)

A similar set of standards is put forward by Richard Dawkins, who endorses:

All the virtues laid out in textbooks of standard methodology: testability, evidential support, precision, quantifiability, consistency, intersubjectivity, repeatability, universality, progressiveness, independence of cultural milieu, and so on. Faith spreads despite a total lack of every single one of these virtues. (1991, p. 4)

Space constraints do not allow me to discuss these restrictions in detail here, but the literature of philosophy of science indicates a multitude of ways in which they are inadequate.[3] I can, however, comment on some of them.

First, the notion of a clear and precise thought is itself unclear and there is simply no hope of normal individuals seriously considering *only* such thoughts, much less keeping all others out of their minds. Some thoughts enter our minds because others express them (as surely Boyer would not deny), so even if we had control of what we think when alone, as social beings we find our cognitive stimuli largely uncontrollable. Second, no major religion depends on clearly inconsistent propositions, if indeed on any that are *internally* inconsistent. Arguably, occasional inconsistencies of certain kinds, say to the effect that someone is 74 years old and was born in the year n (where the numbers do not match) are normal. The Trinity is a special case, but much literature on it shows how inconsistency can be avoided. Third, for much of what we know, say through perception or testimony, there is no need to "consider the evidence," a phrase that suggests some reason for doubt as to whether the proposition in question is true.

My fourth point draws on the difference between *refutability* (liability to being shown flatly false) and *disconfirmability* (liability to being shown improbable to some degree). If these are distinguished, as they should be and indeed are in careful scientific practice, then certain existential propositions, such as the assertion that we will eventually discover at least five new chemical elements, are not refutable despite being testable (and clearly verifiable) scientific hypotheses. Non-discovery, even given a long and hard search, does not entail non-existence. Note, too, that truths of logic and pure mathematics are also apparently irrefutable and that many of the former and some of the latter are non-quantitative.

Much more could be said about deficiencies in the suggested standards for intellectual respectability proposed by Boyer, Dawkins, and others, but here I want to be as forthcoming as possible and explore what may be a rarely stated epistemological principle, but may nonetheless be important in underlying the

---

[3] For critical discussion of the kind of criteria for cognitive acceptability proposed by Boyer and Dawkins, see Audi, 2009.

skepticism about, or a flat rejection of, religious views by many researchers in CSR. The assumption is this:

> *The Causal Criterion of Knowledge*: A belief that *p*, where *p* is the proposition in question, constitutes knowledge only if the possession of the belief cannot be explained except on the basis of causation by the fact that *p*.

Simple illustrations abound. Consider, for instance, perception. My belief that there is printing before me cannot be explained without appeal to causation by that fact, at least in the sense that the state of affairs it corresponds to—there being print here—is an essential cause of my believing this. This causal criterion implies that if, on the basis of CSR, we can causally explain religious beliefs without assuming that they are causally based on facts corresponding to their content—say facts concerning actions by supernatural beings—then these beliefs do not constitute knowledge. Even if an assumption of this criterion or some similar one is not the main epistemological basis of the skepticism found in so much CSR literature, it is well worth exploring.

For ordinary perceptual knowledge, this causal criterion seems to hold, as for many other kinds of empirical knowledge, but what of my future-directed knowledge that I am going to raise my left arm? The relevant fact lies in the future and so does not cause me to believe I will raise my arm. It is true, however, that my *intention* to raise my arm might cause both that *and* my belief that I will raise it (as noted in Goldman, 1967). A natural response is to widen the principle to something like:

> *The Causal Explainability Criterion of Knowledge*: A belief that *p* constitutes knowledge only if the possession of the belief cannot be explained except on the basis of causation by the fact that *p* or some fact that is causally responsible for both that belief and the fact that *p*.

Even if this revision enhances plausibility, what are we to say of knowledge of causal facts or indeed of causal laws? Are causal facts, say that my releasing a pen in midair caused it to fall, themselves explained by other causal facts or perhaps by nomic facts, such as a gravitational law? But are laws causes? They may entail and even explain other laws, but they do not seem to be, properly speaking, causes. Even if they can be construed as causes, other difficulties remain for this explainability criterion. I want to consider one difficulty in particular.

How should we explain beliefs that constitute *a priori* knowledge, the kind that is non-empirical and grounded in reason rather than experience, most notably perception? How is the fact that nothing is both round and square causally connected with the belief constituting knowledge that nothing is both round and square? We presumably believe and know this truth on the basis of understanding the proposition. But propositions are not causes, nor are the necessary relations among abstract entities that apparently ground this kind of truth. If causation is crucial here, that is apparently because, when believing that this proposition constitutes knowledge, the *understanding* of the proposition causally grounds the belief in question, where understanding is a psychological property that may be taken to have at least causal sustaining power (Audi, 2008). Now, however, our epistemological principle will again need revision. We might hold, for instance:

> *The Causal Reliability Criterion of Knowledge*: A belief that *p* constitutes knowledge only if the belief cannot be explained except on the basis of a causal connection to something that reliably indicates the fact (hence the truth) that *p*.

For instance, understanding an *a priori* proposition may *indicate* truth, though beliefs of *a priori* propositions are not causally explained by the facts by virtue of which they are true or by causes of those facts (which are not themselves causally explainable). But now one might note that the causal relevance principle does not rule out (though it of course does not rationally require) maintaining that the fact that God, for example, created the physical universe is needed to explain people's believing the proposition that God did this.

To be sure, the causal reliability principle might seem to rule out many religious beliefs constituting knowledge *on* the assumption, which many writers in CSR make, that religious beliefs, or at least all the supernatural ones, can be explained without appeal to anything that reliably indicates their truth. Moreover, assuming or presupposing this or something close to it can explain why so many writers in CSR take their naturalistic explanations of the genesis and resilience of religious beliefs to undermine the justifiability of those beliefs.

At least three possibilities should be mentioned here. The first is that God might have created not only the universe but also patterns of events that may suffice to explain religious beliefs naturalistically. Then the fact of creation, or at least certain facts about its character, might be needed for any *ultimate* explanation of people's holding religious beliefs. Roughly, the formation and persistence of the relevant beliefs might be the terminal elements in causal chains tracing back to the creation. The second possibility is *explanatory overdetermination*: the existence of two independent explanations for a phenomenon. Even if there are naturalistic causally sufficient conditions for a religious belief, there can still be a supernaturalistic sufficient condition. This could occur if God has power to produce—or causally guarantee the occurrence of—natural events even when there already exist causally sufficient conditions for them. This possibility is compatible with God's creating the world with causal forces operating, but does not require this to be so, since God could exercise power over the world even if it has always existed. The third possibility arises as to the plausible assumption that the universe is not a deterministic system (an assumption in accordance with leading theories in quantum mechanics). If not, then, for an event that is not determined naturalistically by antecedent events under the laws of nature, divine action might be needed to explain why it, rather than some alternative event, occurred.

The second and third possibilities raise many difficulties and need not be discussed now. But it is important to mention them in order to indicate the limitations of what might seem an unassailable epistemological principle. As to the first possibility, many scientifically oriented thinkers will doubt that a non-embodied person is even possible or at least doubt that such a being could have causal power over the physical world. But although these doubts can be defended with some plausible arguments, these arguments are at best inconclusive.[4]

There is a further consideration that also influences many scientists and many philosophers in assessing the idea of divine action as an explanatory factor: simplicity. Here is a principle that is a version of Ockham's Razor:

The Principle of Explanatory Simplicity: Other things equal, the simpler of two competing explanations is more likely to be correct.

A corollary would be that where a phenomenon can be explained by appeal to naturalistic factors alone, which we must in any case countenance in giving explanations, then, all other things being equal: (1) an alternative explanation by appeal to supernatural factors is to be rejected; and (2) an explanation appealing to a supernatural overdetermining cause is not to be affirmed.

One problem here is to explicate simplicity. Another is to show that naturalistic explanations provide a simpler *overall* account of the data to be explained than can be achieved under a theistic view that provides ample space for scientific inquiry.[5] It should also be noted that if the principle of explanatory simplicity is true, that principle itself apparently cannot be non-circularly

---

[4] For defense of a Cartesian conception of mind, see Swinburne (2004) and for discussion of the possibility of embodiment for deity, see Audi (2011).

[5] For example, Swinburne (2004) provides an account of simplicity. For discussion of the epistemic status of simplicity principles, see Chapter 10 of Audi, 2011.

confirmed empirically and, in any case, might admit of theistic explanation. Arguably, the universe could have been created with governing laws that are in some sense simple and, harmoniously with this, people could have evolved with an intuitive preference for—with a kind of "mental tool" favoring—simplicity precisely because behavior in accordance with true generalities is more likely to be conducive to survival than behavior in accordance with falsehoods.

A final appropriate point here is that the epistemological implications of CSR should not be discussed only in connection with knowledge. The concept of justification is quite different. Justified beliefs, unlike beliefs constituting knowledge, need not be true, as may be seen both in everyday life and in the history of science, and clearly the justifiedness of a belief, though an intellectually creditable status, does not entail that it constitutes knowledge. Indeed, in my view, rationality is also a respectable status in a belief, and rationality is normatively more permissive than justification. One way to see this is to note that each is in part to be understood by contrast with its contrary, and the contraries of each are manifestly different in normative status: irrationality is a characteristic that most of us may hope never to instantiate; being on some occasions unjustified is a common condition of virtually all human beings. We can be unjustified in a conclusion that most rational individuals would reach given the same evidence, and many thinkers have concluded that this has been their status, sometimes even with true hypotheses rationalized overenthusiastically. But even those of us who are sometimes unreasonable rarely if ever sink to irrationality—the kind of thing manifested by superstition or foolish prejudices. Perhaps minimal rationality is achieved when irrationality is avoided, but justification requires more—not merely avoiding blatant error, for instance, but having a solid supporting basis. In any case, avoiding irrationality for beliefs of propositions that are difficult to subject to experimental or ordinary observational testing is easier than avoiding being unjustified in holding such beliefs. It is important to see this in appraising religious cognitions. Even if one reasonably considers their basis insufficient for justification, one may not infer from this alone that they are irrational. However, even a belief's being justified has no simple causal relation to the facts that determine whether or not it is true, and the same holds even more clearly for rationality.[6]

None of these points leads to a conclusion about whether one or another religious belief is in fact justified or indeed rational. But if the epistemological perspective I have presented is sound, we might conclude that whatever skeptical

---

[6] Discussion of the relation of justification to knowledge is provided in Chapter 11 of Audi (2010).

implications the findings in CSR may have for the possibility of religious knowledge, the case for these elements equally supporting skepticism about justification is weaker, and if the target of skepticism is rationality in religious cognitions rather than its stronger cousin, justification, the case is weaker still.[7]

***

Research in CSR indicates much about the dynamics of certain kinds of religions and something about the role of those religions in facilitating the kind of coordinated social existence required for the survival of any human society threatened by natural forces and anti-social human tendencies. CSR makes fruitful use of the notions of intuition and agency detection, and of such reinforcers of social cohesion as the costliness of religious affiliation. The overall results of its investigations suggest that religions of at least certain kinds may significantly contribute to the internalization of moral norms that are important for the social coordination needed for human survival. The overall inquiry conducted in CSR is plainly methodologically naturalistic, making no metaphysical commitments other than those required by scientific investigation. But even where researchers in CSR have resisted making such metaphysical presuppositions as that a non-embodied person is flatly impossible, some of them have apparently not resisted epistemological presuppositions that lead to skepticism toward or wholesale rejection of supernaturalistic views. These epistemological presuppositions are open to serious objections and need further exploration, but they are in any case philosophical views that are at least not fully evaluable by scientific inquiry. Fruitful scientific research in CSR, moreover, does not require them. If this chapter clarifies those points and widens the territory for discussion between CSR and related areas of philosophical inquiry, it will have succeeded.[8]

References

Atran, S., 2002. *In Gods We Trust: The Evolutionary Landscape of Religion*. Oxford: Oxford University Press.

---

[7] In Chapters 1–2 of Audi (2011), rationality and justification are compared and contrasted, are connected with knowledge, and are shown to bear on skepticism.

[8] This chapter has benefited from discussions with Justin Barrett, Michael Murray, Jeffrey Schloss, and Roger Trigg, and I also want to thank an anonymous reader for the Press.

Atran, S. and Norenzayan, A., 2004. Religion's evolutionary landscape: counterintuition, commitment, compassion, communion. *Behavior and Brain Sciences*, 27, pp. 713–70.

Audi, R., 1994. Dispositional beliefs and dispositions to believe. *Nous*, 28(4), pp. 419–34.

———. 2008. Intuition, inference, and rational disagreement in ethics. *Ethical Theory and Moral Practice*, 11, pp. 475–92.

———. 2009. Science education, religious toleration, and liberal neutrality toward the good. In: H. Siegel (ed.), *The Oxford Handbook of Philosophy of Education*. Oxford: Oxford University Press, pp. 333–57.

———. 2010. *Epistemology: A Contemporary Introduction to the Theory of Knowledge*, 3rd edn. London: Routledge.

———. 2011. *Rationality and Religious Commitment*. Oxford: Clarendon Press.

Barrett, J.L., 2007. Is the spell really broken? Bio-psychological explanations of religion and theistic belief. *Theology and Science*, 5(1), pp. 57–72.

———. 2008. Why Santa Claus is not a god. *Journal of Cognition and Culture*, 8(1–2), pp. 149–61.

———. 2009. Cognitive science, religion, and theology. In: J. Schloss and M. Murray (eds), *The Believing Primate: Scientific, Philosophical, and Theological Reflections on the Origin of Religion*. New York: Oxford University Press, pp. 76–99.

Bealer, G., 1998. Intuition and the autonomy of philosophy. In: M.R. DePaul and W. Ramsey (eds), *Rethinking Intuition*. Lanham, MD: Rowman & Littlefield, pp. 201–39.

Bergstrom, B., Moehlmann, B. and Boyer, P., 2006. Extending the testimony problem: evaluating the truth, scope, and source of cultural information. *Child Development*, 77(3), pp. 531–8.

Boyer, P., 2001. *Religion Explained: The Evolutionary Origins of Religious Thought*. New York: Basic Books.

Dawkins, R., 1991. Viruses of the mind. *Center for the Study of Complex Systems*. Available at: www.cscs.umich.edu/~crshalizi/Dawkins/viruses-of-the-mind.html.

Goldman, A.I., 1967. A causal theory of knowing. *Journal of Philosophy*, 64(12), pp. 357–72.

Huemer, M., 2005. *Ethical Intuitionism*. Basingstoke: Palgrave Macmillan.

Johnson, D.D.P. and Kruger, O., 2004. The good of wrath: supernatural punishment and the evolution of cooperation. *Political Theology*, 5(2), pp. 159–76.

Ketelaar, T., 2004. Lions, tigers and bears, oh God! How the ancient problem of predator detection may lie beneath the modern link between religion and horror. *Behavior and Brain Sciences*, 27, pp. 740–41.

Sosa, E., 1998. Minimal intuition. In: M.R. DePaul and W. Ramsey (eds), *Rethinking Intuition*. Lanham, MD. Rowman & Littlefield, pp. 257–69.

Sosis, R. and Alcorta, C., 2004. Is religion adaptive? *Behavior and Brain Sciences*, 27, pp. 748–9.

Sosis, R. and Bressler, E.R. 2003. Cooperation and commune longevity: a test of the costly signaling theory of religion. *Cross-Cultural Research*, 37(2), pp. 211–39.

Swinburne, R., 2004. *The Existence of God*, 2nd edn. Oxford: Oxford University Press.

Chapter 3

Whose Intuitions? Which Dualism?[1]

Steven Horst

Recent research in Cognitive Science of Religion (CSR) has produced what seem to be conflicting assessments of our concepts of and beliefs about supernatural agents such as God, spirits, and the soul. Paul Bloom has described both children and adults as "intuitive dualists" who understand humans and non-human animals to be composed of two entities: a body and a soul. But Pascal Boyer and Justin Barrett describe concepts of supernatural beings, including the soul, as "minimally counterintuitive," and trace their memorability and cultural transmission to this very feature.

After describing the accounts themselves, I shall address two issues. First, the crucial terms here—"dualism" and "intuition" (and their variants)—have been used in many ways in ordinary language, in philosophy, and in psychology. I shall attempt to bring greater philosophical clarity to the implicit use of these terms by researchers in CSR. Second, with the terminology clarified, I shall assess whether the two views are really as incompatible as the initial characterizations might suggest.

The Accounts

Several psychologists and anthropologists have recently suggested cognitive and developmental mechanisms whereby humans might acquire concepts of and beliefs about such supernatural[2] entities as God, gods, spirits, ghosts, and souls, and in the possibility of continued personal existence after bodily death. Such accounts are generally neutral on the questions of whether such beliefs are true

---

[1] This research was pursued with the help of a grant from the John Templeton Foundation and Oxford University's Cognition, Religion and Theology Project. Thanks to Stewart Guthrie, Paul Bloom, and Justin Barrett for reading drafts of this chapter.

[2] I recognize that this term is controversial in anthropology and has no equivalent in many languages and cultures. I have employed it here as the most efficient way of summarizing a category embracing God, gods, spirits, souls, etc.

or justified, and of whether anything in reality corresponds to such concepts. However, on these accounts, the possession of such beliefs and concepts can be explained without recourse either to special external causes (supernatural or otherwise) or to special cognitive or developmental mechanisms: the accounts treat the emergence of concepts of, and beliefs in, supernatural entities as explainable in terms of ordinary psychological (social, evolutionary) mechanisms studied in other contexts.

Stewart Guthrie and (Hyperactive) Agency Detection

Stewart Guthrie (1980; 1993) pioneered this line of research with his observation that it is both empirically evidenced and evolutionarily plausible that animals would develop mental modules that detect agents and/or traces of agency. Like any detection systems, such modules would be capable of producing false positives, and because the costs of false *negatives* in the form of failure to detect agents (e.g. predators) are often quite high, we might reasonably expect such systems to be highly sensitive, with low response thresholds, and hence biased towards false positives. In a later formulation of Guthrie's view, Barrett (2004) dubbed this the Hypersensitive Agency Detection Device theory, or HADD. HADD is thus an evolutionary hypothesis about how one or more modules sensitive to traces of agency might have arisen as adaptations, and why people around the world are so ready to see a world full of various types of agents.

HADD may explain why we are prone to attribute agency more often than it is present, but it does not explain why we conceive of, and form beliefs about, specifically *supernatural* agents. The hypersensitivity of an agency detection system that was an adaptation for predator detection, for example, might plausibly be expected to result not in beliefs about supernatural entities, but in the formation of beliefs that hidden predators of known types are nearby (a hidden tiger rather than a ghost or demon). Alternatively, it might trigger a general fight or flight reaction without producing particular beliefs at all. In neither case would it explain the formation of concepts of supernatural beings. Moreover, the very evolutionary plausibility of HADD makes it likely that agency-detecting mechanisms would not be confined to the human species, but would appear quite broadly in the animal kingdom. By contrast, to the best of our knowledge, concepts of supernatural agents are found uniquely among the human species, or at most are weakly evidenced only in our nearest relatives, the chimpanzees, as well.[3]

Paul Bloom, Core Knowledge Systems, and Intuitive Dualism

Developmental psychologist Paul Bloom (2004; 2007) reached conclusions similar to those of Guthrie through psychological rather than evolutionary considerations. Cognitive and developmental psychologists have recently suggested that the human mind possesses early-appearing and developmentally canalized "Core Knowledge Systems" (CKSs) that are attuned to particular domains: contiguous and cohesive solids, agents, numerosity, and spatial geometry. (For a literature review, see Spelke and Kinzler, 2007.) These different CKSs appear to operate independently and on distinct principles, activated by different types of stimuli and allowing distinct inferences and expectations. For example, Objects—capitalized to denote the proprietary sense of things conceptualized by the Core Object System—are understood as passing from rest to motion only through contact interaction, whereas Agents are understood to move of their own initiative. Moreover, these CKSs are dissociable: Core Agency representations can be activated without Core Object representations, and vice versa. While adult cognition involves cognitive bootstrapping beyond these CKSs, it is shaped by them, and we tend to return to them under pressure.

Bloom suggests that this dissociability provides a straightforward explanation of our propensity (already found in young verbal children) to believe that mind and experience continue after death, and also of our ability to conceive of beings other than ourselves that are Agents but not Objects. The dissociability allows us to think of something as an Agent without thinking of it as an Object, and when we do so, we apply only the rules of the Core Agency System and not the Core Object System. When a child does this, the expectations of the Agency System, but not the Object System, are activated. As a result, the child does not find it surprising when things constituted as Agents violate the rules of the Object System, such as by apparently moving from place to place without passing through the intervening spaces.

This provides a candidate explanation for how concepts of Agents that are not Objects—such as ghosts or Cartesian souls—might originate, and why such

---

[3] I am thinking here of the display male chimpanzees make to waterfalls and thunderstorms, which some have speculated might be seen as protoreligious. I take this as weak evidence for the possession of supernatural concepts by chimpanzees and it is at most a behavior found in a single species closely related to our own.

concepts need not cause cognitive dissonance or otherwise violate the child's intuitions about how things ought to behave. But Bloom also goes further than this, claiming that children (and adults) naturally think of humans and animals as each consisting of two things: a body and a soul or mind, and hence that we are "intuitive dualists." This seems to require more than the mere dissociability of Core Systems. Dissociability of Object and Agency Systems allows us to think "Agent" without thinking "Object," but Bloom's intuitive dualism, like Cartesian dualism, seems to involve the stronger claim that we cannot think of a thing as being *both* Object and Agent.

Boyer, Barrett and Minimally Counterintuitive Concepts

Anthropologist Pascal Boyer and psychologist Justin Barrett approach the explanation of supernatural concepts and beliefs in a more comprehensive way, considering not only psychological mechanisms that might underlie religious cognition and the evolutionary processes that might have formed them, but also how concepts of supernatural agents are transmitted and become entrenched through psychological and cultural processes (cf. Boyer, 1994; 2001; 2008; Barrett, 2004; 2008). Unlike Guthrie and Bloom, they assume that concepts of disembodied agents are the products of *alterations* performed upon pre-existing concepts of natural, embodied agents like humans or animals. At a very young age, we possess cognitive schemas for such things as animals and other humans, which include elements for representing their thoughts and actions, as well as their bodily states. Moreover, we possess not only species-level concepts like DOG, but also superordinate concepts such as ANIMAL, which Boyer calls *Ontological Categories*. These Ontological Categories, such as ANIMAL, PERSON, PLANT and INANIMATE_OBJECT, serve a further function as *templates* from which subordinate concepts (like DOG, OAK, or ROCK) can be formed.

Boyer suggests that we view Ontological Categories as analogous to *form documents* in which some information is filled in, but other spaces are left blank, to be filled in with particular types of information. The ANIMAL Category, for example, might encode such information as that animals have parents of the same species, have a species-typical physiology, eat some particular diet, move of their own power, pursue the things they want, and die. When a new animal kind is encountered, a concept for it is coined by copying the ANIMAL Category and filling in such things as physiological characteristics, manner of reproduction, diet, and means of locomotion as the information becomes available.

The Ontological Category of ANIMAL implies, by default, possession of both bodily properties (e.g., physiology) and psychological properties (e.g., desires and perhaps beliefs). However, it is possible to coin concepts from a Categorical template that *violate* one or more of its default rules. It is possible, for example, to form a concept of a bird whose parent is an elephant or one that does not die as other animals do, but renews its youth through self-immolation. Such concepts are, in Boyer's terminology, *counterintuitive*, in the specific sense that they violate rules of a particular Category. Moreover, Boyer and Barrett argue that there is a degree of counterintuitiveness that maximizes potential for memory and social transmission. Specifically, *minimally counterintuitive* concepts, which violate only one rule, are more memorable and more easily transmitted than concepts with more rule violations, or none at all.

The concepts of supernatural beings that figure in the world's religions, they argue, are comprised mostly of such minimally counterintuitive concepts: agents (ANIMALs or PERSONs) that lack bodies or possess super powers, PLANTs or INANIMATE_OBJECTS that can perceive human actions and/or act in ways that affect the welfare of human beings, etc. The fact that such concepts are minimally counterintuitive, they argue, gives them the right profile to be good candidates for memory and transmission. And the fact that minimal counterintuitiveness can come in many forms allows this explanation to be applicable across a wide variety of *particulars* of religious concepts. We can easily form such concepts through violations of single Categorical rules, and they are memorable and easily transmitted, but the particulars of *what* concepts are formed, and what beliefs are formed that employ those concepts, depend upon many additional factors, and hence we find a large degree of cultural variation, albeit within boundaries that are predictable from the Ontological Categories themselves.

An important feature of this account is that concepts of agents without bodies, such as God and the soul, are taken to be generated from a Categorical template (ANIMAL or PERSON) whose default assumptions include embodiment. Concepts of bodiless agents can be formed and used, but they start out and remain counterintuitive with respect to their Category of origin.

Summary of Views and Transition

We may summarize the views I have attributed thus.

Paul Bloom

> BLOOM1: Children possess distinct and dissociable mental models for thinking about Objects and Agents.
> BLOOM2: The dissociability of these systems allows children to conceive of Agents without also thinking of Objects and, in particular, to think of a particular thing as an Agent without also thinking of it as an Object.
> BLOOM3: Children think of individual animals and people as each consisting of *two things*: a body and a soul. Children are thus "*intuitive dualists.*"
> BLOOM4: The Core Systems for Object and Agent are not *lost* as we gain more adult forms of cognition, and so even adults have deeply rooted cognitive models which treat bodies and Agents as distinct things, with different types of properties, *even if* they have acquired *additional* models that treat, say, animals as having both mental and physical properties.

Pascal Boyer/Justin Barrett

> BOYER1: In addition to garden-variety concepts, we (children and adults) possess *Ontological Categories* such as ANIMAL which can serve as something like *schematic templates* for the generation of new concepts.
> BOYER2: Such schemas involve implicit knowledge, and license inferences that do not need to be learned separately for each generated concept, e.g., that animals move of their own volition, eat, have characteristic physiologies, die, and reproduce after their kind.
> BOYER3: However, it is possible to generate concepts that *violate* one or more of the expectations of the schema from which they were derived.
> BOYER4: Such concepts are then *counterintuitive* in the specific sense that they violate the categorical expectations of a particular Ontological Category.
> BOYER5: Ontological Categories like ANIMAL do not change, and hence,
> BOYER6: Counterintuitive concepts *remain* counterintuitive (at least with respect to their Category of origin).

BOYER7: *Minimally* counterintuitive concepts are particularly likely to gain a lasting place in the conceptual repertoire.
BOYER8: Supernatural concepts are minimally counterintuitive concepts.

These claims involve views on *dualism* and *intuitions*, two ideas that have substantial philosophical histories. Moreover, at least on the surface, the two theories seem to reach conflicting assessments regarding whether concepts of and beliefs in agents without bodies are "intuitive" or "counterintuitive." I hope, in the remainder of this chapter, to make first steps in bringing greater philosophical clarity to the debate.

Intuition

The word "intuition" has a long history in philosophy and psychology, with usages distinct both from one another and from those of ordinary language (cf. Horst, 2013 for a more extensive discussion). There is, however, a feature that unites most of them and that is crucial to our discussion here. Intuition is generally contrasted with explicit reasoning. Intuitive beliefs are those that simply "pop out" as self-evident, without our being able to trace back a chain of reasoning that produced or justified them. In early modern philosophy, "intuitive knowledge" was thus contrasted with demonstrative knowledge. And in contemporary cognitive psychology, we find a similar distinction between Kahneman's Type 1 and Type 2 processes (2011; see Table 3.1). This seems a natural construal of Bloom's claim that beliefs about Agents with Bodies are "intuitive": they arise spontaneously as we perceive and interpret the world rather than being products of deductive or hypothetical reasoning.

This literature is generally about beliefs rather than concepts, though the distinction might be extended to differentiate common-sense concepts acquired through inexplicit learning with those that are products of explicit theorizing. However, in ordinary speech, calling a concept "counterintuitive" often suggests something different: namely, that it strikes us as somehow peculiar or perhaps causes cognitive dissonance. While theoretical concepts sometimes have this feature (as in the cases of curved space or particles without determinate locations), they need not do so. This sense, which implies cognitive dissonance, seems to be more the sense in which Boyer and Barrett's account views supernatural concepts as "counterintuitive." And this usage might be extended to beliefs that either

Table 3.1 Dual System Theory. Characteristics of Kahneman's two types of processes. Derived from Kahneman, 2011

System 1	System 2
Unconscious reasoning	Conscious reasoning
Judgments based on intuition	Judgments based on critical examination
Processes information quickly	Processes information slowly
Hypothetical reasoning	Logical reasoning
Large capacity	Small capacity
Prominent in animals and humans	Prominent only in humans
Unrelated to working memory	Related to working memory
Operates effortlessly and automatically	Operates with effort and control
Unintentional thinking	Intentional thinking
Influenced by experiences, emotions, and memories	Influenced by facts, logic and evidence
Can be overridden by System 2	Used when System 1 fails to form a logical/acceptable conclusion
Prominent since human origins	Developed over time
Includes recognition, perception, orientation, etc.	Includes rule following, comparisons, weighing of options, etc.

(a) employ counterintuitive concepts or (b) join together two concepts in a fashion that produces the relevant kind of cognitive dissonance.

At first glance, at least, it seems as though the apparent disagreement between the two theories may be an illusion based on different uses of the word "intuitive" and its variants. We might thus expect there to be concepts and beliefs that are produced through inexplicit means, yet produce cognitive dissonance, and that are hence "intuitive" in the first sense but "counterintuitive" in the second. However, while all of the writers involved might acknowledge this possibility, they do not seem to agree on the question of whether supernatural concepts and beliefs are instances of it. On Bloom's view, children do *not* find anything odd about the idea of Agents without Bodies and adults at the very least *need* not do so. For Boyer and Barrett, however, the mind *does* treat such ideas as odd, and this perceived oddness is precisely what accounts for their memorability and easy transmission. Bloom thinks that the mind treats the concept of a soul as *routine*, whereas Boyer and Barrett think that the mind treats it as *peculiar*.

While I think that there is genuine disagreement here, we can also find deeper connections between the two accounts. One way to begin is with Boyer's observation that a concept is counterintuitive only with respect to something else: say, the concept of a ghost with respect to the Category HUMAN. One possibility this opens up, which I shall return to later, is that a concept might be counterintuitive with respect to one Category but not another. But, more basically, Boyer's account situates most of our concepts within a larger framework (in this case, superordinate Categories) that already encode a good deal of understanding about the world. When a person encounters a new type of animal, the ANIMAL category delineates things that must be true of it *qua* animal (either specifically or in the form of a blank slot that needs to be filled in—all animals eat *something*, but species have their own distinctive diets) and it at least implicitly excludes other possibilities. Similarly, the CKSs that underlie Bloom's account contain a robust set of expectations about how Objects and Agents "must" behave, and violations of these expectations trigger a kind of cognitive dissonance.

Each account thus assumes the existence of what we might, in very general terms, call *mental models* of particular domains of phenomena. Such models provide frameworks for representing particular kinds of things, properties, relations and changes, and license particular patterns of inference. They may thus be described as involving proprietary representational systems and inference rules. (It is a more complicated question as to whether their operation involves the *application* of inference rules or whether this is merely an instrumentally useful description.) And this, in turn, suggests an account of what makes some thoughts "intuitive" and others "counterintuitive." *A thought is intuitive if its truth is implied by the model.* Because it is simply "read off" the rules of the model, it seems obvious and perhaps even necessarily true, and does not require explicit cogitation. Moreover, it may be produced simply by the dynamic principles built into the model in its normal operation, and hence occurs spontaneously. Conversely, *a thought that violates rules of a model thereby causes cognitive dissonance and is experienced as counterintuitive.* There are, of course, a great number of thoughts that fall into neither category: thoughts that are permitted by the model but not required by it. In ordinary language, we might also tend to style such thoughts "intuitive" in the weak sense that they are *not counterintuitive*. But for the purposes of careful analysis, it is better that we find some third term. *I shall thus say that a thought is permissible with respect to a model M if it can be formulated in the representational system employed by M, and is neither intuitive nor counterintuitive with respect to M.*

The Counterintuitiveness of Agents without Bodies in Barrett and Boyer

One distinctive claim of the Boyer/Barrett account is that supernatural concepts are minimally counterintuitive, in the sense that they violate only one expectation (or at most a very few) of the Ontological Category from which they are derived. The ANIMAL Category has default settings anticipating that things to which it is applied will be both thinking and embodied. Denial of the first results in a concept like ZOMBIE. Denial of the second results in concepts of SOUL, GHOST, GOD, ANGEL, etc.

It is less than completely clear how such supernatural concepts relate to other things in a person's conceptual space. Boyer and Barrett suggest that they remain connected in some fashion to their original Ontological Category and hence remain counterintuitive (that is, counterintuitive-relative-to-that-Category). This, however, involves an empirical hypothesis whose status as such may be hidden by a verbal ambiguity. In one sense, it is obvious that if a concept is *ever* counterintuitive with respect to a Category, it is so *always*. In other words, given the precise contents of both concept and Category, whether the concept violates Categorical rules is a matter of logical/semantic fact. But it is quite another question whether a concept remains somehow *psychologically* tethered to a Category that served as its template.

Consider, for example, the concept WHALE. Before Aristotle, everyone assumed that whales were fish, so perhaps the concept WHALE was originally formed using the superordinate concept FISH as a template. Perhaps when Aristotle first observed that whales breathe through their blowholes rather than gills, his concept WHALE briefly became a counterintuitive variation on FISH. But what ultimately happened was that the concept was reassigned to a different superordinate concept, MAMMAL. It seems plausible to me that at some point, Aristotle's concept WHALE was no longer *psychologically* tethered to FISH, though of course the fact that it contains the information that whales breathe air still makes it logically/semantically counterintuitive with respect to FISH. Similarly, one might initially assume that coral is a kind of INANIMATE_OBJECT, such as a rock, but then learn that it is made up of many small animals. Arguably the concept CORAL is then transplanted from one Ontological Category to another.

It seems a plausible hypothesis that, for some individuals and some cultures, some or all of their supernatural concepts may seem to form a class of their own, to be cut free from their original Categorical templates, and understood to be members of some distinct superordinate class or classes, such as GODS, SPIRITS, SOULS, or indeed SUPERNATURAL_ENTITIES. Like Boyer and Barrett's proposal to the contrary, this is an empirical hypothesis, and thus finding a way to test these hypotheses constitutes a research agenda for the psychologists and anthropologists.

The extensions of Ontological Categories would seem to overlap. There is very likely an Ontological Category that applies only to humans and not other animals. But the categories HUMAN (or PERSON) and ANIMAL are both applicable to individual human beings. (We do sometimes contrast human/animal, man/beast, and the like. But arguably this is a result of a cognitive illusion based on the recognition of distinct Categories. When we think about the Categories, as opposed to the instances, we are disposed to assume that the extensions are disjoint.) Moreover, at some point, we have a superordinate concept like PERSON that is applied paradigmatically to humans, but could also be applied to intelligent aliens and machines, or to ghosts, demons, or other spirits that have intellects and personalities but are not organic.

The implicit ontology of the Boyer/Barrett psychology is neither materialist nor dualist. It is not materialist because it allows for concepts of and belief in beings that do not have bodies. Moreover, the Ontological Category of ANIMAL is decidedly *not* the same thing as that of material substance in materialist philosophy. (If anything, it is closer to Aristotelian metaphysics, though Aristotle viewed each species of living thing as a distinct substance kind, even though it has several levels of superordinate categories above it.) The implicit ontology is not substance dualist because it allows for things (e.g., living humans and some non-human animals) to be both thinking things and material things, whereas substance dualism holds that minds and bodies form two mutually exclusive classes of things. Moreover, some of the supernatural concepts seem to require that one and the same thing can undergo a change in its status, as when a living person becomes a ghost or ancestor spirit. And, indeed, not all of the supernatural concepts are of agents without bodies: some (like tree or river spirits) result from *attaching* the idea of thinking to an Ontological Category (PLANT or NATURAL OBJECT) whose default settings disallow thinking.

The relation between the Boyer/Barrett psychology and *property* dualism is more complicated. It is complicated, in part, because of the unresolved question of the status of learned superordinate categories like SUPERNATURAL_BEING. But it is also complicated by the fact that Boyer and Barrett seem to accept the idea that, in addition to Folk Biology, children also possess a Folk Psychology or Theory of Mind and a Folk Physics. It is unclear whether they think that these, like Folk Biology, should be viewed as having distinctive ontological categories (MIND, MATERIAL_OBJECT) and, if so, what the relation of these might be to one another and to that of ANIMAL. Given that the extensions of MIND and MATERIAL_OBJECT each overlap with that of ANIMAL, the implicit ontology of these classes should not be viewed as a substantival metaphysics with mutually exclusive sortal categories. (The alternative would be to hold that children employ several conflicting ontologies.) But it does invite the interpretation that our *understandings* of animals, material things, and minds come in the form of separate ways of *representing* different types of *properties* of things, each of which has its own characteristic relations and inferential potential. This possibility, however, would seem to call for more experimental exploration into such questions as whether priming a subject on one Category disposes him or her to reject the properties of another Category.

The Boyer/Barrett psychology is also unlike most philosophical metaphysics in that it treats the characteristic properties of a Category (or of a non-Categorical schema) as *defeasible* rather than as necessary essential properties of things in that Category. This is not necessarily a problem for the theory, as it may well be that it is traditional metaphysics that has pursued the wrong path in concentrating on necessary and sufficient conditions. Alternatively, theoretical metaphysics may be substantially different from folk classification precisely in this regard—that is, a regimentation of the criteria for inclusion in a class from defeasible default values to necessary and sufficient conditions may be a characteristic mark of the transition from folk classification to philosophical metaphysics.

Officially, Boyer holds: (1) that counterintuitiveness is always relativized to a Category (or perhaps to non-Categorical schema); and (2) that supernatural concepts need to be explained through a multi-factor account. Nonetheless, one might worry that the emphasis on minimal counterintuitiveness, combined with the claim that supernatural concepts remain connected to, and counterintuitive with respect to, a single Ontological Category, may bias the account toward treating supernatural concepts as "counterintuitive" in a more global sense, as things that are abidingly "odd" in ways that other concepts are not. In particular, to the extent that the mind possesses separate resources for Theory of Mind or Bloom's Core Agency, which do not require embodiment, it seems likely that the status of a particular concept as *seeming* intuitive or counterintuitive may depend on how the subject has recently been primed. Likewise, if supernatural concepts arise *after* Theory of Mind is in place, where is the justification for holding that a given concept, in the mind of a given child, was based on the Category ANIMAL rather than MIND? Perhaps Boyer and Barrett believe that Theory of Mind is itself descended from the Ontological Category ANIMAL, but both this and the question of the etiology of a given concept in a given mind would seem to be empirical questions that I, at least, have not seen satisfactorily addressed.

Bloom and Intuitive Dualism

Bloom claims that children (and adults) are "intuitive dualists," and appears to use the terms "dualist" and "Cartesian dualist" more or less interchangeably. This, of course, should not be taken to mean that either babies or indeed most adults understand and endorse the fine points of Cartesian metaphysics. Rather, it should be taken as a claim that the implicit ontology of our way of representing human beings is, as it were, a psychologized counterpart of Descartes' formal metaphysical views. However, we must at the very least note the familiar philosophical distinction between substance dualism and property dualism. And, indeed, this distinction will prove significant in the analysis of Bloom's claims. (For a more detailed critique of Bloom's dualism and that of Descartes, see Hodge, 2008.)

The central theoretical supposition of Bloom's account is that the Core Agency and Core Object Systems are dissociable, and hence that they present no barriers to conceiving of something as an Agent but not an Object. This does, indeed, provide an explanation as to why concepts of and belief in agents without bodies need not cause any cognitive dissonance—that is, why they might be permissible rather than counterintuitive. In addition, it suggests the possibility (incompatible with Bloom's own stated view) that the ability to identify things that trigger the Object and Agency systems as *the selfsame object* may need to be *learned*, with an early stage at which the two systems operate independently without binding into a single object-representation. Moreover, the separate inferential patterns that reside in the two systems would seem to result in something akin to a property dualism, at least insofar as the inferential relations for mental and physical properties are independent.

However, Bloom's claim that children are *substance* or *Cartesian* dualists goes beyond this, and is not entailed by the core elements of the theory. Substance dualism claims that a single thing cannot be both a soul and a material object. Similarly, Bloom claims that people *think of* people and animals as consisting of two separate things—body and soul—and hence implies that we cannot think of the same thing as being both thinking and embodied. In other words, both souls without bodies and material objects without souls would be intuitive, and things that have *both* mental and bodily properties would be counterintuitive. (Indeed, it is not clear that, in Bloom's view, they would even be conceivable.) Yet this is not entailed by the Core Systems account. Dissociability allows for concepts like HUMAN to be *permissible* rather than either intuitive or counterintuitive.

The dissociability of the Agency and Object systems is *compatible* with the possibility that people can *also* bind their representations together as representations of a single object, even if they *need not* do so. The logic of dissociability is:

Not(necessarily(Mx → Bx)) and not(necessarily(Bx → Mx))

(Where Mx = "x has mental properties" and Bx = "x has bodily properties".) But the logic of substance dualism is:

Necessarily((Mx → not (Bx)) and (Bx → not (Mx)))

In particular, "Mx and Bx" is compatible with dissociability, but not with substance dualism.

Second, even if it is not possible to bind together representations of the Agency and Object systems as representations of the selfsame object, it may nonetheless be the case that, past a very early developmental stage, humans gain *other* representational frameworks which *do* allow representations of things that can have both physical and mental properties. Indeed, if there is a Categorical representation of animals or human beings whose default expectation is that they are both thinking and embodied, this possibility is confirmed.

Bloom may nevertheless be correct in saying that children and perhaps even adults (always) think of humans and animals as consisting of two things—a mind and a body—even if this is not a straightforward consequence of dissociable Core Knowledge systems. With respect to adults, however, this claim strikes me as implausible. I at least *seem* to be able to think of the same person as both thinking and embodied. What seems more plausible to me is the weaker claim that in adulthood we continue to have modes of thinking in which we can think of each type of property without the other, and that this may bias us towards thinking of mind and body as distinct entities, at least under certain conditions. This is compatible with our also having modes of thinking that allow us to think of humans and animals as simultaneously thinking and embodied. Indeed, I tend to share Boyer and Barrett's view that Folk Biology *requires* us to think of animals and humans in this way—that is, when we think of them *as* animals or *as* humans. What would be needed to establish Bloom's stronger claim would be experiments that debunk all claims to the effect that humans *ever* think of humans or animals as at once thinking and embodied.

One clarification that might help to untangle the problem is the following: there are really several separate questions here:

1. Can we think of an individual as being both Agent and Object *within a single Core System*? The answer to this, given the characterization of the systems, is *no*.
2. Can we simultaneously represent what is in fact the same individual as an Agent (using the Agency system) and as an Object (using the Object system) (that is, without recognition that the two systems are representing one and the same thing)? Nothing in the characterizations of the systems either implies or precludes this.

Can we do the same while also binding the two representations together *as* representations of the selfsame individual? I think the answer to this is, quite plausibly, *yes*. There would seem to be two ways in which this might take place. First, it might take place through something like the neural phase binding through which we connect such things as color and shape information in perception. Second, even if Core Systems are modular, they might provide *outputs* that can then be connected in a domain-general mental faculty that has resources for logical connection (for example, a language-like faculty such as Fodor's "Language of Thought").

Questions for Further Research

The preceding considerations suggest some questions that should be of interest both to psychologists and to philosophers.

The idea that we possess several dissociable systems for conceptualizing and reasoning about the world, and the further idea that these systems may either have different (perhaps incompatible) implicit ontologies, or at least bias the mind toward different ontological assumptions, are quite alien to the ways that philosophers tend to go about metaphysics (and sometimes, more problematically, the ways we assume that the mind always thinks about the world) in terms of standard logics and a global Language of Thought. It also raises questions about whether any of us really possesses something like a single, comprehensive, consistent world-view. Such issues are, of course, relevant to religious cognition. But they are not unique to it. They may arise from the interactions of such species-typical systems as Core Knowledge, Folk Biology, Folk Physics, and Folk Psychology. And they may be found in the apparent mismatches between scientific theories like General Relativity and Quantum Mechanics as well. Moreover, the possibilities thus raised bear a distinct resemblance to many philosophical paradoxes, in which different ways of thinking about a matter lead to different, and sometimes contradictory, conclusions. I have hopes that discussions of a cognitive architecture containing multiple mental models may shed light on many such puzzles. (For initial discussions of such a Cognitive Pluralism, see Horst, 2007; 2011.)

While the Core Knowledge hypothesis and the Folk Theory hypothesis each posit domain-specific forms of cognition, the relationship between the two could be made clearer. Core Knowledge has generally been supposed to be evidenced in studies of children much younger than those who demonstrate mastery of Folk Biology or Folk Psychology. There is a possible methodological difficulty in drawing too firm a conclusion from this, as tests for the latter involve language. However, the failure of three year olds who can communicate with language to pass the false belief attribution test suggests that there are at least some aspects of the Folk Theories that are later-appearing than Core Systems, even though they seem to be developmentally canalized (Perner and Ruffman, 2005). But what is the relationship between, say, Folk Psychology and Core Agency? Does the one *replace* the other? Or do they exist side by side, as I have suggested here? Moreover, is Folk Psychology achieved by bootstrapping up from Core Agency?

Another set of questions concerns the logical and semantic relations between different models. To what extent does any pair of them have conflicting implicit rules? It seems important to Boyer's theory, for example, that the ANIMAL Category has default assumptions of both thinking and embodiment. Yet the child also possesses a Folk Physics that attributes physical but not mental properties (yet can be applied to living beings), and a Folk Psychology that may not encode a need for bodily properties (which can be applied to humans and some non-human animals). The details of the models imputed to children matter here for our ability to assess what kind of "intuitive ontology" to attribute to children. The fact that the history of philosophy contains many recurrences of a few basic types of ontologies—materialist, Aristotelian/vitalist, dualist, idealist—may turn out to have an explanation in the stock of basic ways of thinking about the world that we are endowed with through canalized developmental processes. We may, in fact, all possess mental building blocks that, when developed in particular ways, dispose us toward more than one ontological view. This suggests that there might be an important avenue of research into how priming may affect manifestations of "intuitive ontologies," and likewise how particular learning pathways might be more or less conducive to particular ontological biases.

Another question, mentioned above, is that of what happens to a concept that starts out as counterintuitive with respect to the Category from which it is formed when it becomes cognitively entrenched and routinely used, and when several such concepts seem to form a natural class, like SPIRIT. Logically speaking, they remain counterintuitive with respect to their parent Category. But does that Category remain, psychologically, as the superordinate Category for them? Or is there, as it were, a transfer of residence to a different Categorical neighborhood?

Immanuel Kant, the great-grandfather of the cognitivist turn in philosophy, was interested in the epistemological implications of that turn—particularly in how it might unveil possibilities of synthetic *a priori* knowledge on the one hand and dialectical illusion on the other. It seems natural for philosophers to ask whether today's more empirically informed cognitive accounts lend themselves to such questions as well. However, a modernized Kantian inquiry would have to take note of two important ways in which contemporary cognitive theories differ from Kant's. First, whereas Kant's account of cognitive architecture posited a single faculty of understanding, characterized by the 12 categories, and applicable to all thoughts, the theories we have seen here involve multiple domain-specific ways of thinking, with their own (sometimes conflicting) internal rules. Second, these various models appear in a developmental order, and it is clear that at least some of them approximate the world only very roughly.

References

Barrett, J.L., 2004. *Why Would Anyone Believe in God?* Walnut Creek, CA: Alta Mira Press.

———. 2008. The naturalness of religious concepts: an emerging cognitive science of religion. In: P. Antes, A. Geertz, and R.R. Wayne (eds), *New Approaches to the Study of Religion: Textual, Comparative, Sociological, and Cognitive Approaches*. Berlin: Walter de Gruyter, pp. 401–18.

Barrett, J.L., Richert, R.A. and Driesenga, A., 2001. God's beliefs versus mother's: the development of natural and non-natural agent concepts. *Child Development*, 71(1), pp. 50–65.

Bloom, P., 2004. *Descartes' Baby: How the Science of Child Development Explains What Makes Us Human*. New York: Basic Books.

———. 2007. Religion is natural. *Developmental Science*, 10, pp. 147–51.

Boyer, P., 1994. *The Naturalness of Religious Ideas*. Berkeley, CA: University of California Press.

———. 2001. *Religion Explained: The Evolutionary Origins of Religious Thought*. New York: Basic Books.

———. 2008. Religion: bound to believe? *Nature*, 455, pp. 1038–9.

Guthrie, S., 1980. A cognitive theory of religion. *Current Anthropology*, 21(2), pp. 181–203.

———. 1993. *Faces in the Clouds: A New Theory of Religion*. New York: Oxford University Press.

Hodge, M., 2008. Descartes' mistake: how afterlife beliefs challenge the assumption that humans are intuitive Cartesian substance dualists. *Journal of Cognition and Culture*, 8, pp. 387–415.

Horst, S., 2007. *Beyond Reduction: Philosophy of Mind and Post-reductionist Philosophy of Science*. New York: Oxford University Press.

———. 2011. *Laws, Mind and Free Will*. Cambridge, MA: MIT Press.

———. 2013. Notions of intuition in the cognitive science of religion. *The Monist*, 95(2), pp. 377–98.

Kahneman, D., 2011. *Thinking, Fast and Slow*. New York: Farrar, Straus & Giroux.

Perner, J. and Ruffman, T., 2005. Infants' insight into the mind: how deep? *Science*, 308, pp. 214–16.

Spelke, E.S. and Kinzler, K.D., 2007. Core knowledge. *Developmental Science*, 10(1), pp. 89–96.

Chapter 4
Explaining Religion at Different Levels: From Fundamentalism to Pluralism

Aku Visala

It is understandable that those who advocate a novel scientific approach to some phenomenon have high hopes and expectations for its usefulness and explanatory power. This is the case with writers in the Cognitive Science of Religion (CSR). Candidly speaking, we can say that some CSR writers are adamant in proving that their approach is more 'scientific' than other approaches to religion and that it will finally solve age-old mysteries about religion by turning them into 'empirically solvable problems'.

Pascal Boyer, a pioneer of CSR, displays this enthusiasm when he writes in *Religion Explained* that:

> There cannot be a magic bullet to explain the existence and common features of religion, as the phenomenon is the result of aggregate relevance – that is, of successful activation of a whole variety of mental systems. Indeed, the activation of a panoply of systems in the mind explains the very existence of religious concepts *and* their cultural success *and* the fact that people find them plausible *and* the fact that not everyone finds them so *and* the way religion appeared in human history *and* its persistence in the context of modern science. (Boyer, 2001, p. 298)

In this one passage, he claims that CSR is capable of answering the following questions about religion:

1. Why religious concepts exist in the first place.
2. Why religious concepts are so widespread in human populations.
3. Why people find religious concepts plausible and hold them true.
4. Why some people do not find them plausible and do not hold them true.
5. How religion emerged.

6. Why religion persists even in modern societies where modern science provides 'a more efficient way of thinking about the world' (Boyer, 2001, p. 49).

According to Boyer, all these questions are not only answered by CSR, but the answers are more comprehensive and scientific than all previous answers. Furthermore, he maintains that whereas these questions used to be mysteries, they can now be addressed as scientific problems that can be resolved through empirical study (Boyer, 2001, p. 48). Finally, he thinks that these questions can be answered by invoking psychological mechanisms. It is our cognitive apparatus and its interactions with the environment that explain why we have certain ideas instead of others.

Even for a book aimed at popular audiences (as *Religion Explained* is), these are bold claims. It is clear that CSR has made good empirical progress in the last 10 years or so since the publication of *Religion Explained*. New studies are constantly being published and many of the hypotheses advocated by Boyer in 2001 have been replaced by more sophisticated ones in 2014. But even today, we have no guarantee that all of the above outlined questions will be answered by attention to the cognitive underpinnings of religion. Why even think that they can be answered with the tools of CSR?

At least one reason, it seems to me, is a commitment to the idea that cultural (and hence also religious) phenomena have sufficient psychological or cognitive causes. If cultures and religions are 'nothing more than' sets of mental and public representations, as many cognitive anthropologists and scholars of religion claim, their features must be explicable in terms of cognitive processes and their environments. This is indeed what Boyer and others seem to be saying: given naturalism, we should believe that there is nothing more to culture than psychological phenomena. In other words, naturalism cannot allow cultures or religions to float free from individual human minds that entertain them. Thus, we should maintain that cultures and religions consist of mental representations that are in turn explained by the various ways in which our cognitive systems process information.

In what follows, I will be arguing that even if it is the case that cultures and religions consist only of mental representations, it does not mean that explanations of cultures and religions should always be given at the level of cognitive processes that produces these representations.

My argument will proceed in two stages: first, I will reconstruct the former view – a view I will be calling *Explanatory Fundamentalism* (EF); second, I will present some standard critiques of such a view and point to a possible alternative that I call *Explanatory Pluralism* (EP). My proposed alternative framework grows out of views that have already been discussed by some CSR researchers themselves (e.g., Pyysiäinen, 2009). This is especially the case with respect to Robert McCauley and his explanatory pluralism. The argument is that instead of adhering to some robust naturalist metaphysics, we should adopt a more pragmatic approach to explaining religion. Causal explanations do indeed float relatively free of the material constituents of their targets and explainers. This makes the EF commitment to reduction of all causal explanations of culture to its lower-level components (mental representations) dubious.

Before I go on, one caveat: what follows is a distinctively philosophical exercise, that is, a meta-level analysis of some possible philosophical underpinnings of CSR. At no point will I argue that there is something fundamentally wrong with CSR theories themselves. Instead, my argument is that although some of the CSR research might be motivated by and interpreted in terms of EF, EF has certain philosophical problems and that there are plausible alternatives available. One of these plausible alternatives is EP, which both satisfies the aims of the CSR and avoids at least some of the problems of EF.

Explanation: The Basics

The basic question to be addressed here is a seemingly simple one, namely, what is it to explain religious phenomena causally? Those who are familiar with the history of the study of religion can easily come up with different answers. Some have attempted to explain religious phenomena as encounters with the sacred, while others have referred to the social function of religion and, finally, some have dismissed explanation altogether and claimed that religion needs to be understood rather than explained (Preus, 1996).

We can begin by noting that explanation is a two-part relation. With respect to any given explanation, we can ask the following questions:

1. What is being explained (target)?
2. What does the explaining (explainer)?
3. How is the explainer connected to the target?

The target of an explanation in the case of religion is not a simple object, but a set of phenomena conceptualised in a certain way. As many representatives of CSR also admit, religion as a category is too broad and vague to be explained as a whole (Boyer, 1994, pp. 29–37). Thus, explaining religion requires concepts that we can use to slice 'religion' into smaller and better-defined bits. We can call these conceptualisations of the target *explanatory frames*.[1]

In CSR, the explanatory frame with respect to religion is constructed in terms of psychological and cognitive theories. Boyer suggests that we should not presume that 'religion' is a homogeneous category at all, but rather a collection of different kinds of activities, events, concepts and representations. As there can be no single explanation for representations of things as diverse as rituals, god-concepts, religious specialists, misfortune and so on, there cannot be a single 'theory of religion'. It is not an entity called 'religion' that is being explained here, but rather certain features of human psychology and behaviour. Ideas about non-observable agents and their communications with ordinary humans, beliefs that a non-physical component of a person survives death, and rituals associated with non-observable agents are all cross-culturally widespread in human populations. This, of course, does not constitute a definition of religion, nor does it aim to do so, but rather it gives us a set of psychologically identified phenomena for the explanatory endeavour to begin to address.

Questions 2 and 3 sometimes overlap, but it is useful to distinguish them conceptually. As I mentioned earlier, explainers such as experiences of the sacred and social structures have been proposed. In CSR, the explainers are the cognitive mechanisms underpinning all transmission of cultural information, including religious information. By their relatively invariant operations across different cultures, they drive cultural and religious information towards certain forms. They are the factors that drive the selection process of cultural evolution.

This leads naturally to the question as to how the explainer explains the target. Generally speaking, the most common case is a singular causal explanation where the explainer event makes the target event more likely or even necessary. In such cases, the *relata* are events and the causal relationship can be either necessary or more or less statistical. But in the case of CSR, we are not talking about singular causal explanations. What is being explained by CSR is a general human disposition to prefer religious concepts and information by invoking certain features in the operation of pan-human cognitive systems. In this sense, CSR explanations resemble psychological explanations: they do not refer to singular events, but rather to mechanisms with parts that produce the target disposition.[2]

---

[1] The notion of explanatory frame comes from Garfinkel, 1981.
[2] For an account of psychological explanation along these lines, see Cummins, 2000.

Explanatory Fundamentalism

Now that we have an overview of how CSR conceptualises its target phenomenon and how it plans to explain it, we can look more closely into what kind of desiderata writers in CSR have for good explanations. Generally speaking, they emphasise something they call 'causal explanation', but their formulations of it are relatively vague. Consider the following passage where Boyer criticises hermeneutical approaches to religion. He writes:

> The hermeneutic stance is based on the fundamental premise that phenomena of meaning cannot be the object of explanation because they cannot be causally related to other, notably physical phenomena. Against this framework, the 'naturalised' view of cultural phenomena is based, precisely, on the assumption that 'meanings', or in less metaphysical terms, thought events and processes, are the consequence and manifestation of physical phenomena. (Boyer, 1993, p. 8)

Here the contrast is between 'thought' as independent of physical causes and 'thought' as a product of the physical operations of the brain. A causal account of thinking would therefore explain how human thoughts are caused by the operations of cognitive systems in human brains. It is the connection between the mind and the brain that makes causal explanation of thought, culture and religion possible.

Later Boyer continues:

> What is new about the cognitive science 'paradigm' is that it makes at the least the *principle* of the connection intelligible, by observing that the rule-directed manipulation of tokens of abstract symbols by machines of whatever nature (mechanical, electronic or biological) can simulate some regularities in thought processes. In other words, the shift to 'physicalist' or materialist interpretation of cognition is made possible, because cognitive science has at least a minimal 'causal story' to explain how thought processes can be actualised in material processes, as well as some practical implementations of that story. (Boyer, 1993, p. 9)

Boyer's argument is directed against those who think that psychology or biology has no explanatory relevance whatsoever with respect to human culture and behaviour. Cognitive science can explain thinking because our physical brains cause thinking. Although Boyer is quite cautious in his claim that 'cognitive science has at least a minimal causal story', he seems to have in mind a certain explanatory frame. This explanatory frame conceptualises the target of its explanation (thinking) and the explainer (brain) and their connection (some physical mechanism) in terms that are compatible with *physicalism*. By physicalism, I mean here something like the following claim: everything that exists is composed of entities and processes that can be described and explained by ideal physical science. From this it follows that all explanations are either clearly physical explanations or reducible to such in one way or another. In what follows, I will be calling this the *physicalist constraint for causal explanation* (PCE).

Compared to Scott Atran, Boyer's remarks look merely suggestive. Atran also insists that the correct way to conceptualise religion and explain it is in terms of PCE. He writes that:

> Naturalism in cognitive anthropology describes the attempt to causally locate the commonsense objects of study – cultures – inside the larger network of scientific knowledge. This approach posits no special phenomena, ontologies, causes, or laws beyond those of ordinary material objects and their inter-relationships. It studies the structure and content of representations, both private and public, and their variously patterned distributions within and between human populations. (Atran, 2002, p. 10)

The PCE can be clearly seen here: it is assumed that there are natural 'ontologies, causes, or laws' of 'normal material objects' that contrast with purportedly vague cultural or social phenomena. A proper causal explanation of any given socio-cultural phenomenon should proceed in terms of the PCE. This leads to the replacement of various explanatory frames of the socio-cultural sciences with the explanatory frame of *ideal* natural sciences.

Later Atran develops the same theme further:

> Cultures and religions do not exist apart from the individual minds that constitute them and the environments that constrain them, any more than biological species and varieties exist independently of the individual organisms that compose them and the environments that conform them. They are not well-bounded systems of definite clusters of beliefs, practices, and artifacts, but more or less regular distributions of causally connected thoughts, behaviors, material products, and environmental objects. To naturalistically understand what 'cultures' are is to describe and explain the material causes responsible for reliable differences in these distributions. (Atran, 2002, p. 10)

Here again we can see the tendency to reduce relevant explanatory factors to the constitution of the target of the explanation and the explainer. The argument seems to go like this: since cultures and religions are ultimately not 'entities' outside the mind and the environment where the mind is situated, the explainers of cultures and religions must be something material in human minds and their environments.

To be fair, there are at least two ways to interpret the remarks of Boyer and Atran. According to the first interpretation, what is being argued for here is simply that the results of cognitive sciences in general and cognitive psychology in particular might be relevant for explaining some general tendencies in cultural evolution and such an approach cannot be ruled out *a priori*. If this is what is being argued, then I can see no problem with it. What I will be saying about EP will simply elaborate upon and deepen what Boyer and Atran are saying already. But it seems to me that a stronger argument is (at least implicitly) being made. According to this argument, as we have seen, there are sufficient psychological causes for all facts about cultural evolution and those causes can be discovered by cognitive science. This stronger argument is the one that I will seek to criticise.

Naturalisation in the Making

A philosopher might ask where this emphasis on 'psychological causes' comes from. There seems to be an underlying assumption here that has to do with the connection of the target of an explanation and the explainer. The assumption is that the explainer is connected to its target via a chain of physically describable connections. That is, there must be some kind of 'push-pull' physical interaction at work in causal explanation. If cultures and religions consist of representations in the human mind and the mind is composed of the physical brain, then cultures and religions are to be explained by the physical interactions going on between the brain and its physical environment, that is, psychological causes.

This emphasis on PCE and material causes seems to be motivated by fear of 'vague' entities or 'higher-level' causal laws that do not fit neatly into physicalist ontology. The assumption seems to be that socio-cultural sciences are populated by such non-physicalist entities and a kind of 'scientific reform movement' is needed to put things back in their proper place.[3]

This scientific reform seems to be motivated by a philosophical programme that I will be calling *strict naturalism*.[4] In short, the basic idea is that the world

---

[3] For criticisms of CSR along these lines, see, e.g., Cho and Squier, 2008a; 2008b.

[4] Sometimes also called ontological naturalism, reductive (or eliminative) physicalism, reductive naturalism or hard naturalism.

is a physically closed system and thus everything in it (including religion) can be sufficiently explained in terms of physics or terms reducible to physics. The natural sciences provide us with knowledge of these physical causes and effects: all other forms of inquiry are either reducible to the sciences or suffer elimination.[5] With respect to religion and the study of religion, this programme requires that religion must have an explanation in terms of natural sciences (or an explanation that is reducible to natural sciences). It also includes the idea that academic disciplines dealing with human culture, societies, behaviours and religions must be unified with the natural sciences with respect to methods and ontological assumptions.

CSR writers seldom make such wide-ranging philosophical claims, although they can be implicit in their works, as we have seen. Others, however, have been more explicit. Edward Slingerland, for instance, claims that the study of religion should adopt a more naturalistic attitude than before because social constructivism, with which the contemporary study of religion has been associated, has made the study of religion parochial and uninteresting to scientists (Slingerland, 2008a; 2008b). Social constructivism is mistaken, Slingerland argues (along the lines of Boyer and others), because it implies that social and mental realms are causally independent of natural realms, such as physics and biology. Slingerland's antidote is the idea that human beings are physically constituted: human thoughts and mental life are physical events in the brain and as such are susceptible to the causal explanations of biology and psychology. For Slingerland, Darwinism is the key to providing a proper foundation for the study of religion: because our bodies and minds are the products of evolution, the products of our minds, that is, ideas and cultural artefacts, are the products of evolution as well. Slingerland thus calls for the *embodiment* of the humanities and a rejection of the implicit dualism between mind and body. It follows from this that the study of religion should work towards *vertical integration*,[6] namely, unifying scientific knowledge under a single causal and mechanistic scheme. This unification would also entail that our 'ideal science' ought not to contain any intentional or socio-cultural causes.

Consider also the following passage in which Dan Sperber, a key influence on both Boyer's and Atran's theoretical stances, reflects on the notion of causal explanation. According to him, an explanation is:

---

[5] On varieties of naturalism, see Kitcher, 1992; Rosenberg, 1996; Flanagan, 2006.

[6] The idea of vertical integration (or conceptual integration) was coined by the evolutionary psychologists Leda Cosmides and John Tooby. See Cosmides, Tooby and Barkow, 1992, pp. 1–6.

mechanistic when it analyses a complex set of causal relationships as an articulation of more elemental causal relationships. It is naturalistic to the extent that there is good ground to assume that these elementary relationships could themselves be further analysed mechanistically down to some level of description at which their natural character would be wholly unproblematic. (Sperber, 1996, p. 98)

The idea seems to be that 'higher-level' causal relationships are problematic from a scientific point of view and that there is an 'elemental level of causal relationships' that can be used as a basis for analysing the more problematic relationships. In other words, there are 'fundamental causal relationships' that are examined in natural sciences and 'problematic causal relationships' that are ultimately dependent on these elemental relationships if they exist at all. So not only is there a fundamental level of description of physical reality from which all other descriptions are ultimately derived, but the actual explanatory work is done by this fundamental level. Presumably, if an otherwise explanatory theory in some 'higher-level' discipline is not analysable in terms of some 'lower-level' discipline, then this constitutes a *prima facie* case against the 'higher-level' theory.

Problems for Explanatory Fundamentalism

Now, there are several problems with EF. I am not saying that EF is impossible to defend, but rather I am saying that CSR is not obliged to adopt it. However, if CSR writers (or others) want to commit themselves to EF, they should be prepared to give a philosophical defence of it, not simply assume it to be true.

The biggest problem with PCE and EF is that they are unable to identify those causal relationships that are relevant for explaining a given phenomenon. For each given phenomenon to be explained, we have numerous physical interactions that are irrelevant for the purposes of explanation. What we want is not a description of all physical interactions that temporally precede the effect and contribute to its emergence, but rather an account of *explanatorily relevant* causes. We need an explanatory account that describes those causes we need to identify, that is, those that are relevant for answering our question.

Let us take a singular causal explanation of an event as an example. Suppose that there is a car crash. If we ask why the car crashed, a decent answer might be that the car crashed because the driver was trying to avoid hitting a cat on the road and hit a tree instead. Given that there actually was a cat on the road, this sounds like a perfectly good explanation for the car crash. Now the fundamentalist will want to say that this is all fine for the time being, but *ultimately* what causes the car to crash are the physical interactions of the physical constituents of the cat, the car, the environment and the driver preceding the crash. But the critic of EF will immediately answer as follows: well, what specific physical interactions of all physical interactions really explain the event? This is known as *the problem of causal relevance*. For each given phenomenon to be explained, we have numerous physical processes that are irrelevant for the purposes of explanation. We can see this if we imagine different kinds of scenarios: the cat can have a different physical constitution (different colour, size, etc.) or the car can be different in its constitution and so on, but these do not affect the outcome. Most microphysical facts about the crash are totally irrelevant for causally explaining why the crash happened. They might be relevant in explaining something else, such as why the cat was there in the first place or why this particular car needs, say, 20 metres to stop while travelling at a speed of 50 kilometres per hour in conditions C. What we want is not a list of all physical interactions that have to do with the car crash, since such an account would not really explain anything – it would be 'too true to be any good'. Instead, we need an explanation that picks out the most relevant causal factor, and this might not have anything to do with anything describable or explainable in terms of physical interactions. I will return to this important point later.

What is happening here is not an endorsement of some sort of emergentist ontology, but instead a decoupling of causal explanation from strong ontological assumptions. The opponent of EF will continue the attack and claim that even if it is the case that the cat, the car and the driver are all completely physical in constitution, it does not follow that the answer to the question as to why the car crashed should be given in terms of physical interactions or terms ultimately reducible to physical terms.

What this suggests is that even in trivial cases such as our car crash, what we want from a good causal explanation is that it reveals the most relevant causal relationship(s) with respect to our question. And this/these most relevant relationship or relationships need not be described in terms of PCE. This is because there seems to be a real explanatory connection between the crash and the cat on the road that 'floats free' from most of the physical constituents of the crash.

This point has been acknowledged in contexts where the behaviour of complex systems is being explained. Even in many domains of physical sciences, there are several instances of explanation that do not deal with constituent physical processes, even though it is usually thought that complex systems consists of physical parts. When, for instance, thermodynamics explains the behaviour of gases, explanations do not refer to trajectories of individual molecules, even though it is widely recognised that gases are just collections of individual molecules, but rather to general laws of the behaviours of such collections of molecules and their environmental conditions. This is even truer in biology or economics, where complex systems are sometimes explained without any reference to individual physical processes underlying these complex systems. Thus, it seems that such 'higher-level' phenomena have at least some explanatory independence of their physical constituents, if not ultimate ontological independence.[7]

What the critic of EF is saying here is that causal relationships do not require an ultimate physical connection between the explainer and the target, nor do causal explanations need to conceptualise the explainer and their target in terms that are translatable to physical terms. Even if we accept the claim that cultures and religions *consist* of mental and public representations alone, it does not follow that the causal explanation of cultures and religions should necessarily be given in terms of cognitive mechanisms and their environments.

Broad Naturalism

The explanatory pluralist view is indebted to a view we might label *broad naturalism*.[8] Basically, the broad naturalist position involves a denial (or at least a rephrasing) of the main claims of EF. It argues for some form of non-reductive or emergent materialism according to which the natural world is physically constituted, but includes complex entities and processes that cannot be explained by physical sciences or explanations reducible to physical explanation or any lower-level description.[9] Thus, the advocates of non-reductive materialism usually deny the explanatory completeness of physics. In this scheme, mental states, for instance, can be seen as relatively independent of the physical states that realise them in the sense that they can have true 'causal power'. A similar analysis can be extended to cultural and social phenomena as well, which do indeed consist of physical parts, but cannot be explained in terms of their parts. One way of fleshing out this view is to argue for *multiple realisation*. The basic idea is that complex states (e.g., mental states, socio-cultural phenomena) can be instantiated by multiple different physical states. As a consequence, multiply

---

[7] For a short overview of the problems of PCE, see Woodward, 2003.
[8] Sometimes called non-reductive naturalism or emergent materialism. Goetz and Taliaferro (2008) consider John Searle and Jerry Fodor as prime examples of broad naturalism.
[9] For an energetic defence of emergent materialism, see Clayton, 2004.

realised states are not identical with the physical micro-states that compose them. Further, the broad naturalist can claim that not only are the higher-level states multiply realised by lower-level states, but that the higher-level states have a relative ontological and explanatorily independence from the lower-level states.

Jerry Fodor, the champion of this view, argues that the special sciences study phenomena that are multiply realised functional states of physical systems. Fodor remains a materialist in claiming that nature is completely materially constituted, but he also claims that mental states are multiply realised in different brain states. As a consequence, mental states (or theories about them) need not be explicable in terms of physical sciences. What is true of mental states is also true of phenomena that are studied in other special sciences: societies, for example, can be described as having true empirical generalisations without the possibility of such generalisations being reduced or even related to psychological, biological or physical theories. This is because concepts and theories in social sciences identify states of affairs that can be realised by different configurations of lower-level structures (Fodor, 1974).[10]

The central problem of broad naturalism is to make sense of the complexity of nature and the supervenient relation between higher- and lower-level structures: we must have some kind of an idea of how autonomous wholes of complex entities and regularities emerge from simpler structures and regularities. The problem is that although many philosophers and scientists agree that higher-level structures are emergent and supervene on lower-level physical structures, there is no generally accepted account of how this might happen. This leaves broad naturalism in an awkward position: it is constantly in danger of lapsing into either strong physicalism or some form of dualism or ontological pluralism.[11]

Explanatory Pluralism

However, recent theories of causal explanation and inter-theoretic relationships have given new life to the broad naturalist position (Horst, 2007; Hohwy and Kallestrup, 2008; Raatikainen, 2010). Instead of strong forms of ontological emergence, the broad naturalist can defend the idea that at least causal explanations can be relatively independent of each other in different sciences. Our conclusion in the last section was that explanatory frames along the lines of PCE are problematic. Is there an alternative available?

---

[10] For discussion, see Clayton and Davies, 2006.
[11] For discussion, see Wilson and Craver, 2007.

It seems to me that there exists a possibility for *explanatory pluralism* along the lines of an updated broad naturalist position. Ultimately, EF is the claim that explanations need to either reduce to one bottom level or be eliminated. This principle is then used to bludgeon those whose explanations do not seem to reduce and show how one's own explanation is more likely to reduce and is therefore better than others. EP, on the other hand, is a view according to which explanations seek their own level independently of the ultimate ontology of entities, events and processes. It seeks out real causal dependencies between events and processes, and postulates entities and processes that explain phenomena in terms of these dependencies.

EP is based on a different notion of causal explanation from EF. In EF, the PCE reigns supreme: the explanatory work is ultimately done by the material or physical relationships between the explainer and the target. In EP, causal connections are understood in terms of counterfactual relationships. This approach has had many pioneers,[12] but writers such as James Woodward (2000; 2003) have recently developed it further.[13] The basic idea behind these *interventionist* or *contrastive theories* of causal explanation is that when we are looking for a causal explanation, we are seeking causal relationships that are explanatorily relevant for our question. Causal explanations are thus answers to 'how' or 'why' questions. We get to the explanatorily relevant causal connections by looking for difference-making factors between two incompatible scenarios.

The assumption that explanations are answers to questions makes it possible to specify the target of a causal explanation more precisely than before. This is because questions include *contrast spaces* that limit the alternative answers. Consider the following famous example. The bank robber Willie Sutton was serving time in prison and the prison chaplain with the intention of reforming him asked him why he robbed banks. Sutton replied: 'That's where the money is.' The point of the example is to show that although both ask the same question, their contrast spaces are different. The prison chaplain wants to know why Sutton robs in general, whereas for Sutton, the issue is why banks are better places to rob than some other places. These questions can be reformulated as what-if-things-had-been-different questions to reveal the relevant contrasts. Sutton's question is: 'Why does Sutton rob banks rather than other places (like supermarkets or private homes)?', whereas the chaplain's question is: 'Why does Sutton rob banks rather than not robbing anything?' When we look at these

---

[12] For earlier agentual theories of causation, see von Wright, 1971. A classic treatment of the pragmatics of explanation is van Fraassen, 1980.

[13] A useful history and an overview of these theories is Woodward, 2008.

formulations, it is easy to see that they require different answers: to explain why Sutton robs banks rather than supermarkets is a different task from explaining why Sutton robs banks rather than living a decent life.

The interventionist account of causal relationships is based on the idea of counterfactual support. The existence of a causal relationship can be determined through intervention: if we change the cause variable, we get change in the effect variable. If we are able to manipulate the cause, have co-variance in the effect and can determine that the variance in the effect is not caused by some other factor, then we can infer that there really is a causal relationship between the cause and the effect. In this analysis, causality is ultimately a relationship that holds in different counterfactual conditions. Causal claims therefore take the following form: 'X, rather than not-X, causes Y, rather than not-Y in condition W.'

When we are looking for an explanation, we are looking for a causally relevant contrast for the cause variable that is appropriate for our effect variable contrast (Craver, 2007, pp. 82, 202–11). Variables X and Y are capable of taking on determinate values. Talk of events or processes can be translated into the vocabulary of variables: events can be seen as variables that have only two values, 0 or 1, and processes can be seen as variables that can take on any value in a continuum. When the relationship between variables X and Y remains stable in specified conditions, we can safely deduce that the relationship between them is causal.

There are several important points that we have to make about this analysis. First of all, the interventionist account does not require an account of a physical chain of events that would link the cause to the effect. Of course, an account of the precise mechanism(s) that relate the change in cause variable to the change in effect variable would increase the plausibility and comprehensiveness of the explanation, but such an account is not necessary in principle. What is necessary for the existence of a causal relationship is that we can produce change in the effect factor by producing change in the cause factor. This point about physical connections generalises over descriptions of causes and effects as well: the descriptions of causes and effects need not be given in 'physical' (or some other predetermined set of) terms. It is enough that descriptions include states, processes or events that we can change in principle. Furthermore, we need not think that we must be able to produce an intervention in the actual world in order to demonstrate the existence of a causal relationship. It is enough that we can have an idea of what an intervention might look like – an ideal intervention. In many cases, causal claims cannot be tested in laboratory settings; this is especially true in the social sciences, where the targets of explanations are macro-level events that are impossible to replicate in the laboratory (revolutions or economic recessions, for instance). However, this does not prevent us from formulating explanations involved in interventionist terms (Craver, 2007, pp. 93–100).

Returning to the car crash example, then, we can say something like this. When we seek to explain why the car crashed, we can have different contrasts or counterfactual scenarios. We can ask why the car crashed at time t rather than time t_1, or why the car crashed into a tree instead of a wall. The car crash is therefore not a simple event to be explained by specifying its microphysical antecedents. To be exact, the question we have been asking would be something like this: 'What made the difference between the car crashing or not crashing?' It was not the microphysical details (whatever they might be), but simply the fact that there was a cat on the road. In other words: 'There was a cat on the road rather than elsewhere and that caused the car to crash rather than not crash in conditions W.' Therefore, in explaining why the car crash happened (instead of not happening), the explanation automatically seeks its own level of description – a level that answers the question.

Explanations Seek Their Own Level

The conclusion reached just now can be summarised by the claim that explanations seek their own level. Explanations, at least if understood along the lines that I suggested earlier, are answers to what-if-things-had-been-different questions. As such, their explanatory frames float relatively free of the physical constituents of the target and the explainer. Alan Garfinkel puts this point strongly in the following passage of his *Forms of Explanation*:

> So the fact that something materially 'is' something else does not mean that we can reduce the explanations involved. From the point of view of explanation there is a relative independence from the nature of the substrate. A macrostate, a higher level state of organization of a thing, or a state of the social relations between one thing and another can have a particular realization ... But the explanation of the higher order state will not proceed via the microexplanation of the microstate which it happens to 'be'. Instead, explanations seek their own level, and typically this will not be the level of underlying substratum. (Garfinkel, 1981, p. 59)

To take just one example to further highlight my point here, consider the difference between explaining individual instances of religious belief and action and explaining population-scale similarities. Suppose we want an answer to the question of why John believes rather than disbelieves in God. Recall that when we are looking for a causal explanation, we are looking for the factor that makes a difference in the case we are explaining. We could answer the question by saying that John believes in God because he has a normal human brain (which includes a normal cognitive architecture). In one sense this is surely right because if John did not have a brain, he would certainly not believe in God. However, this answer seems somehow unsatisfactory because all humans have brains and not all humans believe in God. We are looking for the factor that makes the difference in John's case and having brains does not seem to be it. Suppose that John had a strong religious experience when he went to church two weeks ago. This experience would be an exceptionally good candidate for a causal explanation of John's belief in God because it would reveal the factor that made the difference in John's case.

When we disconnect explanation from PCE as EP suggests, then in the case of John's belief in God we can simply say that this explanation in terms of cognitive mechanisms does not give us an answer to our question. Cognitive mechanisms are surely among the causes of John's belief in God, but they are not explanatorily relevant for our question (that is, why does John believe, rather than not believe, in God?). In contrast, suppose that we want to explain why beliefs about non-natural agents are more or less human universals rather than particular to one cultural tradition. Notice that the causes this time are sought on a completely different level than in the previous case. Cognitive mechanisms that create *biases* might be good candidates for causes of this kind: a mechanistic, constitutive explanation that would explain how the psychological capacity for religion works on the basis of its structure might give us our answer at the proper level.

Pluralism in Interdisciplinary Relationships

EP also has consequences for how we should think about the relationship of theories and disciplines. As we have seen, EF and PCE motivate attempts to unify socio-cultural sciences with natural sciences. In contrast, models along the lines of EP, such as Robert McCauley's model of inter-theoretic relationships, emphasise that poor inter-level mapping, that is, difficulties in reduction, do not constitute a reason to abandon an explanatory hypothesis (McCauley, 1986; 1996; 2007).

EF comes with a strong metaphysical component that guides theory development and interpretation of results, whereas EP puts its money on the practical and experimental success of explanations and emphasises the partiality of our explanations. McCauley writes: 'For the explanatory pluralist, all explanations are partial explanations; all explanations are from some perspective, and all explanations are motivated by and respond to specific problems' (McCauley, 2007, p. 150). In a nutshell, McCauley's explanatory pluralism claims that the reduction or elimination of established scientific theories or disciplines is highly unlikely, as established disciplines have usually uncovered relatively stable causal relationships. If theories in some discipline do in fact work, that is, if they give answers to the questions that the discipline is seeking, then the lack of reduction should cause no particular problem. It follows that constraints of theory development should flow both ways: from the bottom up (as in EF), but also from the top down. Disciplines should seek to build bridges between their theories and theories of neighbouring disciplines. In such cases, constraints coming from higher-level disciplines should also affect the lower-level disciplines.

One interesting feature of McCauley's EP is that it distinguishes between *inter-level contexts* and *intra-level contexts*. In one single analytic level, we get theoretical evolution that can occasionally turn into theoretical revolution when new theories replace (eliminate) or radically reformulate (reduce) previous theories. Physical sciences, for instance, have seen several scientific revolutions where new theories have radically changed and sometimes eliminated old theories' concepts. In situations of elimination, new theories usually explain the same data as old theories, but more elegantly or broadly, and thus incorporate old theories into a larger framework, as in the case of Newtonian mechanics and the theory of general relativity. However, in inter-level contexts, revolutions or reductions of this kind seldom happen. It is more common that theories persist in different analytical levels, even in the case that theories in neighbouring levels do not map onto each other at all. Although it is possible that theories in neighbouring analytic levels might constrain each other quite strongly – as in the case of thermodynamics and statistical mechanics, for instance – and thus have extensive inter-level mapping, this is not a necessary state of affairs. And even in these cases where neighbouring theories are closely related, there is seldom a reduction involved.

In the light of EP, we might see CSR as an attempt to create useful links between ultimately autonomous analytic levels. In other words, we could understand CSR theorising as an attempt to create inter-level connections and inform theorising in both behavioural sciences by pointing out how the study of religious phenomena might provide new material for psychological theories and in the study of religion by providing more psychologically plausible assumptions about the human mind. But this does not mean that the study of religion should become part of psychology or vice versa. Thus, if we make the move from EF to

EP, we should not commit CSR to some general metaphysical theory of what causes of religion qualify as proper causes in the study of religion. Inquiry into religious phenomena can proceed in a piecemeal fashion, more 'locally' than 'globally', and it can be based on the usefulness of different kinds of explanations rather than *a priori* commitment to a possible set of 'psychological' causes. EP would also entail that theories about religion and other phenomena describable at the socio-cultural level do not need to map onto theories about cognition, nor need they fear elimination because of this. Psychological theorising can inform socio-cultural theorising and vice versa, but it is not reasonable to demand complete inter-theoretic mapping.[14]

Concluding Remarks

In conclusion, I offer some remarks about the scope of CSR in the light of EP. EP suggests that we do not yet know how relevant for explaining religion CSR results are. On the one hand, it is clear that CSR has made empirical progress in the last decade: in particular, the studies on the development of folk psychology, intuitive dualism and intuitive teleology show promise and are well grounded in theories and methods of developmental psychology. On the other hand, we do not know how explanatorily relevant these findings are for our questions about religion.

EP challenges us to focus more on our questions about religion. Instead of committing ourselves to the idea that all religious phenomena must have sufficient cognitive causes, we must look at our questions more carefully. What exactly are the questions we are asking about religion and its origins? What kind of questions should we expect the CSR to answer? Answers to these questions are not obvious and crucially depend on our general metaphysical views. What is obvious, however, is that if we look at the situation in the light of EP, we should be careful in distinguishing our ontological assumptions from our attempts causally to explain cultural, psychological and religious phenomena.[15]

---

[14] For a more comprehensive argument along these lines, see Visala, 2011.
[15] The author would like to thank the Cognition, Religion and Theology project, its members, Roger Trigg, Justin Barrett, David Leech, Emma Cohen and the late Nicola Knight at the University of Oxford, and its funder, the Templeton Foundation, for financial and mental support in preparing this chapter.

References

Atran, S., 2002. *In Gods We Trust: The Evolutionary Landscape of Religion*. Oxford: Oxford University Press.

Boyer, P., 1993. Cognitive aspects of religious symbolism. In: P. Boyer (ed.), *Cognitive Aspects of Religious Symbolism*. Cambridge: Cambridge University Press, pp. 4–47.

——. 1994. *The Naturalness of Religious Ideas: A Cognitive Theory of Religion*. Berkeley, CA: University of California Press.

——. 2001. *Religion Explained: The Evolutionary Origins of Religious Thought*. New York: Basic Books.

Cho, F. and Squier, R., 2008a. Reductionism: be afraid, be *very* afraid. *Journal of the American Academy of Religion*, 76, pp. 412–17.

——. 2008b. 'He blinded me with science': science chauvinism in the study of religion. *Journal of the American Academy of Religion*, 76, pp. 420–48.

Clayton, P., 2004. *Mind and Emergence: From Quantum to Consciousness*. New York: Oxford University Press.

Clayton, P. and Davies, P. (eds) 2006. *Re-emergence of Emergence: The Emergentist Hypothesis from Science to Religion*. Oxford: Oxford University Press.

Cosmides, L., Tooby, J. and Barkow, J., 1992. Introduction: evolutionary psychology and conceptual integration. In: J. Barkow, L. Cosmides and J. Tooby (eds), *The Adapted Mind*. New York: Oxford University Press, pp. 3–15.

Craver, C., 2007. *Explaining the Brain: Mechanisms and the Mosaic Unity of Neuroscience*. New York: Oxford University Press.

Cummins, R., 2000. 'How does it work?' versus 'what are the laws?': two conceptions of psychological explanation. In: F. Keil and R. Wilson (eds), *Explanation and Cognition*. Cambridge, MA: MIT Press, pp. 117–44.

Flanagan, O., 2006. Varieties of naturalism. In: P. Clayton (ed.), *Oxford Handbook of Religion and Science*. New York: Oxford University Press, pp. 430–52.

Fodor, J., 1974. Special sciences (or: the disunity of science as a working hypothesis). *Synthese*, 28, pp. 97–115.

Garfinkel, A., 1981. *Forms of Explanation: Rethinking Questions in Social Theory*. New Haven, CT: Yale University Press.

Goetz, S. and Taliaferro, C., 2008. *Naturalism*. Grand Rapids, MI: William B. Eerdmans.

Hohwy, J. and Kallestrup, J. (eds) 2008. *Being Reduced: New Essays on Reduction, Explanation, and Causation*. New York: Oxford University Press.

Horst, S., 2007. *Beyond Reduction: Philosophy of Mind and Post-reductionistic Philosophy of Science*. New York: Oxford University Press.

Kitcher, P., 1992. The naturalists return. *Philosophical Review*, 101, pp. 53–114.

McCauley, R., 1986. Intertheoretic relations and the future of psychology. *Philosophy of Science*, 53, pp. 179–99.

——. 1996. Explanatory pluralism and the co-evolution of theories in science. In: R. McCauley (ed.), *The Churchlands and their Critics*. Oxford: Blackwell, pp. 17–47.

——. 2007. Reduction: models of cross-scientific relations and their implications for the psychology-neuroscience interface. In: P. Thagard (ed.), *Philosophy of Psychology and Cognitive Science*. Amsterdam: Elsevier, pp. 105–58.

Preus, J.S., 1996. *Explaining Religion: Critique and Theory from Bodin to Freud*. Atlanta, GA: Scholars Press.

Pyysiäinen, I., 2009. Reduction and explanatory pluralism in the cognitive science of religion. In: I. Czachesz and T. Bíró (eds), *Changing Minds: Religion and Cognition Through the Ages*. Leuven: Peeters, pp. 15–30.

Raatikainen, P., 2010. Causation, exclusion, and the special sciences. *Erkenntnis*, 73, pp. 349–63.

Rosenberg, A., 1996. A field guide to recent species of naturalism. *British Journal for the Philosophy of Science*, 47, pp. 1–29.

Slingerland, E., 2008a. Who is afraid of reductionism? The study of religion in the age of cognitive science. *Journal of the American Academy of Religion*, 76, pp. 375–411.

——. 2008b. *What Science Offers to the Humanities: Integrating Body and Culture*. Cambridge: Cambridge University Press.

Sperber, D., 1996. *Explaining Culture: A Naturalistic Approach*. Oxford: Blackwell.

Van Fraassen, B., 1980. *The Scientific Image*. Oxford: Clarendon Press.

Visala, A., 2011. *Naturalism, Theism and the Cognitive Study of Religion: Religion Explained?* Aldershot: Ashgate.

Von Wright, G.H., 1971. *Explanation and Understanding*. London: Routledge & Kegan Paul.

Wilson, R.A. and Craver, C., 2007. Realization: metaphysical and scientific perspectives. In: P. Thagard (ed.), *Philosophy of Psychology and Cognitive Science*. Amsterdam: Elsevier, pp. 81–104.

Woodward, J., 2000. Explanation and invariance in the special sciences. *British Journal for the Philosophy of Science*, 51, pp. 197–254.

Woodward, J., 2003. *Making Things Happen: A Theory of Causal Explanation*. New York: Oxford University Press.

——. 2008. Causality and manipulability. *Stanford Encyclopedia of Philosophy*. Available at: http://plato.stanford.edu/entries/causation-mani.

Chapter 5

HADD, Determinism and Epicureanism: An Interdisciplinary Investigation

Robin Attfield

In this chapter, I introduce a key tenet of the Cognitive Science of Religion (CSR), with a view to testing it by reference to relevant phases of the history of philosophy and relevant facts from those phases. The relevant facts consist in beliefs about agency and purposes, most particularly those held in the ancient world. While CSR is largely concerned with non-reflective beliefs or intuitions, I will be assuming there is a close enough connection between non-reflective and reflective beliefs for theories of CSR to be testable by reference to the latter, as well as what they tell us about the former. (The close links between non-reflective and reflective beliefs are explained by Justin Barrett in *Why Would Anyone Believe in God?* (2004, pp. 2–17).) This process of testing allows, if I am right, divergent appraisals of deterministic and non-deterministic versions of at least one theory of CSR.

First, it may be useful to present a recent summary of the primary claims of CSR, and thus to introduce the hypothesis of humanity's Hypersensitive Agency Detection Device (HADD). Theodore Brelsford summarizes three primary claims of CSR as follows:

1. *Beliefs should be understood as attempts to rationalize intuitive sensibilities* (in other words, beliefs derive most naturally from reflection on intuitions).
2. *Intuitive sensibilities are governed by unconscious mental processes* (thus, intuitions are outcomes of mental processes, but those processes are largely unconscious, automatic, and instinctual in accordance with certain structures of mind).
3. *These unconscious mental processes and structures of mind are the result of long periods of evolutionary experience* (thus, structures of mind that shape unconscious mental processes that govern intuitive sensibilities on which

beliefs are based are themselves shaped by human experience in the world over many millennia) (Brelsford, 2005, pp. 174–91).

For present purposes, this summary will serve as encapsulating the general claims of CSR, to which the HADD hypothesis is a leading contribution.

Intuitions would presumably include non-reflective assumptions, which in much ordinary discourse are referred to as "feelings" or, often, as "beliefs". But such intuitions are to be distinguished from the "beliefs" specified in the first article of this summary, since the beliefs mentioned there are clearly reflective beliefs, as Brelsford makes clear, of which examples might be the religious beliefs specified in creeds, or the political beliefs specified in party constitutions.

HADD itself, to follow Justin Barrett's summary in *Agency Detection/ HADD*, "is set off by various ambiguous environmental stimuli such as the apparently goal-directed movement of objects, etc., and when triggered, HADD produces beliefs in unseen agents who are presumed to be the causes of such ambiguous stimuli" (Barrett, 2008a). It is held by Stewart Guthrie (who effectively devised the theory in large part, without devising the name or the acronym: Guthrie, 1993) to be adaptive, since the fact that our ancestors had "a strong perceptual bias to interpret ambiguous events as caused by an agent" made it "far less likely that" they "would have ended up as a predator's kill. It would have been much less costly for our ancestors to have detected too much agency in their environment than too little" (Barrett, 2008a, p. 1). We should also note that the relevant stimuli are apparently goal-directed movements and the like; this accounts for the focus both in Guthrie's writing and in the present chapter on teleological phenomena and beliefs.

HADD normally operates unreflectively by giving rise to non-reflective beliefs from which reflective beliefs are formed in ways depicted by Barrett in the opening chapter of *Why Would Anyone Believe in God?* (2004, pp. 2–17). Accordingly, people's reflective beliefs can supply a reasonable (if indirect) test of claims about it. The HADD hypothesis would be more readily confirmed if these beliefs standardly have the character of hypersensitive or hyperactive commitment to agency or purposiveness in the face of ambiguous phenomena, whereas significant departures among beliefs from such commitment, if they are to be found, might call for the hypothesis to be reinterpreted, or even possibly to be modified or discarded.

Accordingly, history can supply a reasonable test of the HADD hypothesis (as Guthrie effectively agrees, by dedicating considerable space to historical evidence of the human tendency to detect agency and purposiveness, not least in philosophy). The history of philosophy in particular supplies a relevant area of investigation, since it includes much reflection about agency, purposiveness and their scope. Indeed, Guthrie goes so far as to claim that the evidence available from Greek philosophy supports his theory of religion, since "Greek philosophy, though growing away from Greek religion, keeps the latter's fundamental anthropomorphism" (1993, p. 157). As we shall see, there is considerable reason to question and to qualify this claim.

Stances have differed enormously about how far the world is purposive. Aristotle, to cite a widely influential figure of the fourth century Before the Common Era (BCE), is to be found at one extreme of the relevant spectrum. For him, everything has a *telos* or purpose. The suggestion is not that everything was made by an external agent and operates to fulfil the purpose or perform the function thus bestowed on it, much as human artefacts do. Rather, it is that everything has an inbuilt goal or purpose that governs what it is, and largely governs how it behaves, even though there is no conscious recognition of this on the part of the item in question. This is the view that most people hold about living organisms, with their natural tendencies of growth; Aristotle's view, however, is that all this applied to inanimate entities too, such as mountains, the sea and the stars (Gottlieb, 2001, pp. 233–9).

Aristotle was far from the first to adopt such a view. For instance, Aristotle's fifth-century predecessor Socrates relates in *Phaedo* (97b–99d) that he turned at one stage to the philosophy of Anaxagoras of Clazomenae because he wanted to know why things were as they were, and the latter taught that everything was ordered by mind. But Plato goes on to say that he came away disappointed because Anaxagoras failed to explain how things were ordered for the best, and rested content with mere mechanical explanations of astronomical and meteorological phenomena. Thus, Socrates assumed that everything is how it is for a purpose, rather as Aristotle was later to teach. Or at least the Socrates of Plato's dialogue assumed this—and this passage is widely held to be historically reliable.

To cite one further influential philosopher, Thomas Aquinas, in the thirteenth century, employs the supposed fact that everything behaves as if directed toward a goal or target in an argument connecting the world to God. Commentators differ about what this means, some of them interpreting him as meaning little more than that inanimate objects behave as if governed by the laws of nature (Kenny, 1969, pp. 96–100; Ward, 1982, p. 100). But on any interpretation his assumption is that there is some kind of aim, goal or purpose in the behaviour of material objects in general. Aquinas was in many matters a follower of Aristotle, and Aristotle's views may have predisposed him to make this assumption, but as he was arguing to a conclusion that importantly diverged from Aristotle's theology, he cannot be presumed to be adopting Aristotle's metaphysical views about purposiveness unamended in the premise of his argument. Thus, he may be construed as holding some form of belief in universal purposiveness of his own.

Very large numbers of other people have been influenced by the beliefs of Socrates, Aristotle and Aquinas, and so far the history of philosophy appears to illustrate just what we should expect if the HADD hypothesis is true, for all these people either concluded or assumed that everything is and does what it is or does for a purpose, whether conscious or unconscious, external or inbuilt. Indeed, Guthrie's text could easily lead the reader to suppose that this is the whole story, at least up to the early seventeenth century, for he writes about the ideas of Francis Bacon (1561–1626 CE): "final causes really belong only to humans; that is, only humans set and work towards goals. Bacon thus rejects teleology, and seems the first to do so" (1993, p. 159). However, in a note that reads like an afterthought, which was never integrated with his main text, he adds, on the strength of a personal communication from Bernard Gilligan, that "the pre-socratic atomists and the later Greek and Roman Epicureans 'emphasised a non-teleological view of nature'" (Guthrie, 1993, p. 237). (Here "later" must mean "later than the pre-socratics" rather than referring just to the later of the Epicureans, for the Epicureans were anti-teleological from the outset.)

Thus, the teleological tendency just illustrated from Socrates, Aristotle and Aquinas comprises only part of the story, albeit a large part. For there was also an opposing tendency, which originated even earlier than Guthrie's note suggests, and thus from almost as long ago as the period for which we have literary records. It may well have originated among the Milesian pre-socratic philosophers of the sixth and fifth centuries BCE, Thales, Anaximander and Anaximenes, whose naturalistic explanations of astronomical and meteorological phenomena appear to exclude theological ones, and may have continued in the work of their successor, Anaxagoras of Clazomenae, the fifth-century philosopher whose failure to supply teleological explanations so disappointed Socrates. Certainly Anaxagoras' reputed proneness to debunk religious explanations and to supply naturalistic ones in their place already indicates that he took this kind of position. But in any case, an anti-teleological approach is manifest in the work of the Sicilian fifth-century philosopher Empedocles (492–c. 434 BCE), who probably wrote his works before the atomists (whom Guthrie mentions) did.

Empedocles held that the survival of the species is due to natural selection from among a whole range of randomly generated creatures, fantastical and otherwise, many of which were ill-fitted to survive. Aristotle, who of course strongly disapproved of this theory, presents it in *Physics* 198b29–32 (Wright, 1981, pp. 212–14). Charles Darwin was later to notice and quote a parallel passage of Aristotle as conveying a faint foreshadowing on the part of Empedocles of his own theory of evolution by natural selection; as Darwin put it: "We here see the principle of natural selection shadowed forth" (Darwin, 1968, pp. 53–4). (Empedocles' anti-teleological theory was cited by Aristotle in these passages so as to refute it in favor of a purposive theory.) It should be recognized that Empedocles also believed that history is a cosmic struggle between Love and Strife, and that Aphrodite (or Love) cunningly created the eye (Sedley, 1998, p. 20). But this is figurative language, and Love and Strife seem to have been impersonal forces; Empedocles does not seem to have imputed purposiveness, let alone design, to either of them. On the contrary, his accounts of biological phenomena turn on contingency and chance, a feature of his views unaffected even by his belief in reincarnation.

Empedocles' younger contemporary, Democritus (c. 460 to c. 370 BCE), believed that all material phenomena result from the chance interplay of the movements of indestructible atoms colliding blindly in void space (Gottlieb, 2001, pp. 94–108). Democritus wrote many books, but only small fragments survive. However, his anti-teleological ideas were taken over by the founder of Epicureanism, Epicurus (Gottlieb, 2001, pp. 283–308), and embodied in a systematic philosophy and way of life which formed a significant minority position in the Greco-Roman world from the time when Epicurus founded his Garden in Athens around 300 BCE until the Emperor Justinian closed down all the non-Christian philosophical schools in 529 CE (Gottlieb, 2001, p. 346). For example, St Paul encountered Epicureans at Athens (Acts 17:18). The Epicureans may have been retiring, but they were not obscure; among the more prominent ancient Epicureans were the Roman poets Horace and, before him, Lucretius, while Virgil was to have contacts with the Epicurean school of Philodemus (Sedley, 1998, p. 64). Many of their writings have been discovered in a house buried in volcanic ash at Herculaneum, almost certainly the library of Philodemus' school (Sedley, 1998, p. 65); the texts are still being reconstructed. Meanwhile, other prominent Roman Epicureans included Cassius, Caesar's assassin, and possibly Caesar himself (Sedley, 1998, pp. 64–5). Thus, if we include the period of Empedocles, Anaxagoras, and Democritus, there was a vigorous and continuous anti-teleological tradition, well-known to (at least) cultured contemporaries, for an entire millennium of the ancient world. Moreover, this tradition died not through lack of support, but because it was closed down by imperial edict. Indeed, a variant of this tradition was to become a live option again when soon after 1600, Gassendi, a contemporary of Bacon, saw fit to revive ancient atomism.

Cosmic purposiveness, as we have seen, was explicitly rejected by the Epicureans. Since the metaphysical works of Epicurus are lost, we can turn in this connection to Lucretius, who expresses this theme with great clarity and versatility.

Thus, in Book V of *De Rerum Natura*, David Sedley has recently argued that at lines 124–234 Lucretius gives a point for point reply to a key passage (29e–30e) in Plato's *Timaeus*, which at the time was the teleologists' bible, and that this systematic reply echoes an earlier parallel reply in a lost work of Epicurus. Here Lucretius argues "that the world cannot be alive ... that the gods cannot have created it, for lack of either a motive or a model to give them the idea ... and that it is not good enough to be divine handiwork" (Sedley, 1998, p. 153). There is, Lucretius holds, no need to accept atomism before drawing these conclusions; most of the earth is in any case useless to humanity, and even what is left can only be cultivated with great effort and great difficulty: "by no means has the nature of things been fashioned for us by divine grace; so great are the flaws with which it stands beset" (V, 198–9).

Lucretius did apparently believe in the gods, but makes it clear in his opening book that the gods have no interest in humanity and live an untroubled life far away from our world (I, 44–9). What troubles human life is in fact religion, which Epicurus had heroically resisted (I, 62–79). Religion generates atrocities such as the sacrifice of Agamemnon's daughter Iphianassa (otherwise known as Iphigeneia); such, he adds, are the evils that religion could prompt: "tantum religio potuit suadere malorum" (I, 101).

Lucretius proceeds to criticize Empedocles' four-elements theory (I, 716–829), plus Anaxagoras' belief in many indivisible elements, or homoeomeries (1, 830–920), after presenting his own account of atoms, void, and molecules, which adopts with appropriate adjustments (just as Epicurus had done) the theories of Democritus. The human soul is held to consist of fine and tenuous atoms (III, 177–230), which at death are dispersed into the breezes of the air (III, 425–44); thus, religious accounts of its nature and destiny are to be avoided.

We should also resist, he goes on to argue, any teleological account of our limbs or our faculties. The eyes were not made for seeing, nor the legs for walking, for sight and walking did not precede the existence of eyes or legs; rather, for each thing that came about, uses were subsequently found (IV, 822–57).

There again, the arrangement of matter into earth, sky, and sea is to be explained in an evolutionary manner, for "not by design did the first-beginnings of things place themselves each in their order with foreseeing mind, nor indeed did they make a compact what movements each should start" (V, 419–21). Instead, atoms came together as they randomly jostled one another across an unlimited time-span, driven by chance impacts and their own weight. This is also how living creatures emerged (V, 422–31).

After a passage on astronomy, in which evolutionary atomism is applied to the sun, moon, and stars, and phenomena such as eclipses, Lucretius advances the Epicurean theory of natural selection. Random processes produced many creatures, some of them monsters incapable of reproduction, and many creatures were thus eliminated (V, 837–77), as were others that failed to feed or breed successfully. However, there never were the kinds of monsters imagined by Empedocles, such as centaurs (half-human and half-horse), for creatures of these kinds would be completely non-viable from the start, with one half reaching old age before the other half was mature enough to reproduce (V, 878–924). So, here, one theory of natural selection is criticized in favour of another. A possible explanation is that Lucretius and the Epicureans in general wanted to avoid the ridicule aimed by Aristotle at Empedocles' monsters, which he depicts, quoting Empedocles, as "ox-children man-faced" (Sedley, 1998, p. 20), and sought to present a more cogent account of biological origins that avoided both Empedocles' far-fetched imaginings and the purposefulness of Aristotle's story.

Thus, Lucretius advanced a comprehensive and more or less consistent anti-teleological account of the world, which addressed both physics and psychology, astronomy and geology, biology and psychology, perception and epistemology, and of course religion and theology. Indeed, he went on to supply a theory of the origins of human society and culture (V, 925–1457) and of apparently mysterious events such as the great plague of ancient Athens (VI, 1138–286). The overall impression was that there was nothing in human life that would not yield to an Epicurean and anti-teleological explanation.

Opponents could resist his theories, for example, with regard to consciousness and also to ethics. But even those who were not fully persuaded were often impressed, as was Cicero. Indeed Cicero, in dialogues such as *De Natura Deorum* (Sedley, 1998, p. 67) and *De Finibus* (Sedley, 1998, p. 162), includes a spokesperson of the Epicureans as well as one for the Stoics, and one for his own, more sceptical, academic view. Later, Christian writers of the patristic age found themselves troubled by Epicurean atomism; works of theirs routinely included attacks on Epicureanism, as in Tatian's *Address to the Greeks*, Justin Martyr's *Hortatory Address to the Greeks*, and Irenaeus' *Against the Heretics* (Cook, 1996).

When atomism was rediscovered in the seventeenth century, it was combined by scientists such as Robert Boyle and Sir Isaac Newton with a belief in a purposive creator, and this development could perhaps be cited by Guthrie in support of his position. However, even if we set aside the anti-teleological beliefs of many Darwinists from the publication of *The Origin of Species* in 1859 to the present, the millennium of anti-teleological theories (and related beliefs) in the ancient world may well give us pause before endorsing his view of the philosophy of that period as anthropomorphizing, for anthropomorphism was fairly consistently avoided and indeed explicitly rejected by the Epicureans.

But here a reply should be considered that might be adduced by supporters of Guthrie. For, strangely enough, Lucretius opens his poem with an invocation to Venus as the mother of the descendants of Aeneas and the goddess of spring, of fertility, and of peace. She is urged to distract her partner Mars, the god of war, from disturbing the peace of the Romans and of Lucretius' patron, Memmius (I, 1–43). Lucretius seems here almost to be subverting his own anti-religious message and can in any case be accused of instantiating the very anthropomorphizing tendency that he has here been cited as opposing and contriving to avoid. (We have already encountered a parallel problem for Lucretius' anti-teleological predecessor, Empedocles.)

Nor is Venus the only deity whom Lucretius invokes. For he also calls upon the Muses of Helicon for their support, praising his poet-predecessor Ennius for bringing them first from Greece to Italian shores (I, 117–19; IV, 1–5). But the Muses were goddesses, and invocations in their regard amount to further requests for assistance made to supernatural agencies.

As if these problems were not enough, it could be added that Lucretius also addresses (more than once) the founder of Epicureanism, Epicurus, as a cosmic hero who has dared to defy the wrath of heaven in his endeavor to bring humanity a message of tranquillity (I, 62–79; III, 1–30). The charge here is not of anthropomorphism, for Epicurus was a human in the first place, but of virtual deification, when Epicurus is raised to the rank of mythological heroes such as Theseus, Perseus or Hercules.

The charge, then, could be that despite his anti-teleological reasoning and conclusions, Lucretius had as active a HADD as anyone else and displayed it despite himself at all kinds of moments, some appropriate and some less so. His official beliefs may have been anti-teleological, but his intuitive beliefs or intuitions were as anthropomorphizing as Guthrie suggests were those of ancient philosophy in general. (Guthrie (1993) actually purports to find anthropomorphizing in Lucretius when, at p. 55, he represents Lucretius as attributing "chance images of people and animals in rocks and clouds to the 'generative powers of Nature'"; this charge will be treated here as part of the accusation that Lucretius' treatment of Venus, the goddess of fertility, is an example of an anthropomorphizing tendency.) It could be added that if such was Lucretius, then inquiry into the lives of other opponents of teleology would be likely to find them equally torn between teleological intuitions and their critical rejection, and thus no exceptions to Guthrie's generalization about ancient philosophy any more than Lucretius was. Indeed, this would all be consistent with the conclusions of Deborah Kelemen and Evelyn Rosset, whose recent research suggests that adults as well as children display a "promiscuous teleology" (an indiscriminate tendency to resort to purposive explanations) when it comes to explaining natural phenomena, whether biological or non-biological, at least when required to respond without time for reflection (Kelemen and Rosset, 2009, pp. 138–43).

These various objections need to be considered through literary criticism of Lucretius' poetic form as well as of his philosophical message; such an approach proves to be necessary to sift through the possible defences of Guthrie that have just been introduced.

Let us begin with the adulation of Epicurus. Here we need to remember that Lucretius had chosen to present his message in hexameter verse, the medium of heroic poetry such as Homer's *Iliad*. So his poetic medium could have seemed to demand a hero. Besides, the tradition in which he wrote required there to be a mentor and guide in the quest for truth, just as Odysseus has Tiresias as a guide when he visits the underworld in the *Odyssey*, and Aeneas was to have the Sibyl and then his late father Anchises as guides when he does the same in Virgil's *Aeneid*, and just as Dante was going to have in Virgil when he visits the underworld in *The Divine Comedy*. Further, Lucretius' praise of Epicurus is for resisting religion and thus liberating humanity (I, 62–79), and so the heroic role that Lucretius bestows on him itself serves to underline his anti-religious message. Admittedly, Lucretius refrains from mentioning the three other founders of Epicureanism whom other Epicureans often mentioned (Sedley, 1998, pp. 67–8), but this reflects not a tendency to anthropomorphize but, as Sedley expresses things, a rather "fundamentalist" approach implicit in his own interpretation of Epicureanism, in which the original founder is lionized to the exclusion of all others (Sedley, 1998, pp. 62, 71–2). I conclude that the objection based on Lucretius' adulation of Epicurus does not assist Guthrie's case.

When we turn to Lucretius' invocation of the Muses, we need to bear in mind the requirement, perceived through most of the ancient world, for poets to seek inspiration from these patron deities of art and culture, or rather to go through the motions of seeking such inspiration. Such had been the approach of the pioneer of didactic poetry (the form that Lucretius was entering), namely Hesiod. And so persistent was this approach that it was observed even by the arch-rationalist among Greek philosopher-poets, Parmenides. (Its persistence is also borne out by the fact that even the Puritan poet John Milton observed this convention by opening his *Paradise Lost* with the words: "Sing heavenly Muse.")

Yet Parmenides could hardly have really believed in the separate existence of the goddess from whom he claims a revelation, for according to his official stance everything is a single entity, spatially and temporally continuous, without any gaps or distinctions (Gottlieb, 2001, pp. 52–64); his allusions to the goddess are just a literary formality. Similarly, Lucretius can hardly have held that the Muses were distinct existences, either dwelling on mountains such as Helicon or Parnassus, or resident in Italy, after being brought there by his predecessor Ennius, for he held that what we should believe about the gods is that they live in the spaces between worlds and are in any case utterly unconcerned about humanity. Lucretius had the problems of conveying philosophy in Latin and in verse, and relates how he used to stay up at night devising a vocabulary to this end (1.136–45). In these circumstances it is understandable that he goes through the motions of pretending to seek inspiration from the Muses, despite his likely disbelief that they would answer his requests. (At most, his apparent belief in the Muses involved a temporary and partial suspension of disbelief, which left that deep-seated disbelief unchallenged.) Thus, his invocation of the Muses is best construed as a literary device or gesture to satisfy people's expectations in a didactic poet, and gives no significant comfort to supporters of Guthrie.

To turn now to his invocation of Venus, many of the same points could be deployed again as have been raised about the Muses, and certainly his praise of the prolific fertility of the natural world need not be construed in any way as belief in nature's purposefulness, granted his explanations of birth and growth in terms of random atomic and molecular processes. However, the opening passage of Lucretius' poem serves to introduce some additional layers of explanation. One of his aims in this passage was to persuade patriotic readers to read on and benefit from the lessons that his poetry was to entice them to learn. His opening address to Venus, as the mother of the Romans, manifestly assisted this purpose.

But there is a further explanation of his opening passage, proposed by David Furley and recently revised by Sedley. Venus and Mars are Latin equivalents of the Love and Strife of Empedocles' poem about the nature of the universe, which may well have had a similar title to that of Lucretius. Furley took the view that Lucretius wanted to be seen as imitating Empedocles because of the esteem in which he and his poem were held, and because Lucretius regarded him as an anti-teleological predecessor (Furley, 1989, pp. 14–26). Sedley, however, doubts whether Lucretius had all this in mind, in view of his criticisms of Empedocles. According to Sedley, what Lucretius was consciously imitating, and wanted to be seen to be imitating, was Empedocles' poetical form, for establishing this kind of pedigree was going to help him secure the attention of his cultivated readers. This is why his poem, like that of Empedocles, opens with an apparent appeal to the goddess of love (Sedley, 1998, pp. 21–8). But in fact Lucretius no more believed in the agency or purposiveness of Venus than he believed in that of the Muses, and to be on the safe side, he rapidly went on to explain the true nature of the gods, as ideal exemplars of tranquillity and carefreeness, in a passage already cited above. Lucretius, then, was writing in a society widely and deeply saturated by religion, and had to compromise with it by observing some of the conventions in order to secure a hearing. But there is no reason to believe that he took his own invocations literally. Thus, there is no need to invoke promiscuous teleology to account for Lucretius' treatment of Epicurus, of the Muses or of Venus, for in all these cases the best explanations lie in his purposes as an author, a poet, a philosopher, and a propagandist.

There is oddly a similar problem where Guthrie treats Darwin's willingness to write of natural selection as an anthropomorphizing tendency. Alfred Wallace, for example, warned Darwin against this practice (Guthrie, 1993, pp. 173–4). However, Darwin reasonably replied that such a criticism was based on taking literally what he had written figuratively (Guthrie, 1993, p. 174). Writing like this had allowed him to compare artificial selection, with which his readers were familiar, with natural selection, but rather than natural selection being an additional agency, it simply amounted to whatever happened when the recognized laws of nature operated without interference. This is, I suggest, an entirely credible response and may indicate that Guthrie was scraping the bottom of the barrel in questioning it. We should not be surprised when causal factors are metaphorically represented as agencies and should be prepared to distinguish between those writers whose mention of agencies is just a literary device (as with both Lucretius and Darwin) and those who believe that the agencies they mention make a genuine difference as distinctive, non-fictitious and quasi-personal agencies (as most religious believers do about the gods of their belief).

Granted, then, that the possible reply made on Guthrie's behalf that Lucretius himself is guilty of anthropomorphizing, despite small grains of truth, largely fails, there is nothing left to consider of the argument that if Lucretius was guilty of this, then so too probably were the other ancient anti-teleologists, short of evidence in individual cases to the contrary. Thus, the phenomenon of ancient anti-teleology remains something with which the HADD theory has to be reconciled one way or another, insofar as it predicts commitment to personal or other kinds of agency not only at the intuitive level, but also to some degree at the level of rational reflection.

How much, we may inquire, does the HADD theory predict about our propensity to adopt teleology? Much depends on whether the HADD thesis is adopted in a deterministic or a non-deterministic version. (Both of these seem possible stances, on the strength of Theodore Brelsford's summary of CSR and subsequent avowal that while its theories can be adopted in a deterministic form, they need not be so held.) I am here using "determinism," as Peter van Inwagen does, to mean "the thesis that the past determines a unique future" (van Inwagen, 1983, p. 2), or more precisely that "there is at any instant exactly one physically possible future," where "physically possible" means what is possible given the actual past and the laws of nature (van Inwagen, 1983, p. 3; see further Attfield, 2012, pp. 216–49). Much depends on whether the version adopted is deterministic (in its own sphere), because the more deterministic the version adopted is, the more unremitting and invariant an anthropomorphizing tendency it predicts, and the closer it is to predicting a single outcome and no other, for, subject to qualifications shortly to be mentioned, just one outcome (or future) is represented as possible by an unqualifiedly deterministic theory.

Admittedly, even if a deterministic version of HADD is in question, agency detection will not take place in all circumstances on the part of all human beings. Propensities are not triggered in all circumstances—for example, solubility is not always manifested by solutes becoming dissolved in solvents, for there may already be a saturated solution of that solute, and beyond that point, the solubility of the solute makes no difference to what happens next. Also, a propensity could fail to be manifested if a countervailing factor is present—for example, however soluble a solute may be, it will not be dissolved in an otherwise suitable solvent if the solvent gets evaporated before the process of solution can take place. However, once suitable circumstances for HADD to be operative are in place, we can reasonably expect agency detection to be manifested, unless there are countervailing factors by which it is outweighed or rendered impotent, and in the absence of unsuitable circumstances and of such countervailing factors, we can reasonably expect agency detection to take place, given a deterministic interpretation of HADD, at least at the intuitive level of unconscious beliefs and impulses, and on many occasions at the level of conscious beliefs as well. For a deterministic HADD, like any other deterministic tendency, allows, in suitable circumstances and in the absence of obstacles, for one outcome only.

The HADD hypothesis would, further, have been adopted in a deterministic version if HADD were understood both to be hard-wired and irresistible in a wide range of normal circumstances. Let us then assume that such an interpretation has been adopted, in order to explore the implications, and to investigate whether the history of philosophy in particular bears out the hypothesis thus interpreted.

If HADD is a hard-wired and irresistible propensity, then the hypothesis can be argued to be put in doubt itself by the evidence of the anti-teleological thought of Epicureans, as well as by that of their successors in believing in natural selection, the Darwinians of the last century and a half. For this thesis in this form would lead us to expect that even if Epicureanism were ever to be put forward at all, it would fail for lack of a following, unless potential adherents were subjected to a powerful training in anti-teleological theory, and that maybe the same applies to Darwinism too. For would-be adherents would be continually torn between their reflective anti-teleological beliefs and their own unreflective HADD-induced intuitions, and these reflective beliefs themselves could only be maintained through conscious mental exertions and deliberate resistance to the intuitive beliefs that they would be unable to prevent themselves from forming and finding in themselves like uninvited alien presences day by day. In such a context their anti-teleological beliefs would be unstable and unlikely to prove enduring except in the hardiest of individuals.

Thus, the millennium-long ancient history of Epicureanism, as the dominant doctrine of a relaxed and friendly community, counts quite strongly against any deterministic version of the HADD hypothesis, sufficiently, I suggest, to require that such a version be significantly modified, to say the least. It even counts against such a version being amended, but only slightly, to allow for occasional cases of HADD-blindness, with the HADD tendency being irresistible wherever it is operative, but missing in isolated individuals. For the history of ancient anti-teleological beliefs involves not isolated individuals but a concerted and continuous community and culture (in the form of Epicurean communities), which at times recruited significant proportions of the people with whom it came into contact.

However, if the hypothesis instead concerns a tendency (whether hard-wired or not) that is resistible, then it is arguably compatible with the history of philosophy, including the powerful but minority millennium-long presence of Epicureanism and its equally anti-teleological predecessors. For the Epicureans and the other anti-teleologists could have harboured HADD-like tendencies, but resisted them (plus whatever intuitive beliefs these tendencies might have inclined them to accept) through deploying the various objections and arguments presented above. Indeed, their resistance at the reflective level could have produced anti-teleological beliefs which could have become second nature and habitual even at the intuitive level, as long as their HADD was not producing irresistible agency-detecting beliefs at this level. I have no wish to endorse such anti-teleological arguments wholesale, for I have argued in favour of design arguments elsewhere (Attfield, 2006). The point is rather that this kind of HADD hypothesis is not falsified in the way that deterministic kinds apparently are, predicting as they do that people with anti-teleological beliefs would be hopelessly self-divided between anti-teleological reflections and irresistible agency-detecting intuitions that would return as soon as the thinker attempted to neutralise or expel them.

Certainly, the writings of Lucretius could even be held, in view of his invocations of deities and of a hero, to give this hypothesis (in a non-deterministic form) some small measure of support, for these episodes, including his invocation to Venus, could be regarded as manifestations of an intuitive HADD which Lucretius firmly resisted (as in Book I: 44–9, the passage about the dispassionate nature of the Gods) at least at the level of the reflective beliefs about the world that he took seriously. Further, his resistance, echoed in that of most members of the Epicurean community and tradition to which he belonged, may well reflect a widespread human ability certainly to resist the adoption of avoidable teleological beliefs at the reflective level and, quite possibly, to build up a culturally instilled habit (approaching a second nature) of resistance to the adoption of intuitive agency-detecting responses (to ambiguous stimuli) even at the level of unreflective intuitions, assumptions, or beliefs, natural and instinctive as these intuitive responses may be.

As was mentioned above, the HADD hypothesis would be the more readily confirmed if people's beliefs recurrently have the character of hypersensitive or hyperactive commitment to the presence of agency or purposiveness in the face of ambiguous phenomena, whereas significant departures among beliefs from such commitment, if they are to be found, might call for the hypothesis to be reinterpreted, or even possibly to be modified or discarded. The anti-teleological beliefs of the ancient world (as well as those of the modern world) can be seen as significant departures from such commitment, but would only require the HADD hypothesis to be modified if it were held in a deterministic form which would predict their non-occurrence, at least on this scale and with this persistence, all other things being equal. Rather, they call for a suitable interpretation of the HADD hypothesis (to avoid this difficulty), involving it being held in a non-deterministic form, in which HADD is resistible, certainly at the reflective level, and even to some degree at the intuitive level. (I have attempted to explain in greater detail in another paper (Attfield, 2010, pp. 465–83) what is meant by "non-deterministic" in connection with versions of CSR and indeed of Darwinism, with some indications of forms that at least non-deterministic Darwinism might take.) In this form, the hypothesis is compatible with other factors, including critical reasoning, influencing at least people's reflective beliefs and, quite possibly, with people becoming able (maybe through years of cultural training) to avoid adopting agency-detection assumptions at the intuitive level as well.

This view receives all but explicit support from Justin Barrett, the originator of the HADD formula: "CSR's claim that religious beliefs derive from (unconscious) intuitions arising from basic evolved structures of mind need not imply complete determinism, since intuitions need not be seen merely as fixed outcomes of structures of mind but as capable of being consciously reformed or overridden via intentional reflection and practice" (Barrett, 2008b, p. 2). Thus, Barrett's considered view favors a non-deterministic interpretation of CSR, and therewith of the HADD hypothesis, including its bearing on human intuitions.

Accordingly, HADD can be reconciled with the facts of the history of philosophy I have recounted, or at least with those that I have selected, as long as it is understood in a non-deterministic version. And this finding tallies with the account of CSR of Theodore Brelsford (with which this chapter opened), who, in holding that CSR need not be deterministic, effectively denies that determinism is implicit in CSR. At the same time, it involves some not inconsiderable modification of Guthrie's claims that the anthropomorphizing tendency of which he writes has historically been close to ubiquitous.

References

Attfield, R., 2006. *Creation, Evolution and Meaning*. Aldershot: Ashgate.

———. 2010. Darwin's doubt, non-deterministic Darwinism and the cognitive science of religion. *Philosophy*, 85(4), pp. 465–83.

———. 2012. *Ethics: An Overview*. London and New York: Continuum/Bloomsbury.

Barrett, J.L., 2004. *Why Would Anyone Believe in God?* Lanham, MD: AltaMira Press.

———. 2008a. *Agency Detection/HADD*. Oxford: Philosophical Summary for Cognition, Religion and Theology Project. Available at: http://www.icea.ox.ac.uk/labs/projects/cognition-religion-and-theology/archive-of-cognitive-science-of-religion-methods/hadd.

———. 2008b. *Broad Doctrinal Implications of CSR for Religion and Theology*. Oxford: Cognition, Religion and Theology Project. Available at: http://www.icea.ox.ac.uk/fileadmin/CAM/cBroaddoctrinalimplicationsofCSRforreligionandtheology.pdf.

Brelsford, T., 2005. Lessons for religious education from cognitive science of religion. *Religious Education*, 100(2), pp. 174–91.

Cook, V., 1996. Epicurean history. Available at: http//:www.epicurus.net/en/history.html.

Darwin, C., 1968. *The Origin of Species by Means of Natural Selection*. Harmondsworth: Penguin.

Furley, D.J., 1989. *Cosmic Problems: Essays on Greek and Roman Philosophy of Nature*. Cambridge: Cambridge University Press.

Gottlieb, A., 2001. *The Dream of Reason*. London: Penguin.

Guthrie, S.E., 1993. *Faces in the Clouds: A New Theory of Religion*. Oxford: Oxford University Press.

Kelemen, D. and Rosset, E., 2009. The human function compunction: teleological explanation in adults. *Cognition*, 111, pp. 138–43.

Kenny, A., 1969. *The Five Ways*. London: Routledge & Kegan Paul.

Sedley, D., 1998. *Lucretius and the Transformation of Greek Wisdom*. Cambridge: Cambridge University Press.

Van Inwagen, P., 1983. *An Essay on Free Will*. Oxford: Clarendon Press.

Ward, K., 1982. *Rational Theology and the Creativity of God*. Oxford: Basil Blackwell.

Wright, M. R., 1981. *Empedocles: The Extant Fragments*. London: Duckworth.

Chapter 6

Understanding 'Person' Talk: When is it Appropriate to Think in Terms of Persons?

Graham Wood

Introduction

This chapter offers a sketch of how insights from evolutionary psychology and cognitive science of religion may contribute to our metaphysical and religious understanding of ourselves and our world.

It will be undertaken in two parts. The first part will describe how distinct and largely independent structures in the mind (modules) generate distinct 'cognitive ontologies': both physical (roughly speaking, representations of physical objects and events) and intentional (roughly speaking, representations of agents performing actions). The second part will describe how these cognitive ontologies can be used to reinterpret the linguistic and conceptual frameworks described by Rudolf Carnap and Willard van Orman Quine. This, in turn, will hopefully give some insight into 'ontological commitments' (in the Quinian sense of the term), to such things as gods and spirits. All this will be approached by asking the following question: when is it appropriate to think in terms of persons? Or, put slightly differently, when is person talk appropriate? I will return to these questions throughout the chapter and thus they will guide our exploration.

Importantly, I will use the word 'person' in a very specific way. I will assume a person is an entity or system that is taken to have intentional states (i.e., beliefs and desires). This characterisation of 'person' is relevant to one particular dimension of religious belief, namely, the belief in the existence of persons that are not directly associated with a live human body. There are a number of forms that such belief could take. For example, the God of classical theism, the forest spirits of the lowland Maya peoples, the spirits that created certain land forms described in the Dreaming of Indigenous Australian peoples, and the spirits of dead ancestors are all persons in the sense I have described, or so I will assume. Thus, while perhaps it is not a standard characterisation of the word 'person', this characterisation will be useful in our analysis of the guiding questions.

Now, the question 'when is it appropriate to think in terms of persons?' might seem a strange question to be asking, simply because the answer (surely) is obvious. It is appropriate to think in terms of persons when there are persons there! But that answer makes two assumptions: the first metaphysical and the second epistemological. First, it assumes realism with respect to persons; realism in the sense that the existence of individual persons is independent of anything anyone thinks about those persons. And, second, it assumes that our talk (or our thought) should be truth tracking. But, in this chapter, I do not necessarily make either of these assumptions. Indeed, one can think of this chapter as an exploration of the questions above without these assumptions in place. To unpack this a little more, consider how two different philosophers, Richard Swinburne and Patricia Churchland, would answer my guiding questions.

Swinburne is a dualist. He believes at the level of ultimate ontology two types of stuff exist. There exist both physical objects and persons at the most basic level of this universe (1991). He is a realist about the existence of persons and physical objects. Thus, talk about persons and physical objects can be truth tracking. There is a fact of the matter, about the existence of persons and physical objects, that our talk or thought can successfully track. So Swinburne endorses talk and thought about both persons and physical objects. Therefore, he endorses two modes of explanation: he endorses both scientific explanation, which involves objects with powers and liabilities, and personal explanation, which involves persons with powers and intentions (incorporating beliefs and desires). So, for him, when is person talk appropriate? Or when is it appropriate to think in terms of persons? When there are persons really there.

Churchland is a monist. She believes that at the level of ultimate ontology, one type of stuff exists: physical stuff.[1] Furthermore, she is an eliminative materialist, who advocates that we should attempt to explain human behaviour without reference to beliefs and desires because these are not part of ultimate ontology as she understands it (1986). She is a realist about the existence of physical objects, but not about persons, at the most fundamental level of this universe. Thus, while talk about physical objects can be truth tracking, talk about persons cannot track the truth (at the level of ultimate ontology). There is a fact of the matter, about the existence of physical objects, that our talk and thought can successfully track, but this is not the case with respect to persons (understood in the sense I have defined). Thus, Churchland does endorse talk and thought

---

[1] Here I ignore the distinction drawn in philosophy between materialism and physicalism, and I use the phrase 'physical stuff' simply to preserve the consistency of the language in the chapter.

about physical objects, but not about persons. So, in contrast to Swinburne, she does not endorse two modes of explanation (when talking or thinking about ultimate ontology). Therefore, her answers to the questions 'when is person talk appropriate?' and 'when is it appropriate to think in terms of persons?' will be different from Swinburne's. For her, when talking and thinking about ultimate ontology, person talk and thought is not appropriate.

Both Swinburne and Churchland are realists about the content of ultimate ontology, and both believe that talk and thought can and should be truth tracking. But they differ on what they assume is the nature of ultimate ontology and thus their answers to the guiding questions of this chapter are different. Churchland does not think that beliefs and desires are part of ultimate ontology, while Swinburne does. They think that if something is part of ultimate ontology, then it is appropriate to refer to that thing in our explanations, but if it is not part of ultimate ontology, then it is not appropriate to refer to it in our explanations. Because Churchland does not think that beliefs and desires are part of ultimate ontology, she does not endorse person talk. Because Swinburne does think that beliefs and desires are part of ultimate ontology, he does endorse person talk.

I question the assumption that explanations should be limited to using language that corresponds only to the entities that comprise ultimate ontology. Why is the appropriateness of talk driven only by whether or not it is tracking the truth of ultimate ontology? One answer might be that the goal of explanation is truth. So, if our explanations use terms such as 'belief' and 'desire' that do not correspond to anything in ultimate ontology, then such terms can only be leading us away from truth, and so should be avoided. But, informed by an evolutionary perspective, I take a different approach to the role of explanation.[2] I don't see it as necessarily tracking the truth; rather, explanations are cognitive representations that we, as evolved organisms, use to survive or more optimistically to thrive. Now, it is certainly the case that in many circumstances, if our explanations do not have some relationship to reality, then they will not help us to survive or thrive. But that does not imply that they have to be strictly true (whatever that might mean).

Thus, I wish to explore the possibility that person talk is appropriate in ways that may or may not track the truth. And to be clear, I am not asserting that truth is irrelevant to our endeavours; rather, I am suggesting that a focus on truth tracking

---

[2] This is a perspective that is gaining acceptance by researchers who adopt an evolutionary or ecological approach to human cognition (e.g., Gigerenzer, Todd and ABC Research Group, 1999; Gigerenzer, 2000).

may not be the best way to determine the appropriateness or inappropriateness of person talk, given our goal of surviving and, hopefully, thriving.

The point that the goal of living is not necessarily furthered by truth tracking cognitive processes is endorsed by a number of evolutionary biologists, for example, Wilson and Lynn:

> Dozens of evolutionists have observed that insofar as beliefs are products of natural selection, either proximally or distally, then they should be designed to enhance fitness, not to perceive the world as it really is ... To begin with genetic evolution ... deception begins with perception. All organisms perceive only the environmental stimuli that matter to their fitness. Our species can see only a narrow slice of the sound and light spectrum, cannot sense electrical and gravitational fields at all, and so on. We also distort what we can perceive, for example, by turning the continuous light spectrum into discrete colors. Perception might not qualify as belief, but if the former is so prone to adaptive distortions, it would be surprising if the latter was not prone as well. (2009, p. 539)

I will assume that truth tracking is, at best, an intermediate goal. The ultimate 'goal' of any organic system, subject to natural selection, is fitness.[3] If truth tracking furthers fitness, then it is appropriate from an evolutionary perspective. But if truth tracking does not further fitness, then it is not appropriate from an evolutionary perspective. And the way in which truth tracking may reduce fitness is related to the efficiency of thinking and talking. Cognitive systems that produce both thinking and talking require energy to run, and this has a metabolic cost to the organism. If the use of simple concepts (e.g., the concept of a person), rather than more complex concepts, increases the efficiency of cognitive processes, then the use of such concepts will be endorsed by natural selection. Thus, it may be more efficient to talk and think in terms of persons independently of whether there are any persons really there or not.

Assumptions

Cognitive science of religion is a relatively new area of research and there is no undisputed set of assumptions that all cognitive scientists of religion accept.

---

[3] The word 'goal' is in scare quotes because (it is assumed) there are no goals in evolutionary processes.

However, here, I will make the following two assumptions.[4] The first is that 'evolutionary analysis' (Samuels, 2000, p. 24) is necessary to understand the cognitive structures and functioning of the human mind, while the second is that the mind is modular, at least to a significant extent.

Biological 'evolutionary analysis' assumes that biological evolution is the causal-historical origin of the structure of biological systems. Evolutionary analysis provides a perspective from which to entertain possible causal-historical accounts of the production of particular organisms (or particular organs within organisms, such as the human brain). Furthermore, adopting evolutionary analysis imposes certain constraints on what we should accept about the structure of the human brain. These constraints can be made explicit by considering the following question: could biological evolution have produced the human brain as it is currently characterised by orthodox psychology? If biological evolution could not have produced the human brain as characterised by orthodox psychology, then this calls into question the assumptions made within orthodox psychology about the structure of the human brain.

Orthodox psychology considers the mind[5] to be a general cognitive system that has a number of features, including: perception, habituation, operant and classical conditioning, imitation, and the basic principles of logic and probabilistic reasoning. These are all *general* cognitive capacities. Any other more specific cognitive capacities, beliefs and practices are the result of learning and reasoning (Mameli, 2007, p. 21). Orthodox psychology assumes that the general features of cognition are the products of evolution, but that many of the more specific cognitive capacities are the product of human culture. So, orthodox psychology assumes that evolution gave us *general cognitive capacities*. However, this assumption is challenged by evolutionary analysis.

Evolution, it is assumed, is a process without foresight that builds upon existing features by random variation. Evolution is an incremental process that proceeds by small variations to pre-existing traits. If this assumption is correct, then the challenge for orthodox psychology is to explain how such a process could have produced the *general* cognitive capacities that we are assumed to have. Evolutionary analysis suggests that general cognitive capacities are not the type of capacities that one would expect evolution to generate (Simon, 1962; Carruthers, 2006, pp. 12–28).

---

[4] I will not argue for these assumptions, but rather take them as a starting point for exploration.

[5] I have moved from talk of the brain to talk of the mind. I make the move for the sake of the narrative of the chapter and I acknowledge that it is a significant move. But the relationship between the brain and the mind is beyond the scope of this chapter.

Thus, evolutionary analysis suggests that the mind is structured differently from the way that has been traditionally assumed within orthodox psychology. Rather than being one general information-processing system, evolutionary psychology assumes the mind is many distinct information processing systems. If a cognitive system were built up gradually by variations upon existing systems, one would expect the cognitive systems to be specialised rather than general. Just as, over evolutionary time, individual species (and the organs within them) get more adapted to the environment in which they exist, we should expect cognitive systems to get more adapted to the informational problems they encounter. In other words, they should become more specialised in response to specific survival situations.

Importantly, just because we cannot specify how an evolutionary process (that is assumed to proceed by small incremental steps) could have resulted in a general cognitive system, this does not prove that evolution could not generate such a system. But advocates of evolutionary psychology assert that we will make more progress in our understanding of the human mind if we assume that small incremental changes have been made to cognitive systems that evolved in response to specific evolutionary challenges, and that such a process would tend to produce specialised cognitive systems, not generalised ones.

Thus, an evolutionary perspective suggests we should be thinking about the structure of the mind differently, as pointed out by, for example, David Sloan Wilson:

> The ability to navigate by the stars or to dead reckon by the sun appear miraculous to us because they exceed our own ability, at least without extensive training. However, our minds are also packed with specialized circuits that enable us to solve our own problems of survival and reproduction as naturally as celestial navigation in birds and dead reckoning in ants. Psychologists should be trying to identify and understand these specialized circuits rather than pretending that human behaviour can be derived from a few law-like mechanistic principles. (2002, p. 26)

Evolutionary psychologists take the view that cognitive structures, like all other structures in the human organism, were produced through a process of evolution, 'to perform specific functions or to solve information processing problems that were important in the environment in which our hominid ancestors evolved' (Samuels, Stich and Tremoulet, 1999, p. 9). The general distinction between evolutionary psychology and orthodox psychology that is relevant here is related to the distinction between general cognitive systems that are capable of processing information in a large number of ways across a large number of domains, and specific cognitive systems that are only capable of processing information in a limited number of ways and only with respect to a limited number of domains.[6]

Adopting this evolutionary perspective leads to the second assumption I will make – that the mind is modular. This concept has been enthusiastically taken up by evolutionary psychologists, such as Leda Cosmides and John Tooby, who hold that the mind is massively modular:

> our cognitive architecture resembles a confederation of hundreds or thousands of functionally dedicated computers (often called modules) designed to solve adaptive problems endemic to our hunter-gatherer ancestors. Each of these devices has its own agenda and imposes its own exotic organization on different fragments of the world. There are specialized systems for grammar induction, for face recognition, for dead reckoning, for construing objects and for recognizing emotions from the face. There are mechanisms to detect animacy, eye direction, and cheating. There is a 'theory of mind' module ... a variety of social inference modules ... and a multitude of other elegant machines. (1997, p. xiv)

The massive modularity hypothesis assumes that most, if not all, of the mind is modular. I will not be assuming the massive modularity of the mind.[7] However,

---

[6] There may be a deeper historical and cultural reason that Western psychology has a tendency to think of the mind as a unified cognitive system. Western philosophy (and psychology) has been deeply affected by Descartes. Cartesian dualism allowed for considerations about the nature of the mind to be unconstrained by any causal-historical understanding of the nature and origins of the human brain. Although Descartes assumed that there was a relation between the mind and the brain, the origins of the brain were taken to be independent of the origins of the mind. This position, I believe, is endorsed today by Swinburne. Swinburne accepts the evolutionary account of the origins of the human brain as an organ within the body of a human. However, Swinburne's dualism (as I understand it) allows there to be an independent origin of the human mind. Thus, the human mind is unconstrained by the historical-causal origins of the human brain. Although I will not argue for it here, the development of orthodox psychology can be understood as the gradual limiting and dividing of a unified Cartesian mind, and in contrast, evolutionary psychology can be understood as assuming that cognition began evolutionarily as specific and fragmented cognitive responses to evolutionary pressure. Thus, evolutionary psychology and orthodox psychology have very different ways of conceptualising the mind.

[7] And furthermore, I will be assuming that the specific 'problems endemic to our hunter-gatherer ancestors' are of no particularly special relevance. I will be applying the attitude of evolutionary analysis to the problem of consciously representing the world from the moment our very ancient ancestor species began representing it.

I will be assuming that there are a significant number of processes in the mind that are modular, and that the outputs of these modules are available to 'central cognition'. A way of understanding the relationship between modules and central cognition is to use the 'two systems' approach to cognition (Stanovich and West, 2000).

Within this approach, it is assumed that there are two ways in which the mind processes information. These two systems are characterised as follows:

> *System 1 (intuition):* fast; automatic; undemanding of cognitive capacity; acquired by biology, exposure, and personal experience.

> *System 2 (reasoning):* slow; controlled; demanding of cognitive capacity; acquired by cultural and formal tuition. (Kahneman, 2002)

For the purposes of this chapter, I will assume that modules are responsible for system 1 cognitive processes and that central cognition is responsible for system 2 cognitive processes.

Yet another way of understanding the relationship between modules and central cognition is to think of modules or system 1 to be employing heuristics (Gigerenzer, Todd and ABC Research Group, 1999; Gigerenzer, 2000). Heuristics can be thought of as 'rules of thumb' that are deployed directly by central cognition, but it is also possible that evolution has created stand-alone (modular) information-processing systems that use fast and frugal computational processes independently of central cognition. The outputs of these system 1 modules then simply present central cognition with their output. The output of these system 1 modules is what central cognition recognises as intuitions.

So in this chapter, I will assume, first, that the structure and function of the mind must be consistent with a biologically evolved mind, and, second, that a significant proportion of the mind is modular in structure.

Person Talk and Object Talk

Taking evolutionary analysis and mental modularity seriously can give us an insight into the structure and functioning of the mind, and into the nature of religious belief. And specifically, it can help us answer the following question: when is person talk appropriate? I will assume for the purposes of this chapter that there are modules in the mind that generate our cognitive representations of the world. Following Cosmides and Tooby, I also believe that each of these modules 'has its own agenda and imposes its own exotic organization on different fragments of the world' (1997, p. xiv). Thus, for example, between the stimulation of the rods and cones in the retina of the eye and central cognition's perception of a bounded physical object, say a ball being thrown toward you, there are a number of modifications that have occurred to that stream of information. These modifications may all occur in one module (sometimes called the 'folk physics' module), but perhaps it is more likely that they occur in a number of modules. One module may be responsible for representing the surface of the ball, such that the ball is considered an object distinct from other objects, and another module may be responsible for predicting the movement of such physical objects through space so that central cognition is able to decide to move your hand so that you can catch the ball.

This approach assumes that a number of modules are actively structuring the representations of the world that are then made available to central cognition.

So, perhaps, the very notion of a physical bounded object may be generated by the set of modules rather than being a real feature of ultimate ontology. Indeed, this is consistent with our contemporary understanding of physical objects. As is pointed out in introductory physics (and metaphysics) classes, the so-called 'solid' mid-sized physical objects with which we interact are not solid at all; they are largely empty space. All this leaves open the possibility that tables and chairs, and buses and bandicoots are not really part of the ultimate ontology. Perhaps they are representations given to us by our modular mind.[8]

At this point it is worth making a distinction between two uses of the word 'ontology'. I use the phrase 'metaphysical ontology' to refer to the ultimate ontology of existence (whatever that might include) and I use the phrase 'cognitive ontology' to refer to the set of representations of entities that are generated by cognitive processes. Given that I am assuming a modular architecture of the mind, there may be a number of different cognitive ontologies that are all created by different modules.

In addition to the set of modules that result in the cognitive ontology representing the physical, I suggest that there is a set of modules that create

---

[8] There is an even deeper level at which this representation of a physical object might be given to us by the modules in our mind. If we embrace the notion that a quantum particle does not have an exact location until it is observed (or, more accurately, before it is observed its location is defined by a probability function), then perhaps the module in the mind is also responsible for the observation that gives mid-sized objects (as sets of quantum particles) definitive location. But I will not pursue this idea any further here. However, I will note in passing that it has interesting parallels with Kant's claim that the concepts of the space and time themselves are not part of ultimate reality.

the cognitive ontology representing the intentional. The intentional involves actions and agents (or, if you like, persons that undertake actions to further their purposes). While there can be a relationship between the outputs and inputs of the modules that create both the cognitive ontology of the physical and the intentional (as I will explain presently), I suggest that the functioning of these sets of modules may be much more independent than has been previously assumed.

To get a sense of what I mean by an intentional action, consider some sensory input that is manipulated by a module such that it represents an event. The representation of the purely physical event will be the output of the set of modules that generate the cognitive ontology of the physical. And that could be the end of the matter, such that the event could just be represented simply as a physical event. However, it might not end there. The representation of the event could become an input to the set of modules that represent the cognitive ontology of the intentional and thus be represented as an intentional event. If this happens, then, rather than only being represented as a physical event, the event is also represented as an intentional action.

If the relevant set of modules has represented an event as an intentional action, then the module itself (or perhaps central cognition) must further represent an agent who could have performed the action. There cannot be *sui generis* 'action' simply because an action, as opposed to an event, does not make sense without an agent to perform it.. Thus, within the relevant set of modules (or perhaps in combination with central cognition), an ontology of the intentional is built that involves actions and agents (persons). Therefore, the set of modules has an input of certain sensory stimuli (that may themselves be the output of a different set of modules – for example, the set responsible for the representation of physical entities) and posits the existence of an intentional cognitive ontology (i.e., agents performing actions) and then the output of that module can be used by central cognition to enable us to act appropriately in response to that representation. Thus, there are two sets of modules that may interact, but equally may process information independently to generate two independent ontologies: one of the physical and one of the intentional.[9]

Notice how this fits with Swinburne's position that there are parallel personal and scientific explanatory schemas. Perhaps Swinburne's personal explanations (that involve the postulation of persons with powers and intentions, incorporating

---

[9] Here I suppose an advocate of a naturalistic world-view will assume that the 'proper function' of the cognitive ontology of the intentional is to attribute intentionality to very particular parts of the cognitive ontology of the physical, namely live humans, and perhaps some other animals. But, as I have said, this chapter is an exploration without making certain assumptions, such as this.

beliefs and desires) have their origin in a set of modules that have generated a cognitive ontology of the intentional, i.e., representations of actions and agents. Similarly, perhaps Swinburne's scientific explanations (that involve the postulation of objects with powers and liabilities) have their origin in the set of modules that has generated the cognitive ontology of the physical, i.e., representations of events and objects. Notice also that this could be the case independently of whether or not persons and objects are part of metaphysical ontology.

On this account, different sets of modules may be operating dependently (e.g., one set taking the output of another set as its own input) or independently. There is no assumption of dependence simply because the sets of modules may have evolved as independent solutions to particular evolutionary challenges. To illustrate this point, think of different sets of modules as different government departments within a nation state that are all largely autonomous and choose to interact with the citizens of the state in their own often unique ways. Now consider dealing with a number of different government departments with respect to the same issue, say, registering a corporation. It is easy to imagine different departments requiring that information be submitted in very different forms. Thus, the information would need to be represented in different ways. Similarly, we should not necessarily expect sets of modules to be coordinated with other sets of modules; rather, each set could generate its own 'exotic organization' on the parts of the world it represents.

Fitness, Not (Necessarily) Truth

Now I wish to return to the claim that the structure and functioning of cognition in biological organisms is determined not by whether or not the cognitive processes generate true beliefs, but rather by whether or not they enhance fitness.

The generation of cognitive ontologies, I claim, is driven by evolutionary selective pressures. If a particular set of stimuli are represented as a physical entity in the cognitive ontology of an organism and as a result of that representation the organism is subject to positive selective pressure, then such representations will tend to persist in the cognitive systems of the descendants of that organism. And, importantly, this persistence is independent of whether or not such physical entities exist in metaphysical ontology. Similarly, if a particular set of stimuli are represented as an intentional entity in the cognitive ontology of an organism and as a result of that representation the organism is subject to positive selective pressure, then such representations will tend to persist in the cognitive systems of the descendants of that organism. And, again importantly, this persistence is independent of whether or not such an intentional entity exists in metaphysical ontology.

Furthermore, I have suggested that the functioning of these modules may be independent of one another. And this independence has important consequences with respect to the guiding questions of this chapter: when is person talk appropriate? And when is thinking in terms of persons appropriate? Therefore, these consequences are worth exploring briefly.

Imagine, for argument's sake, that you endorse the (metaphysical) position that it is appropriate to consider only humans and some other animals to be intentional entities and, furthermore, that once those humans and other animals die, they cease to be intentional entities. If this is your position, you have imposed a hierarchical relation upon the functioning of the set of modules responsible for creating representations of physical entities and the set of modules responsible for creating representations of intentional entities. For example, if there is no representation of a physical entity of a very particular kind, namely the representation of a living human (or other relevant animal), then any output of the set of modules that creates representations of intentional entities is deemed inappropriate. Put more simply, it is deemed inappropriate to use person talk if there is no living human (or other relevant animal) to which the person talk can refer.

The endorsement of this metaphysical position brings with it certain assumptions (assumptions that, for the purposes of this chapter, I neither accept nor reject). First, it assumes that there are mid-sized physical objects, 'out there' independently from our perception of them.[10] And, second, it presupposes that the 'goal' of cognition is truth tracking. Thus, cognition 'gets it right' when cognition represents physical objects as existing when they actually do exist. Similar assumptions are made with respect to persons. First, this approach presupposes that there are persons (intentional systems) 'out there' independently of our representation of them. And, second, it presupposes that the 'goal' of cognition is truth tracking. Thus, cognition 'gets it right' when cognition represents intentional systems as existing when they actually do exist. Furthermore, this position assumes that intentional systems only exist where there is already a particular physical system (a living human or other relevant animal).

With respect to the last assumption made above, notice that there is a hierarchy assumed to hold between the outputs of the modules that create

---

[10] To be clear here, I am not denying the independent existence of the entities that comprise metaphysical ontology, but only the independent existence of the entities that comprise cognitive ontology.

representations of physical entities and intentional entities. But, I suggest, purely from the perspective of evolutionary analysis (and without making the assumptions listed above), there is no hierarchy necessarily imposed upon the functioning of these two sets of modules. These systems could represent the world independently of one another. The set of modules that generated the cognitive ontology of intentional entities can represent any fragment of reality as an intentional system and the set of modules that generate the cognitive ontology of physical entities can represent any fragment of reality as a physical system. Each will be subject to selective pressure, and if the representations lead to reproductive success, then those representations will tend to persist within the cognitive processes of individuals in the population. Again, it is important to stress that the representations that are produced by the cognitive processes within organisms are selected with reference to fitness and these representations may or may not represent the world as it really is. To put it another way, the cognitive ontologies that evolution endorses may or may not have any direct relation to metaphysical ontology.

Metaphysics: Sellars, Dennett, Carnap and Quine

Now I wish to move from cognitive science of religion and evolutionary psychology to philosophy, and I will suggest that the cognitive structures that I have described can be used to understand the origins of a number of important distinctions and concepts within philosophy. I will draw on the work of Wilfrid Sellars, Daniel Dennett, Rudolf Carnap and Willard van Orman Quine, beginning with the distinction Sellars draws between the manifest image and the scientific image of the world:

> Thus although methodologically a development *within* the manifest image, the scientific image presents itself as a *rival* image. From its point of view the manifest image on which it rests is an 'inadequate' but pragmatically useful likeness of a reality which first finds its adequate (in principle) likeness in the scientific image. I say 'in principle' because the scientific image is still in the process of coming into being. (1964, p. 57)

I take the manifest image to be constructed from outputs of modular structures in the mind (system 1), while the scientific image is constructed by central cognition (system 2). If we take the cognitive ontology of physical entities and the cognitive ontology of intentional entities to be the outputs of sets of modules, then these are both parts of the manifest image (called by some 'folk physics' and 'folk psychology'). In contrast, our best science, say, relativity theory and quantum mechanics, are part of the scientific image.

Thus, cognitive ontologies, produced by modular processes, equate to the manifest image of the world, and metaphysical ontology is the ultimate ontology that presumably science is attempting to uncover. And it follows from this that the contents of a cognitive ontology will not have any direct relation to the contents of metaphysical ontology just as the common-sense world of mid-sized physical objects will not have any direct relation to the quantum world.[11]

Dennett endorses the idea that our minds generate the manifest image:

> It is no accident that we have the manifest image that we do; our nervous systems were designed to make the distinctions we need swiftly and reliably, to bring under single sensory rubrics the relevant common features of our environment, and to ignore what we can usually get away with ignoring ... The undeniable fact is that usually, especially in the dealings that are most important in our daily lives, folk physics works. Thanks to folk physics we stay warm and well fed and avoid collisions, and thanks to folk psychology we cooperate on multiperson projects, learn from each other, and enjoy periods of local peace. These benefits would be unattainable without our extraordinarily efficient and reliable systems of expectation-generation. (1987, p. 11)

And although he does not explicitly claim that these 'systems of expectation generation' are modular, such a suggestion would be consistent with his position.

Let us now look in some detail at Dennett's description of taking the intentional stance, the stance in which one attributes beliefs and desires to other entities:

> first you decide to treat the object whose behaviour is to be predicted as a rational agent; then you figure out what beliefs that agent ought to have, given its place in

---

[11] Although it is interesting to note that we sometimes still use concepts generated within the manifest image to represent concepts within the scientific image. To illustrate this point, consider the concepts of a wave and a particle that are both outputs of the cognitive ontology of the manifest image. These concepts are combined (with questionable success) in the concept of 'wave-particle duality' within the metaphysical ontology of the scientific image. This highlights the fact that there are limited resources within the manifest image to capture the notion of light when considered from within the scientific image. The currently accepted option is to attempt to combine two concepts from the manifest image that really do not go together at all! But given that we have no other way of representing the scientific image of light, we make do with what we do have some grasp of from within the manifest image.

the world and its purpose. Then you figure out what desires it ought to have, on the same considerations, and finally you predict that this rational agent will act to further its goals in the light of its beliefs. (1987, p. 17)

Notice that Dennett's language here clearly suggests that taking the intentional stance is something that one decides to do, and this would suggest that it is central cognition (system 2) that takes the intentional stance. And as we will see, both Carnap's and Quine's language also suggest that adopting a certain linguistic or conceptual framework is something one decides to do. And this is where I will take a different approach from Dennett, Carnap and Quine. I suggest that, due to the modular structure of the mind, the apparent decisions they claim that one makes are not decisions in the standard sense of that term; rather, I suggest that these are cognitive ontologies that our modular mind gives our central cognition to think with, in the same way that Sellars' manifest image is given.

So, rather than making a conscious choice to take the intentional stance towards a system, I suggest that the very idea that a system could have an intentional attitude may only be available to central cognition because it has been produced by a module. Think of the module as providing to central cognition the pieces of a jigsaw (the postulation of the existence of particular actions performed by agents, say) that central cognition then constructs into a complete intentional explanatory schema. On my account, if the module (system 1) had not first attributed intentionality to some entity, then central cognition (system 2) could not 'decide' to treat the entity as an intentional agent.

Dennett also considers when it is appropriate to take the intentional stance, thereby providing an answer to the guiding questions of this chapter: when is person talk appropriate and when is thinking in terms of persons appropriate? His answer is that it is appropriate to attribute intentionality to a system if your predictions based on those attributions are successful:

Any system whose behaviour is well predicted by this strategy is in the fullest sense of the word a believer. What it is to be a true believer is to be an intentional system, a system whose behaviour is reliably and voluminously predictable via the intentional strategy. (1987, p. 15)

Now this commits Dennett to a position he calls 'semi-realism', a position that I will not explore in detail here. But for our present purposes, let us take Dennett to hold that the following claim is true: if a system is reliably and voluminously predictable via the intentional strategy (and if no other strategy can give equivalent predictability) then that system really has beliefs and desires (albeit in Dennett's semi-realist sense). So, predictability is the fundamental measure of success for Dennett. The appropriateness or inappropriateness of attributing beliefs and desires to a system is settled by whether or not the system is 'predictable via the intentional strategy'. If a system is predictable (and only predicable) using the intentional strategy, then that system has intentions.

But I resist the assumption that predictability determines the appropriateness or inappropriateness of the attribution of beliefs and desires to a system; rather, I suggest fitness determines this matter. I assume that it is appropriate to attribute beliefs and desires to a system if that attribution enhances the fitness of the organism making the attribution. Or, putting this point in terms of the guiding question of the chapter, it is appropriate to think in terms of persons when such thinking enhances fitness.

Now I wish to move to Carnap and Quine and consider the notions of linguistic (Carnap) and conceptual (Quine) frameworks, and suggest that these frameworks have their origin in the cognitive ontologies that are produced by evolved modules (or sets of modules) in the mind. This modular characterisation is a very different interpretation of these frameworks from the interpretations offered by both Carnap and Quine. I assume they would have supposed that the application of a linguistic or conceptual framework was largely (if not exclusively) the work of central cognition (system 2). But I suggest that much more work is being done by modules (system 1) than I assume they would have supposed.

I will begin by considering Carnap and Quine on what they call internal and external questions with respect to the adoption of both linguistic and conceptual frameworks. Then I will use Quine's idea of ontological commitment to suggest how we might understand ontological commitment to intentional systems. And, finally, I will link these ideas to research in cognitive science of religion and point to how this might explain the positing of the existence of the gods and spirits.

So, to begin, here is Carnap on linguistic frameworks:

> If someone wishes to speak in his/her language about a new kind of entities, s/he has to introduce a system of new ways of speaking, subject to new rules; we shall call this procedure the construction of a linguistic framework for the new entities in question. (1958, p. 206)

Carnap distinguishes internal questions and external questions that one could ask about the linguistic framework. Internal questions are questions relating to 'the existence of certain entities of the new kind within the framework', while external questions are questions 'concerning the existence or reality of the system of entities as a whole'. Consider Carnap on the internal question of how one recognises something as real within the language of things:

> To recognise something as a real thing or event means to succeed in incorporating it into the system of things at a particular space-time position so that it fits together with the other things recognised as real, according to the rules of the framework. (1958, p. 207)

We could take this exact proposition and take him to be referring to a cognitive ontology generated by a module. The only difference would be that rather than the 'rules of the framework' being interpreted as linguistic rules, the rules are representational rules of the internal workings of the module; in this case, perhaps the internal computational rules of the folk physics module. Similarly, we could paraphrase this sentence such that it refers to the cognitive ontology of intentional entities:

> To recognise something as a real person means to succeed in incorporating it into the system of persons within a web of purposes so that it fits together with the other persons recognised as real, according to the rules of the framework.

And again, rather than a set of linguistic rules, the rules in this case would be the set of representational rules of the internal workings of the module, in this case perhaps the internal computational rules of the folk psychology module. If the inclusion of the representation of a particular object or a person in a cognitive ontology of an organism (in conformity with the rules of that cognitive ontology) increased the fitness of that organism, then that incorporation would be endorsed.

Internal questions relate to whether or not to incorporate the representation of some stimulus within a pre-existing cognitive ontology. However, there is also the external question of whether or not to adopt an entire cognitive ontology. So now let us consider Carnap on external questions.

For Carnap, the acceptance of a new language form is not an assertion of the existence of the entities; rather, 'acceptance ... can only be judged as being more or less expedient, fruitful, conducive to the aim for which the language is intended' (1958, p. 214). So, in order to answer whether or not it is appropriate to use the concepts of 'person' or 'physical object' at all, we need to know the use of the concept.

What is the intended use of 'person talk'? To unpack this question, we can return to a response we considered earlier to the following question: when is 'person talk' appropriate? The response was: when there are real persons there! But now we see that there are other ways to consider this question, as indeed Carnap does.

It is appropriate to use 'person talk' when such use furthers the aim for which the language (or, as I would suggest, the cognitive ontology) is intended. So what is the use for which the cognitive ontology is intended? Well, others may assert that the intended use of person talk is to track the existence of real persons, but I suggest that the purpose of person talk is the enhancement of fitness. If the use of the cognitive ontology of persons enhances fitness, then its use will be endorsed by evolution.

Much of this is echoed by Quine:

> As an empiricist I continue to think of the conceptual scheme of science as a tool, ultimately, for predicting future experience in the light of past experience. Physical objects are conceptually imported into the situation as convenient intermediaries – not by definition in terms of experience, but simply as irreducible posits comparable, epistemologically, to the gods of Homer … Both sorts of entities enter our conception only as cultural posits. The myth of physical objects is epistemologically superior to most in that it has proved more efficacious than other myths as a device for working a manageable structure into the flux of experience. (1963, p. 44)

Just as Carnap described the process as a conscious linguistic process, Quine describes it as a cultural process. But again I suggest that this process is going on at a much deeper level. It is going on at the level of cognitive ontologies produced by modules that are in turn produced by evolutionary pressures. Quine describes the concept of a physical object as being an irreducible posit and a convenient intermediary, and this is consistent with the concept of a physical object being generated by the folk physics module and then becoming part of the manifest image.

Now, just as Carnap considered both internal and external questions with respect to the use of a linguistic framework, Quine considers these questions with respect to the use of a conceptual framework. His criterion of ontological commitment is the answer to the internal question:

> [A] theory is committed to those and only those entities to which the bound variables of the theory must be capable of referring in order that the affirmations made in the theory be true. (1963, p. 14)

As the answer to the internal question, this criterion (or the slogan 'to be is to be the value of a variable') is used in 'testing the conformity of a given remark or doctrine to a prior ontological standard' (1963, p. 15). But this does not answer the external question of what conceptual schema to adopt: 'the question what ontology actually to adopt still stands open'. And it is addressed with reference to 'the epistemological point of view. [But t]his point of view is one among various, corresponding to one among our various interests and purposes' (1963, p. 19).

Quine characterises 'physical object talk' as superior to 'god talk' when our purpose is 'predicting future experience in the light of past experience'. But again I suggest that this is merely an intermediate purpose. Evolution is only interested in cognitive systems predicting future experience because (in some or perhaps most circumstances) this enhances fitness, but if other cognitive processes, not focused on prediction, also enhance fitness, then evolution selects them too.

If this is the case, then commitment to an intentional ontology may be appropriate. And this may mean that the cognitive ontology of persons and purposes (or agents and actions) is appropriately applied not only to humans and other relevant animals, but much more broadly too. Thus, from an evolutionary perspective, beliefs about gods and spirits may be appropriate. Of course, an account explaining how beliefs about gods and spirits could enhance fitness is needed, but such accounts exist in the current cognitive science of religion literature (e.g., Wilson, 2002; Schloss and Murray, 2009).

Conclusion

In this chapter I have made two perhaps controversial assumptions: first, that we should understand the structure and functioning of the human mind using evolutionary analysis; and, second, that the mind is to a significant extent modular in structure. Perhaps equally controversially, I have resisted making two other assumptions: a metaphysical assumption (realism with respect to physical mid-sized objects and persons); and an epistemological assumption (the purpose of belief is to track the truth). I have sketched an account of how modules generate cognitive ontologies that may or may not correspond to metaphysical ontology. A module (or set of modules) generates the cognitive ontology of the physical. An independent module (or set of modules) generates the cognitive ontology of the intentional. The entities in the intentional ontology are persons with intentions (purposes) or, if you like, agents performing actions. If an entity is part of your intentional ontology, you then understand the relation of that entity (that person) to other entities (other persons) with reference to intentions (articulated with reference to beliefs and desires). And the intentional ontology of 'persons' is independent of the physical ontology of 'objects' (independent in the sense that an intentional entity does not first need to be a physical entity before it can be represented as an intentional entity) because these two different cognitive ontologies are the outputs of different mental modules (or sets of modules) shaped by distinct evolutionary pressures. The belief in the existence of gods, spirits and human persons can all be understood with reference to the cognitive ontology of the intentional.

Finally, and really only as an aside to the analysis undertaken here, we could, if we so desired, ask whether Sellars' scientific image or Quine's scientific ontology could settle the question of when it is appropriate to use person talk. But, as it happens, it could not settle that question. This would be equivalent to asking the following question: would quantum physics tell me when it is or is not appropriate to believe that there is a chair in front of me? Similarly, quantum physics could not tell me whether it is appropriate or inappropriate to believe that the physical system in front of me has purposes (be that physical system a member of the human species, a forest or the universe). It could not settle the question because such questions, for Quine, are settled by pragmatic factors. Indeed, Quine consulted his own 'interests and purposes' and chose the epistemological point of view (and presumably Sellars' claim that the manifest imagine was 'inadequate' was also informed by his own 'interests and purposes'). But others may have different interests and purposes, and hence judge things from a different point of view. And, furthermore, the metaphysical ontology cannot be consulted to settle questions of what are the appropriate cognitive ontologies unless you have already assumed realism with respect to the entities in question, and that truth tracking is the trumping function of our cognitive systems. Now you may well make these assumptions if making them furthers your own 'interests and purposes', but I will leave that up to you. And, of course, these are the very assumptions that I have abstained from making throughout this exploration. But, in conclusion, it is intriguing to note that, if we accept the Quinean analysis in order to answer these questions, we must consult our own interests and purposes. So, it would seem that one's ontological commitments depend upon one's teleological commitments.

References

Carnap, R., 1958. Empiricism, semantics and ontology. In *Meaning and Necessity: A Study in Semantics and Modal Logic*. Chicago: University of Chicago Press, pp. 205–21.

Carruthers, P., 2006. *The Architecture of the Mind*. Oxford: Clarendon Press.

Churchland, P.S., 1986. *Neurophilosophy: Toward a Unified Science of the Mind/Brain*. Cambridge, MA: MIT Press.

Cosmides, L. and Tooby, J., 1997. Foreword. In: S. Baron-Cohen, *Mindblindness: An Essay on Autism and Theory of Mind*. Cambridge, MA: MIT Press.

Dennett, D., 1987. *The Intentional Stance*. Cambridge, MA: MIT Press.

Gigerenzer, G., 2000. *Adaptive Thinking: Rationality in the Real World*. Oxford: Oxford University Press.

Gigerenzer, G., Todd, P.M. and ABC Research Group, 1999. *Simple Heuristics that Make Us Smart*. New York: Oxford University Press.

Kahneman, D., 2002. Maps of bounded rationality: a perspective on intuitive judgment and choice. Nobel Prize Lecture. Available at: http://nobelprize.org/nobel_prizes/economics/laureates/2002/kahnemann-lecture.pdf.

Mameli, M., 2007. Evolution and psychology in philosophical perspective. In: L. Barrett and R. Dunbar (eds), *Oxford Handbook of Evolutionary Psychology*. Oxford: Oxford University Press, pp. 21–34.

Quine, W.V., 1963. *From a Logical Point of View*. New York: Harper & Row.

Samuels, R., 2000. Massively modular minds: evolutionary psychology and cognitive architecture. In: P. Carruthers and A. Chamberlain (eds), *Evolution and the Human Mind: Modularity, Language and meta-cognition*. Cambridge: Cambridge University Press, pp. 13–46.

Samuels, R., Stich, S. and Tremoulet, P.D., 1999. Rethinking rationality: from bleak implications to Darwinian modules. In: E. Lepore and Z. Pylyshyn (eds), *What is Cognitive Science?* Oxford: Blackwell, pp. 74–120.

Schloss, J. and Murray, M. (eds), 2009. *The Believing Primate*. Oxford: Oxford University Press.

Sellars, W., 1964. Philosophy and the scientific image of man. In: R. Colodny (ed.), *Frontiers of Science and Philosophy*. London: Allen & Unwin, pp. 35–78.

Simon, H., 1962. The architecture of complexity. *Proceedings of the American Philosophical Society*, 106, pp. 467–82.

Stanovich, K. and West, R., 2000. Individual differences in reasoning: implications for the rationality debate. *Behavioral and Brain Sciences*, 23, pp. 645–65.

Swinburne, R., 1991. *The Existence of God*. Oxford: Clarendon Press.

Wilson, D.S., 2002. *Darwin's Cathedral: Evolution, Religion, and the Nature of Society*. Chicago: University of Chicago Press.

Wilson, D.S. and Lynn, S.J., 2009. Adaptive misbeliefs are pervasive, but the case for positive illusion is weak. *Behavioral and Brain Sciences*, 32, pp. 539–40.

Chapter 7

Knowledge and the Objection to Religious Belief from Cognitive Science

Kelly James Clark and Dani Rabinowitz

Belief in gods requires no special parts of the brain. Belief in gods requires no special mystical experiences, though it may be aided by such experiences. Belief in gods requires no coercion or brainwashing or special persuasive techniques. Rather, belief in gods arises because of the natural functioning of completely normal mental tools working in common natural and social contexts. (Barrett, 2004, p. 21)

Part I

Theism is no stranger to attack. In its long and checkered history it has faced a barrage of assaults on its veracity. Some of these challenges, like the problem of evil, remain unresolved. The scientific revolution marked the beginning of a particularly difficult period for theism, with these difficulties intensified by modern science. Today the science vs. theism debate is an industry of its own. In recent years a growing number of atheists have made recourse to some of the findings in contemporary cognitive science to formulate a novel challenge to theistic belief. According to several psychologists, anthropologists, evolutionary theorists, and cognitive scientists, the human mind evolved in such a way that it is naturally drawn towards belief in disembodied, supernatural agents, the God of monotheism being just one such agent. The belief that God exists, according to most defenders of this view, is an accidental byproduct of certain cognitive mechanisms that evolved for rather different adaptive purposes. Richard Dawkins (2006, pp. 200–22) and Daniel Dennett (2006), for example, make use of this research in their case against theism.[1] While neither explicitly claims that in virtue of this research there is something epistemically suspect about the belief that God exists, the innuendo is obvious. Dawkins contends that these findings partly explain why it is that people acquire and maintain the delusion that God exists, while for Dennett, this research "breaks the spell" of religious belief.

---

[1] Atran (2002), Bering (2006; 2011), Bloom (2005), Boyer (2001), and Wilson (2002) are additional examples of this style of argument.

Since no formal arguments are presented, it remains unclear how the research in the Cognitive Science of Religion (CSR) is alleged to undermine the positive epistemic status of the belief that God exists (hereafter, we shall call such attempts "the CSR objection"). Some (e.g., Murray, 2009; and Clark and Barrett, 2010; 2011) have taken up the challenge of proposing different ways in which such arguments could be formulated to the conclusion that religious beliefs are *irrational*. This chapter is a continuation of this line of work, but differs in two respects. First, we consider how the CSR objection might be understood in terms of Timothy Williamson's knowledge-first framework (Williamson, 2000). Second, in light of the significant role that testimony plays in the acquisition and transmission of religious belief, we consider the role that the epistemology of testimony could play in the CSR objection. Section 2 begins with a presentation of the relevant aspects of the CSR research. Thereafter follows a brief explanation of Williamson's claim that safe belief is a necessary condition for knowledge. A treatment of several epistemic terms of art concludes section 2. In section 3 we present two different ways in which the CSR objection can be formulated as an argument to the effect that the belief that God exists is unsafe. We argue that neither version works.

Part II

The Cognitive Science of Religion

Owing to differences in methodologies and research goals, there is no definitive statement of the cognitive and evolutionary psychology of religion. For our purposes it will suffice to draw attention to the work of Justin Barrett (2004; 2009), a dominant figure in the CSR literature. Here is a rough sketch of Barrett's theory.

Human beings are naturally prone to develop a certain class of concepts that Barrett labels "minimally counterintuitive concepts" (MCIs). An MCI is a standard concept that has been augmented in some rather unusual ways such that it becomes attention-grabbing, easy to understand and remember, and has the capacity to feature in the explanation of many events. A "talking shoe" or an "invisible dog" are examples of MCIs. It is not unusual to find disparate groups, in no contact with one another, having many MCIs in common. The concept of a "god" is an example of a common MCI, where a "god" is a disembodied, supernatural agent. Eventually the concept of God developed where that term denotes the God of monotheism.

The mental configuration of human beings also includes an Agency Detection Device (ADD) that disposes us to detect agency in our environment. Because ADD is sometimes triggered on the slenderest of bases (a rustle in the bush, a creaking of the floor), it has been called "hypersensitive." As such, the so-called Hypersensitive Agency Detection Device (HADD) often registers false positives. With respect to evolutionary psychology, possessing such a hypersensitive device has survival advantages, since the speedy and non-inferential detection of an agent in the vicinity (a predator, say, or a potential mate) would have increased one's survival, thus leading to greater reproductive success. Once the presence of an agent is registered, a second mental tool kicks in. This tool, commonly termed "Theory of Mind" (ToM), attributes a mental life to the detected agent, where such attributions typically concern what beliefs, desires or intentions that agent might have vis-à-vis the subject.

At a point in our history some primitive peoples perceived a state of affairs that resulted in HADD triggering a belief in the presence of an agent. With the aid of ToM, the state of affairs made sense by virtue of an agent acting in a particular way with particular intentions. However, only agents with MCI concepts of god-like agents could explain what they had perceived, as no natural explanation adequately accounted for these circumstances. As a result, human beings came to believe that God exists. In some cases the order of explanation is in the reverse—the MCI "God" developed on its own apart from such inexplicable states of affairs. Only much later did certain human beings retroactively understand said states of affairs in terms of God's actions.

Knowledge as Safe Belief

Knowledge, for Williamson (2000), requires avoidance of error in similar cases. The basic idea is that S knows p only if S is safe from error, where being safe means that there must be no risk or danger that S falsely believes p in a relevantly similar case. Knowledge, then, permits just a small margin of error; that is, cases in which S knows p must be buffered by cases of true belief. The relevant modal notions of safety, risk, and danger are cashed out in terms of possible worlds such that a margin for error is created insofar as there is no close world in which S falls into error. Such worlds act as a "buffer zone" from error and thereby prevent the type of epistemic luck that characterize Gettier cases (Gettier, 1963; Shope, 1983). Here is one pertinent formulation of the safety condition:

If in a case α one knows *p* on a basis *B*, then in any case close to α in which one believes a proposition *p** close to *p* on a basis [*B**] close to *B*, then *p** is true. (Williamson, 2009, p. 325)

For example, *S* does not know that it is noon by looking at a broken clock that correctly reads noon, since there is a close world in which *S* falsely believes that it is noon, e.g., a world in which *S* looks at the broken clock at any time other than noon.

Unlike the aforementioned authors, we grapple with the CSR objection in terms of knowledge and not in terms of rationality. There are several reasons for this difference in strategy. First, since those putting forward the CSR objection do not explicitly state that religious beliefs are irrational by virtue of the finding in cognitive science and evolutionary psychology, there is no *prima facie* reason to interpret their challenge in terms of rationality instead of knowledge, especially if knowledge is the more primitive concept of the two.[2] Given the current popularity of explications of knowledge in terms of safe belief, Williamson's safety condition is a natural choice, seeing that he is one of the more influential safety theorists.[3]

Second, most agree that knowledge is non-accidentally true belief. However, there is no consensus to be found among those working on rationality. While some consider rationality to be tied to the degree to which evidence increases the probability of a belief's being true, others see it as a property that supervenes on the reliability of cognitive mechanisms, while yet others deem it to be a kind of self-reflective state. As such, some see rationality as being determined from an external point of view, while others view it from an internal point of view. The concepts of rationality that result from such divergent approaches can be radically different. By concentrating on knowledge as opposed to rationality, we avoid this murky and contested territory.

Third, given that the CSR research concerns the apparently accidental genesis of theistic belief, one natural concern would be that accidentally true theistic belief is unsafe. It would not make sense, then, to formulate arguments against theistic belief on the basis of the CSR research in terms of rationality, for on most accounts of rationality an agent *S* may be rational in believing *p* despite being lucky that *p* is true.

Finally, there is good reason to think that the appropriate norm for assertion and practical reasoning is knowledge and not justified or rational belief

---

[2] For arguments to the effect that knowledge is a primitive concept, see Williamson, 2000, pp. 2–5.

[3] Sosa (1999) and Pritchard (2005; 2009) are the other two influential safety theorists.

(Williamson, 2000, pp. 238ff; Hawthorne and Stanley, 2008). Since theistic belief is often the subject of assertion and, more importantly, influences the way theists go about living their lives, it makes sense to worry about whether theists can know that God exists in light of the CSR research more than whether theists can rationally believe that God exists.

Before commencing our treatment of the CSR objection, two epistemic terms of art need to be addressed. First, there is a distinction between individual epistemology and social epistemology. The first makes normative assessments of a specific agent's beliefs, e.g., that an agent S's belief that p is warranted or rational or justified or known if and only if conditions $C_1, ..., C_n$ are satisfied. The second differs in that normative assessments are made about an entire community's belief(s). We understand the methodology of social epistemology to begin with an assessment of which method or cognitive process a group uses to produce a certain belief and then to judge the epistemic status of that belief, the judgment naturally applying to all agents in that community. An adequate treatment of the CSR objection must take into account this distinction for it is unclear whether CSR objectors have specific theists in mind or intend their remarks to apply to all theists.

Second, knowledge is factive—only true propositions can be known. Without thereby begging the question, it makes little sense for the CSR objection to be framed on the assumption that theism is false, for then it would be trivially true that theistic belief is unsafe. The CSR literature would then be irrelevant to the claim that theistic belief is unsafe. We therefore interpret the CSR objector as making the claim that despite it being true that God exists, one does not know that God exists.[4] Given the conceptual dependence of assertion, practical reasoning, and evidence on knowledge in Williamson's framework (2000, pp. 184ff), such a challenge is a serious one indeed.

Part III

As adverted to earlier, we think that the CSR objection can be formulated into two different arguments to the conclusion that the belief that God exists is unsafe. An independent discussion of each objection follows.

---

[4] The same point can be made with respect to interpreting the CSR objector as claiming that theistic belief is unjustified, where justification is understood as a property supervening on the reliability of a cognitive process.

The Counterfactual Argument

Recall that one does not know it is noon by looking at a broken clock that fortuitously just so happens to read noon correctly. That the agent would have believed it noon even if it were not noon is one way of explaining why agents who look at broken clocks fortuitously reading the correct time are denied knowledge. On similar grounds, the CSR objector might have the following argument in mind:

1) If God did not exist, human beings would still believe that God exists (given that humans are primed to believe in supernatural agents, independent of whether or not such agents exist).
2) Therefore, the belief that God exists is unsafe.

The cogency of this argument turns on the first premise, which is expressed in the form of a counterfactual. There are three reasons why this argument fails. First, those familiar with accounts of knowledge in the post-Gettier period will recognize that the type of counterfactual expressed by (1) above corresponds to Robert Nozick's sensitivity condition for knowledge. According to Nozick (1981, p. 171), an agent S does not know p if it is the case that were p false, S would still believe p. It is now recognized that the sensitivity condition for knowledge is inadequate in several respects.[5] That theistic belief fails to satisfy the sensitivity condition for knowledge in light of evolutionary cognitive science is therefore irrelevant.

Second, the Counterfactual Argument is invalid as it is not the case that if a belief fails the sensitivity condition, it is therefore unsafe; that is to say, a failure of sensitivity does not entail a lack of safety. For example, in some cases sensitivity is the more stringent condition, while in others safety is. The following two points of logic elicit the difference between the safety and sensitivity conditions. When it comes to cases concerning knowledge of the denial of skeptical hypotheses, the safety principle is less demanding than the sensitivity principle. The sensitivity principle requires that the agent not believe p in the nearest possible world in which p is false. As such, no agent can know the denial of skeptical hypotheses, e.g., "I am not a brain in the vat," by the sensitivity test because in the nearest possible world in which the agent *is* a brain in the vat, the agent continues to believe that he is not a brain in the vat.

---

[5] For some reasons counting against the sensitivity condition, see Goldman, 1986, pp. 45–6.

The safety principle, however, permits knowing the denial of skeptical hypotheses. By the safety principle, I count as knowing the everyday proposition p "that I have hands" only if I safely believe p. It follows, then, that if I safely believe p, then there is no close world in which I am a brain in the vat and am led to falsely believe that I have hands. Consequently, if I know that I have hands and I know that that entails that I am not a brain in the vat, then I know that I am not a brain in the vat.

On the other hand, cases can be constructed in which safety is more demanding than sensitivity. Suppose S truly believes p in the actual world, but (i) in the *closest* world in which p is false S does *not* believe p, and (ii) there is a *close* world in which S falsely believes p. In this case S satisfies the sensitivity condition, but fails to satisfy the safety condition. The following case illustrates this point. Unbeknown to Mary, the thermometer she has just purchased is defective and will always yield a reading of 39°C regardless of her temperature. Mary, who is running a fever of 39°C, then uses the thermometer to measure her temperature and it just so happens to correctly read her temperature of 39°C. However, in the nearest world in which her temperature is not 39°C and she uses this thermometer to take her temperature, she is distracted by her son and she doesn't form any belief about her temperature. She accordingly satisfies the sensitivity condition for knowledge. However, there happens to be a non-closest close world in which Mary, who is running a fever of 38.5°C, uses this thermometer to take her temperature and consequently forms the false belief that her temperature is 39°C. Mary thus fails to satisfy the safety condition.

In light of the complicated relationship between the sensitivity and safety conditions for knowledge, with respect to any belief p, it is not the case that failure of the sensitivity condition entails failure of the safety condition. The counterfactual argument is therefore invalid.

A third reason to discount the Counterfactual Argument is a semantic one. According to the standard Lewisian semantics for counterfactuals, a counterfactual with an impossible antecedent is vacuously true (Lewis, 1973, p. 24). For example, the counterfactual (F) "If frogs were numbers, then pigs would fly" is true, but vacuously so. As discussed earlier, we have interpreted the CSR objector as putting forward her objection on the assumption that God exists. On standard conceptions of God's existence, if God exists, he exists necessarily; that is to say, he exists in every possible world. Therefore, by the CSR objector's own lights the antecedent of (1) is impossible. Asserting (1) thus amounts to no more than asserting (F). As such, there is ample reason to discredit the Counterfactual Argument.

The Argument from Testimony Chains

Reliability, as a property of a belief-forming method, comes in different kinds, two of which are important for the purpose at hand—local and global. The latter refers to a method M's reliability in producing a range of token output beliefs in different propositions $P, Q, R, ...$, etc. A method M is globally reliable if and only if it produces sufficiently more true beliefs than false beliefs in a range of different propositions. For example, M could be the visual process and P the proposition that there is a pencil on the desk, Q the proposition that there are clouds in the sky, and R the proposition that the bin is full. If a sufficiently high number of $P, Q, R, ...$ is true, then method M is globally reliable. A method M is locally reliable with respect to an individual target belief P if and only if M produces a sufficient ratio of more true beliefs than false beliefs in that very proposition P. Method M, e.g., the visual method, is locally reliable with respect to the belief P if and only if it produces a sufficiently high ratio of true beliefs about the presence of the pencil on the desk.

According to Williamson, for a belief to count as safe, it must, among other things, be the product of a globally reliable method or basis: "If in a case α one knows P on a basis B, then in any case close to α in which one believes a proposition P^* close to P on a basis close to B, P^* is true" (Williamson, 2009, p. 325). In light of these considerations, the CSR objector might have the following argument in mind:

3) The basis on which the theist believes that God exists is globally unreliable.
4) Therefore, the belief that God exists is unsafe.

According to Barrett, theistic belief arose through the interaction of HADD, MCIs, and other mental tools, ToM in particular. For the sake of simplicity, let us call this set of mental tools HADD+. On the simplifying assumption that these constitute a singular basis of belief, HADD+, so the CSR objector argues, is globally unreliable, as HADD+ generates many false positives. Hence, the doxastic products of HADD+ are unsafe. If the above argument is valid, theistic belief is unsafe.

As discussed earlier, the distinction between individual and social epistemology must be kept in mind when assessing the CSR objection. It is unclear *who* the CSR objector has in mind with this argument. With respect to the contemporary theist, it is controversial whether: (i) said theists come to believe that God exists on the basis of HADD+; or (ii) whether HADD+ is globally unreliable. Concerning (i), some contemporary theists believe that

God exists either via testimony or as the result of an argument, neither of which involves HADD+. With respect to (ii), even were the contemporary theist to believe that God exists on the basis of HADD+, HADD+ is, at least for us today, globally reliable; that is, we form more true than false beliefs about agents in our environments. So the above argument is irrelevant to at least some contemporary theists.

Suppose, however, we concede the truth of (3) for the earliest theists because they were using HADD+ in ways that generated many false positives; that is to say, for these very early theists, their HADD+ may have been globally unreliable. Therefore, with respect to these very early theists, the belief that God exists was unsafe. Given this supposition, the CSR objector might have the following argument in mind:

5) On the basis of HADD+, some primordial human beings came to believe that God exists.
6) In these primordial human beings HADD+ was a globally unreliable basis for belief.
7) Beliefs produced by globally unreliable methods do not constitute knowledge.
8) Therefore, these primordial human beings did not know that God exists.
9) Contemporary theists believe that God exists via testimony chains originating with these primordial human beings.
10) A testimony chain that does not begin with knowledge cannot yield knowledge to the recipient at the termination of that testimony chain.
11) Therefore, contemporary theists don't know that God exists via such testimony chains.

The Argument from Testimony Chains seeks to undermine the epistemic status of theistic belief by identifying its epistemically suspect causal origins.[6]

As has been conceded, (5)–(8) may indeed be true. And given that many contemporary theists believe that God exists via testimony, (9) may be true as well. (10), however, is false. An agent S_2 can safely believe a true proposition p via testimony from an agent S_1 even if S_1 does *not* safely believe p. Consider the following case from Lackey (2008, p. 48). It is plausible that a child knows that modern-day *Homo sapiens* evolved from *Homo erectus* when taught so by

---

[6] It goes without saying that the causal origin of a belief p can be important to the epistemic status of p. For instance, many would hesitate to ascribe knowledge that p to one who acquired that true belief from the say so of a deceived deceiver. See Goldman (1986, p. 52) for a further case demonstrating the importance of a diachronic approach to epistemic status.

her teacher, even though her teacher is a religious fundamentalist who does not believe that evolution is true. In this case the child's belief is safe despite the teacher not believing that modern-day *Homo sapiens* evolved from *Homo erectus* and therefore not knowing as much (on the assumption that knowledge entails belief). Testimony can thus be an epistemically generative process—it may permit the hearer to gain something the speaker lacks.

So much for testimony from one person to another, but what about testimony chains? Might a testimony chain that originates with a person who does not safely believe *p* prevent the person at the termination of the chain from knowing *p*? An extrapolation of the foregoing case proves that safe belief is possible for an agent at the termination of such a chain. Suppose Billy, one of the children in the biology class, tells his best friend Jack that modern-day *Homo sapiens* evolved from *Homo erectus*. We take it that Jack also counts as safely believing that modern-day *Homo sapiens* evolved from *Homo erectus*. And so on. And surely the contemporary theist, relying on the testimony of her parents or community, counts as knowing that God exists even if that testimony chain originated in a primordial ancestor who did not know that God exists. The Argument from Testimony Chains is therefore unsound.[7]

In light of these considerations, the CSR objector may concede that while (10) is not a universally true principle, there are cases in which it does hold and that the genesis of theistic belief according to CSR is just such a case. For example, if I truly believe that the train is about to depart on the basis of testimony from someone who read a departure schedule riddled with mistakes, it seems that my belief does not count as safe. The CSR objector might argue that the contemporary theist is in a similar position if she believes that God exists based on a testimony chain originating in an ancestor who came to believe that God exists on the basis of a globally unreliable method.

There is room to argue, however, that *exceptionally long* testimony chains with unsafe origins exhibit some unique epistemic features. A case can be made for there being a sense in which the primordial human (S_1) is a reliable testifier and as such the contemporary theist (S_n) can safely believe that God exists from a testimony chain originating with S_1 even if S_1 used the globally unreliable HADD+ to arrive at theistic belief. For the sake of argument, consider a case in which S_1 holds a set of beliefs {*P, Q, R,* ...} and that many of these beliefs are

---

[7] We are aware that this is not an uncontentious claim to make as many epistemologists require the speaker to know *p*, among other things, in order for the hearer to know *p*, (e.g., Nozick, 1981, p. 187; Burge, 1993; and Plantinga, 1993, p. 86). But the *prima facie* plausibility that Billy knows that modern-day *Homo sapiens* evolved from *Homo erectus* questions the veracity of the traditional view.

generated by HADD+. S_1 testifies to others a great many of the beliefs she holds overall. Let us stipulate further that P is the belief that God exists and is one of the few true beliefs in the set $\{P, Q, R, ...\}$. According to the CSR objector S_1 is thus an unreliable testifier. Assume further, and not unreasonably, that as time passes, humans develop mentally. As they do, the testimony chains passing along beliefs Q, R, and the other false beliefs in the set "die out" or "dry up" because people come to realize that Q, R, etc. are false. We call this feature of long testimony chains *epistemic winnowing*; individuals and communities do not generally pass along information they deem false. And epistemic winnowing is something we expect others in our community to be committed to.[8] By the time S_n receives the testimony that P from a testimony chain originating with S_1, there are no false beliefs from S_1's mouth that are passed along anymore; if so, from S_n's perspective, at least, S_1 is a reliable testifier.

One can explain this conclusion in terms of safety: there is no close world in which S_n falsely believes P or any other relevantly similar belief by way of a testimony chain originating with S_1. It seems reasonable to us that the case of the contemporary theist who believes by way of such a long testimony chain is the beneficiary of epistemic winnowing. Therefore, even if the testimony chain by which a contemporary theist believes that God exists has an unsafe genesis, the belief held thereby is safe. The Argument from Testimony Chains is thus unsuccessful.

Part IV

We have presented two different ways in which CSR might be used to generate an argument towards the conclusion that the belief that God exists is unsafe. For a number of reasons, each argument fails. This failure does not entail that belief in God is safe, however. That conclusion would require a separate consideration of its own.

References

Atran, S., 2002. *In Gods We Trust: The Evolutionary Landscape of Religion*. New York: Oxford University Press.

---

[8] For the role of one's community in the epistemology of testimony, see Goldberg (2010).

Barrett, J.L., 2004. *Why Would Anyone Believe in God?* Walnut Creek, CA: AltaMira Press.

——. 2009. Cognitive science, religion, and theology. In: J. Schloss and M.J. Murray (eds), *The Believing Primate: Scientific, Philosophical, and Theological Reflections on the Origin of Religion.* Oxford: Oxford University Press, pp. 76–99.

Bering, J.M., 2006. The folk psychology of souls. *Behavioral and Brain Sciences*, 29, pp. 453–62.

——. 2011. *The Belief Instinct: The Psychology of Souls, Destiny, and the Meaning of Life.* New York: Norton.

Bloom, P., 2005. Is God an accident? *Atlantic Monthly*, 296, pp. 105–12.

Boyer, P., 2001. *Religion Explained: The Evolutionary Origins of Religious Thought.* New York: Basic Books.

Burge, T., 1993. Content preservation. *Philosophical Review*, 102, pp. 457–88.

Clark, K. and Barrett, J.L., 2010. Reformed epistemology and the cognitive science of religion. *Faith and Philosophy*, 27(2), pp. 174–89.

——. 2011. Reidian religious epistemology and the cognitive science of religion. *Journal of the American Academy of Religion*, 79, pp. 1–37.

Dawkins, R., 2006. *The God Delusion.* Boston, MA: Houghton Mifflin.

Dennett, D., 2006. *Breaking the Spell: Religion as a Natural Phenomenon.* New York: Viking.

Gettier, E., 1963. Is justified true belief knowledge? *Analysis*, 23, pp. 121–3.

Goldberg, S., 2010. *Relying on Others: An Essay in Epistemology.* Oxford: Oxford University Press.

Goldman, A., 1986. *Epistemology and Cognition.* Cambridge, MA: Harvard University Press.

Hawthorne, J. and Stanley, J., 2008. Knowledge and action. *Journal of Philosophy*, 105(10), pp. 571–90.

Lackey, J., 2008. *Learning from Words: Testimony as a Source of Knowledge.* Oxford: Oxford University Press.

Lewis, D., 1973. *Counterfactuals.* Oxford: Blackwell.

Murray, M., 2009. Scientific explanations of religion and the justification of religious belief. In: J. Schloss and M.J. Murray (eds), *The Believing Primate: Scientific, Philosophical, and Theological Reflections on the Origin of Religion.* Oxford: Oxford University Press, pp. 168–78.

Nozick, R., 1981. *Philosophical Explanations.* Oxford: Oxford University Press.

Plantinga, A., 1993. *Warrant and Proper Function.* Oxford: Oxford University Press.

Pritchard, D., 2005. *Epistemic Luck.* Oxford: Oxford University Press.

———. 2009. *Knowledge*. Basingstoke: Palgrave Macmillan.

Shope, R., 1983. *An Analysis of Knowing: A Decade of Research*. Princeton: Princeton University Press.

Sosa, E., 1999. How must knowledge be modally related to what is known? *Philosophical Topics*, 26(1–2), pp. 373–84.

Williamson, T., 2000. *Knowledge and its Limits*. Oxford: Oxford University Press.

———. 2009. Reply to John Hawthorne and Maria Lasonen-Aarnio. In: P. Greenough and D. Pritchard (eds), *Williamson on Knowledge*. Oxford: Oxford University Press, pp. 313–29.

Wilson, D.S., 2002. *Darwin's Cathedral: Evolution, Religion, and the Nature of Society*. Chicago: University of Chicago Press.

Chapter 8
Assessing the Third Way

Jason Marsh

Introduction

Consider the following view of the world from Simon Blackburn:

> The cosmos is some fifteen billion years old, almost unimaginably huge, and governed by natural laws that will compel its extinction in some billions more years ... We evolved only because of a number of cosmic accidents ... Nature shows us no particular favors: we get parasites and diseases and we die, and we are not all that nice to each other ... That, more or less, is the scientific picture of the world. (2002, p. 1)

This is the contemporary, naturalistic,[1] alternative to traditional religion, and it has become increasingly popular in the academy. But most people are inclined to endorse a more personal view of the world, such as the following theistic view:

> there is such a person as God. God is a *person*: that is, a being with intellect and will. A person has (or can have) knowledge and belief, but also affections, loves, and hates; a person, furthermore, also has or can have intentions, and can act so as to fulfill them. God has all of these qualities ... Still further, he has created the universe and constantly upholds and providentially guides it. (Plantinga, 2000, p. 3)

Now there are cognitive reasons, as we shall see, as to why most people are prone to accept a view like theism over a view like naturalism. But some are not happy with either option and argue for a third way. Indeed, a number of philosophers, convinced that traditional religion is no longer epistemically credible, have

---

[1] Naturalists need not, of course, describe the world in such gloomy terms. Naturalism, however, does seem incompatible with religion as defined by Schellenberg. As he puts it, "if the physical universe and what it spans is all there is, nothing is *unsurpassably* excellent" (2005, p. 27). For more on what naturalism might be committed to, see Goetz and Taliaferro, 2008.

begun to explore more abstract and less personal religious possibilities. The best recent example is J.L. Schellenberg, who in a highly significant trilogy (2005; 2007; 2009) argues that our immaturity as a species, when combined with other arguments, should lead us to adopt a non-believing, skeptical faith in the following generic view, which he calls ultimism:

> The central religious idea, as I understand it, is the idea of a Divine reality, of something ultimate both in reality and in value, in relation to which an ultimate good for humanity and the world may be attained. (Schellenberg, 2012, p. 13)

My task in what follows will be to explore two questions: first, is a generic religious outlook like ultimism likely to be cognitively attractive to human minds and cultures?; and, second, is Schellenberg's ultimism really that much better off, philosophically speaking, than theism? My first conclusion, which draws on recent work in the cognitive science of religion, is descriptive.[2] Unless ultimism gets filled in with agent-based content, there is reason to doubt that it will compete in the marketplace of religious ideas. My second conclusion, which should be of interest to philosophers, is normative: although ultimism may have some epistemic advantages over traditional theism,[3] Schellenberg overstates these advantages. More particularly, one of the things that helps to give ultimism some cognitive traction, namely its commitment to afterlife, reintroduces the problem of evil. This problem, moreover, offers at least *some* persons a way to justifiably reject ultimistic faith. If that is correct, then generic ultimism—our third option—has enough content to raise potentially serious philosophical worries, but may well lack enough content to culturally compete with the major historical religions. Finally, although I will focus on Schellenberg's project here, my claims may have significance for a number of abstract proposals in analytic and continental philosophy of religion.[4]

---

[2] In other words, I am not seeking to use cognitive science of religion to epistemically debunk any religious view. I doubt that the science all by itself has substantive epistemic implications, whether positive or negative. I also acknowledge that some theistic cognitive scientists, like Justin Barrett, see God as working through natural causes.

[3] The main advantage of simple ultimism over more detailed views is that in saying less, it is less likely to say something that is mistaken.

[4] Including John Hick's "The Real" or "Ultimate" (2004), Mark Johnston's view of God (2009), and Philip Kitcher's conception of the transcendent (2012). My claims also have implications, so far as I can tell, for more continental views about the divine, for negative theology, and for theologies that don't see God as a person (i.e., as having intellect and will).

Ultimism: Faith without Details

This chapter is about generic ultimism. To get a better sense of what generic ultimism claims, consider the following passage:

> What we have been discussing so far might be called *generic* ultimism, the idea that there is an ultimate reality of some sort in relation to which an ultimate good of some sort can be obtained. (Schellenberg, 2005, p. 37)

Although many will want to affirm something more than this, Schellenberg is clear that we must keep ultimism's content fairly thin and fairly agent-free. He states:

> It is not to be linked with any particular religious proposition about God or gods that may still have the mud of early evolution clinging to it but instead involves cognitively and conatively aligning oneself with the more general proposition ... that what is deepest in reality (metaphysically ultimate) is also unsurpassably great (axiologically ultimate) and the source of an ultimate good (salvific) ... I call this *ultimism* to distinguish it from theism and other specific "isms." (2009, p. xii)

> ... other religious ideas may be proved false—if my arguments in Part III of *Skepticism* are correct, then this has occurred for the personalist conception already—but it will be harder to reach this conclusion in respect to simple ultimism, because of its greater generality. (2009, p. 28)

These passages are best understood in light of Schellenberg's evolutionary approach to religion. According to this approach, we are still at a very early stage when it comes to religious reflection (a fact that is supposed to trouble both confident naturalists and traditional religious believers). The problem with past religions, we are told, is that they tend to say too much, including things that are bound to be false. Most notably, in ascribing mentality to God, theistic religions are said to make the world predictable,[5] generating all kinds of worries about evil and divine hiddenness. By contrast, non-personal ideas, or even quasi-personal

---

It thus goes without saying that philosophers and theologians should be paying attention to developments in cognitive science—at least, that is, if they care about whether their religious claims are likely to be widely endorsed by non-academics.

[5] Not everyone agrees, of course. Skeptical theism is a view that, in effect, denies that God's ways are predictable. For Schellenberg's critical treatment of skeptical theism, see Schellenberg, 2007, pp. 299–304.

ideas, like generic ultimism are harder to pin down conceptually and are thus harder to predict and disconfirm. This means that if Schellenberg's ultimate turns out to possess some form of consciousness—something he is not firm about either way (2009, p. 48)—it can't be too personal, or behave as though it were too personal, if it is to avoid the main problems associated with classical theism. I will speak more about the tension this creates for Schellenberg in due course, but first I want to explore a more basic question about whether ultimism is likely to be culturally successful as an idea.

Now clearly *some* versions of ultimism are likely to be culturally successful, if only because we are told, somewhat controversially (Keller, 2010), that all major religious traditions are versions of ultimism, endorsing the "central religious idea" mentioned earlier. This is another way of saying that ultimism, in the broadest sense, is really a disjunctive outlook whose disjuncts consist of various possibilities, some of which can be ruled out, while others of which are allegedly true for all anyone knows. Since ultimism permits various religious outlooks, let me clarify that when I speak of ultimism in this chapter, I am interested in the prospects of a highly stripped-down and atheistic version, which, recall, for Schellenberg is the only kind of religious outlook that warrants any kind of faith response at the present time.

Objections to Faith without Details

There are number of worries that might be voiced about ultimism's cultural prospects. One objection is that generic religion is too abstract and lacking in content to permit even non-doxastic faith. Schellenberg refers to this as the Emptiness Objection (2009, pp. 30–35). Another worry is that ultimism, again given its abstractness and somewhat ahistorical character, simply won't seem very appealing to prudent skeptics (Schellenberg, 2009, p. 47) or to anyone at all (2009, p. 48). Although Schellenberg tackles each of these objections, I will develop a variation of the last, suggesting that there is an important worry here that both Schellenberg and his critics have overlooked. The worry is that ultimism won't be very appealing to many since it doesn't have the right kind of content. To properly grasp this feasibility worry, it will not be sufficient to simply reflect on the matter of who might be attracted to ultimism. We also need to say something about how the religious mind works. Doing this will allow us to test Schellenberg's claim that ultimism is "hard to imagine because we have got so used to detailed formulations and the demand for belief" (Schellenberg, 2009, p. xiii). It will also support the hypothesis that simple ultimism is hard to imagine, in no small part, because of the structure of human cognition, which often leads us to automatically form agent-based concepts and to believe that which they represent.

Cognitive Science of Religion: Why the Details Matter to Human Minds and Culture

One of the lessons from the Cognitive Science of Religion (CSR) is that the human mind does not find all religious ideas equally plausible, attractive, or worth spreading.[6] Quite independently of questions about philosophical plausibility, certain concepts and ideas get our attention better than others, which is to say that certain concepts have a good cognitive fit with us; that we are biased toward them. Just as cognition informs and constrains linguistic expression (Chomsky, 1965; Pinker, 1997), something similar can be said about religion. Despite the awesome cultural differences around the world, the space of possible religions radically outstrips the set that people are likely to develop (Guthrie, 1993; Boyer, 2001; Atran, 2002; Barrett, 2004; 2007; Bloom, 2004; 2007; Kelemen, 2004).

Thus, in contrast to popular socio-political accounts of religion, which tend to see religious belief as a merely contingent matter of upbringing, CSR posits that religious belief naturally emerges from various cognitive systems. This is not to say that there is agreement on every detail within CSR,[7] only that there is wide agreement that the human mind is predisposed to affirm some sort of supernatural agency. As Scott Atran puts it: "Supernatural agency is the most culturally recurrent, cognitively relevant, and evolutionarily compelling concept in religion. The concept of the supernatural is culturally derived from an innate cognitive schema" (2002, p. 57).[8] Or to put Atran's point another way, context and upbringing supply much of the content of what is learned, like a ghost's name or particular history. But the kinds of minds we have evolved shape the

---

[6] Naturally, a full understanding of religion would require thinking about not just ideas and belief, but ritual, morality, and religious experience. But I will focus mainly on religious concepts and beliefs here.

[7] Some stress, for instance, that religion was evolutionarily advantageous (since the belief that a supernatural agent is watching might promote honesty and trust within groups), whereas others stress that religion is a byproduct of cognitive capacities that evolved for non-religious purposes.

[8] This does not mean that non-belief in God can never be natural (see Marsh, 2013). It also does not rule out the possibility of naturalists, who deny all forms of supernatural agency.

basic contours of our religious concepts, and constrain the kinds of details they are likely to take on.

Our Mental Tool Kit

Two mental tools or capacities that are often discussed in CSR are as follows.

Hypersensitive Agency Detection Device (HADD)

A mental tool that enables us to detect actual or potential agency in our environments.

Stewart Guthrie (1993) was among the first in the field to note a connection between agency detection and anthropomorphism. As he pointed out, we naturally see faces in clouds and in pretty much everything else, and this has substantial impact on culture and religion. Building on the work of Guthrie, Justin Barrett (2004) stresses that our agency detection systems are hypersensitive in the following sense: since it is better to be safe than sorry in a world of predators, we often over-interpret environmental stimuli and perceive them in mentalistic terms.[9] True, we sometimes realize that our HADD experience is just a false positive ("I guess that noise was just a falling branch"), though in other cases we may develop a lingering sense that "someone" is present or that we are being watched, even where no physical agent can be detected.

Theory of Mind (ToM)

A mental tool that enables us to interpret the behavior and thoughts of others, whether actual or fictional, by attributing mental states to them.

We do not simply wish to know whether an agent is present, but whether she is ultimately dangerous, friendly or indifferent. Knowing these further facts, however, requires having the ability to see into the mind of an agent. ToM—sometimes referred to by Daniel Dennett as the intentional stance (2006, p. 108)—concerns not so much our ability to detect agents, as our ability to form psychological beliefs about them once they have been detected. The focus, in short, is on our capacity to read minds.

This mindreading capacity, though it gives rise to some controversial questions (such as whether we have a corresponding ToM module or what

---

[9] Guthrie tells me that he does not like the term "hypersensitive."

particular theory of mindreading we should adopt),[10] is itself well-established and fundamental to social cognition. In fact, humans who lack it are sometimes said to have a disability greater than physical blindness (Baron-Cohen, 1995). But the capacity to read minds also appears to have important connections to culture and religious belief. Perhaps most notably, where ToM is fully intact, it can inform people's reasoning about supernatural agents. For instance, ToM could encourage an individual to conclude that the divine is angry when lightning violently strikes the earth or to see God as loving when a great event happens.

As might be expected, not everyone can read minds. But this actually helps us to test the connection between ToM and polytheistic beliefs. For instance, one apparent prediction made by CSR is that children with autism—who have impaired ToM or mindreading abilities—are less likely to fully grasp or fully affirm supernatural agent concepts than other children. Recent evidence supports this prediction (Norenzayan, Gervais, and Trzesniewski, 2012).

Design, Dualism, and Theological Incorrectness

In addition to the above capacities, certain information-processing biases make people prone to endorse personal religious ideas. The first bias concerns how we reason about teleology or design. As Deborah Kelemen (1999; 2004) has observed, children are prone to overdetect design in the natural world, a phenomenon she refers to as "promiscuous teleology." For instance, children can find it rather natural to say that mountains are pointy so that animals can scratch themselves, which of course was never taught to them. True, we tame our more extreme teleological judgments as we age, but not entirely it seems. For instance, according to Margaret Evans, even biology and medical students, supposedly familiar with evolutionary explanations, often "misconstrue biological change as a response to an animal's wants or needs" (2000, p. 314). In addition, Alzheimer's patients, having lost semantic knowledge, often revert back to their earlier promiscuous design stance (Lombrozo, Kelemen, and Zaitchik, 2007).

Leaving aside our intuitive creationism, we are also intuitive dualists, at least according to Paul Bloom (2004), who argues that babies start out believing persons to be radically distinct (and indeed separable) from bodies. Bloom's hypothesis, though not uncontroversial among philosophers and cognitive

---

[10] I will not enter into the simulation theory versus theory theory debate, nor will I consider how automatic versus theoretical ToM ability really is. From what I can tell, CSR is not committed to specific ideas about these matters.

scientists, can help to explain a widespread belief in spirit possession and afterlife (Cohen, 2007).

Another aspect of CSR worth mentioning is the tendency to re-anthropomorphize theologically abstract features of the divine, a tendency that is revealed in studies on so-called theological incorrectness (Barrett and Keil, 1996; Barrett and VanOrman, 1996; Barrett 1999). One task explores how subjects remember or rather misremember stories about supernatural agents. The subjects in question, despite their explicit belief that God is timeless and unrestricted in power, implicitly believe that God (or Vishnu, Krishna, Brahman, etc.) acts inside of time and can save only one person at a time. According to Todd Tremlin, the lesson of these and related studies is clear:

> God concepts themselves must stay within specific representation parameters if they are to remain relevant to believers. Abstract theological descriptions of gods are largely ignored in on-line thought, have little staying power in the minds of people, and may not substantially impact how believers think and behave. (2006, p. 123)[11]

Now more needs to be said, to be sure, about how such claims square with people in our culture who profess belief in a higher force or belief in a non-personal divine realm.[12] But we have some reason in the above claims to expect that many such persons, along with theologians who claim that God is not a person, may well ascribe rather specific mental properties to the divine in online thought—such as the property of loving humans or having intelligence or a general awareness of things or acting for reasons. Even if there are some exceptions here, though, we still have reason to think that agent-based religious concepts are more likely to seem intuitive than non-agent based religious concepts, giving them a cultural advantage.

How to Gain a Transmission Advantage

If the above claims are on track, then religious concepts that activate our mental tools and our information-processing biases will in general be more likely

---

[11] Barrett, similarly puts the point this way: "Theologians and religious leaders cannot simply teach any ideas they want and expect those ideas to be remembered, spread, and believed; rather, the way the human minds operate gradually selects only those with the best fit to become widespread" (cited by Tremlin, 2004, p. 30).

[12] Schellenberg made this point to me.

to become widespread and cultural than religious concepts that do not. But what do particularly well, it seems, are concepts that violate some of our basic assumptions about the natural world. These minimally counterintuitive (MCI) concepts are ordinary, even mundane, concepts from our physical environments, albeit with an important ontological twist (Boyer, 2001). To borrow a common example, walking dogs are not all that exciting or memorable on their own. Take a dog that walks through walls or that can talk, however, and now you have an interesting mix between the mundane and the memorable. This is not to say that successful narratives maximize on counterintuitive properties. Having too many violations will likely just amount to cognitive overload, canceling out memorability. (To consider another non-original example, an invisible dog that walks through walls, experiences time backwards, and only exists on Tuesdays threatens to be massively counterintuitive, rendering it much less likely to spread than even purely ordinary concepts.)[13] The idea is rather that stories about MCI agents are especially fit to become successful—particularly, it should be added, when those stories explain important events or facts in personal terms, such as why people have a certain disease or who made the animals (Boyer, 2001, p. 78).

Claims like these have led Pascal Boyer to argue for two theses: first, most of the world's religious concepts, along with many important works of fiction, concern MCI agents (Boyer, 2001);[14] and, second, MCI religious concepts are typically more memorable than non-MCI religious concepts. Others have corroborated Boyer's basic views about transmission (Atran and Norenzayan, 2004).

Finally, it might be thought that non-theistic religions like Buddhism are the obvious counterexample to the kinds of claims made by CSR. But this is not actually so clear. Leaving aside the claim that Buddhism makes up a relatively small portion of the religious demographics, Buddhism is not, historically speaking, so agent-free. For example, according to Ilkka Pyysiainen (2003), many strands of Buddhism pass the MCI test. As Pyysiainen notes Buddha (and certain Buddhas), while human, have been widely thought to (a) be born in heaven, even in a virgin birth; (b) have radiant skin upon death; (c) appear in

---

[13] I owe this example to Justin Barrett.

[14] As Boyer puts it: "Persons can be represented as having counterintuitive physical properties (e.g. ghosts or gods), counterintuitive biology (many gods who neither grow nor die) or counterintuitive psychological properties (unblocked prescience). Animals too can have all of these properties. Tools and artifacts can be represented as having biological ones (some statues bleed) or psychological ones (they hear what you say). Browsing through volumes of mythology, fantastic tales, anecdotes, cartoons, religious writings and science fiction, you will get an extraordinary variety of different *concepts*, but you will also find that the number of *templates* is very limited and in fact contained in the short list above" (2001, p. 78).

various forms; and (d) perform miracles. In saying this, to clarify, Pyysiainen is not making a negative normative pronouncement about the value or plausibility of non-MCI versions of Buddhism. The point is just that (i) non-MCI religions in general have notably fewer adherents than MCI religions; and (ii) this demographic difference is unsurprising in light of CSR.

Cultural Implications for Atheistic Religion

I have suggested that supernatural agent concepts are cognitively easy to process and that, all other things being equal,[15] this gives them a competitive advantage over non-personal religious concepts. This in turn gives us reason to think that generic ultimism, which is not clearly an MCI religion[16] and which does not activate various mental tools and habits of mind, will be at a competitive disadvantage to much traditional religion. But there is more. Since generic ultimism is compatible with a huge range of open-ended possibilities and since we are not exactly supposed to believe in the reality it describes, this raises another cognitive risk: simple ultimism, especially in Schellenberg's skeptical context, might be even more difficult to process than other abstract religious outlooks, which would be bad for cultural transmission.

These claims incline me to think it is somewhat likely, and not just an interesting epistemic possibility, that simple ultimism won't compete with traditional religion any time soon. However, suppose that I am mistaken in raising this strong version of the cultural challenge—say because theories within CSR are still immature and open to question.[17] Even so, a weaker version

---

[15] I say "all other things being equal" since other factors besides those described by evolutionary and cognitive science can of course have bearing on how successful an idea is (e.g., wealth, media, military power, etc.). I suspect that these various factors would in reality only add to the cultural challenge against ultimism, but that is for another time.

[16] One objection that has been raised to me is this: couldn't generic ultimism itself be an MCI concept? That is, couldn't it be seen as a kind of twist on ordinary theism, creating a new MCI concept out of an old (familiar and less exciting) MCI concept? In response, I have no reason to think that MCI concepts work this way or to think that people are becoming all that bored with standard MCI religious concepts (even many non-believers find them fascinating, after all). MCI concepts interest us, it seems, because of their anthropomorphic features and, in many cases, because of the personal way they violate our expectations about how natural objects work. See note 14.

[17] Although there is something to this "prematurity objection," it is important to distinguish between the cognitive biases and trends we have been discussing and large-scale theories that seek to explain religion as a whole. Even though particular theories of religion

of the cultural challenge would remain, one that is still very much of interest. The weaker challenge is that we have interesting, and initially promising, lines of empirical evidence that ultimism will have a hard time competing with various traditional religions.

To clarify, neither of the above cultural challenges rules out the possibility that generic ultimism might take off someday. We do not know what humans or post-humans will think in 5,000 years, never mind in five million years, after all, and Schellenberg's aims in evolutionary religion are big. In addition, we must remember that Schellenberg's intended audience very much includes religious skeptics. Perhaps such skeptics, who already reject traditional religion, will be more open to ultimistic faith than others—though this possibility could easily be overstated.[18] What seems clear, in any case, is that when it comes to most people in the near future, generic ultimism may be hard to sell.

Why Ultimism May Do Better Cognitively than Naturalism

We will soon discuss more epistemic matters. But before doing so, it is important to stress something that could easily be missed by our previous discussion: namely, that generic ultimism and its entailments does have something going for it, cognitively speaking, something that may well render it more cognitively natural to many than, say, metaphysical naturalism. Two things in particular stand out. First, there is existential theory of mind.

Existential Theory of Mind (EToM)

A generic explanatory system that allows individuals to perceive or to think they perceive meaning in various life events, including tragedies.

According to Jesse Bering (2002), human beings in general, including nonbelievers, often feel that life's events take place as part of a grand and purposeful narrative—many feel that their lives in some sense go in the way they are supposed to and that things will work out in the end. In the words of Bering: "I define EToM, in a purposively general sense, as a biologically based, generic explanatory system that allows individuals to perceive meaning in certain life

---

(like supernatural punishment theories or memetic theories, etc.) might be undermined with future research, the basic cognitive trends that we have been describing seem less vulnerable to disconfirmation. Thanks to Schellenberg for raising the objection in question.

[18] After all, many religious skeptics still want theism to be true, with many others wanting nothing to do with religious ideas or faith of any kind.

events (e.g. 'I was in a bad car accident when I was a teenager *because* I needed to learn that my life is fragile')" (2002, p. 4). Now compare this with Schellenberg's claims about ultimism:

> Consider, for example, how our lives can sometimes seem fragmented, resisting significant unity; we may lose focus and despair of fundamental order and meaning. But as we saw earlier, it is written into ultimism and its entailments that there is a fundamental pattern of meaning and order in things ... How fearful (i.e., worthy of fear) are the illnesses that beset me? ... I am having faith that ultimately all will be well. (2009, pp.40–41)

Schellenberg's claims seem interestingly analogous to EToM experiences, something that arguably counts, cognitively speaking, in its favor.[19]

The second factor that helps to give ultimism some cognitive traction is its somewhat surprising commitment to afterlife. This move seems to be good news, religiously speaking, but I want to stress that it is also good news from the standpoint of cognitive and cultural fitness (Bering and Bjorklund, 2004). Of course, claims about afterlife, like claims about EToM experiences, would seem to be even more natural if we postulate an intentional, parent-like structure behind reality bringing it all to pass. But the point here is that cognitive fit comes in degrees and that, even as things stand, simple ultimism offers us something.[20]

Epistemic Implications: Afterlife and Evil

Now that we have introduced the topic of life after death, let me raise a normative puzzle about ultimism, afterlife, and evil. The puzzle is that Schellenberg's concession of afterlife, although it helps to give ultimism some cognitive traction, re-introduces the problem of evil. To put the point somewhat crudely, if we can be confident enough in our value assessments to derive afterlife in response to horrendous evils, by which I mean life-ruining evils, why can't we be confident enough to say that some of these evils would not likely arise in the first

---

[19] Aside from being widespread, EToM experiences arguably increase subjective wellbeing (Marsh 2014a), which is also presumably an important selling point

[20] Perhaps an afterlife might be easier to imagine if Schellenberg were to explicitly affirm the existence of souls, preserving our intuitive dualism. Then again, dualism is philosophically controversial. To minimize the chances of metaphysical error, perhaps Schellenberg may wish to entertain not just dualist theories of afterlife, but also some physicalist possibilities as well (Leslie, 2007).

place? Stated more precisely, atheistic defenders of ultimism and afterlife owe us a plausible explanation of the following claim:

> Asymmetry: we can see clearly that ultimism entails the reality of an afterlife for those who experience horrendous or life-ruining evils, but we cannot see clearly that ultimism entails (or even provides much evidence) that these same evils wouldn't arise in the first place.

Asymmetry can seem highly implausible and some will no doubt reject it on intuitive grounds. But to see why Asymmetry is philosophically questionable, it is important to distinguish Asymmetry from the following weaker claim:

> Weak Asymmetry: we can be more confident, given a generic ultimistic framework, in our ability to reason about afterlife in response to evil than we can in our ability to reason about whether there should be horrendous evil in the first place.

Perhaps we have reasons to endorse this weaker principle. In fact, the way Schellenberg defines ultimism lends support to Weak Asymmetry. Recall that it is part of the definition of ultimism that human beings can achieve their greatest possible good, which entails that people have at least the chance to do so. This means that if someone's life is damaged and cut extremely short on account of some horror, such an individual must, given ultimism, experience an afterlife in order to have her chance to flourish. It does not mean that there must be no severely damaged individuals to begin with. Nothing in the definition of ultimism, more generally, implies the latter claim.

I will grant this line of reasoning for the sake of argument (though some may wish to question the logical compatibility between ultimism and evil). The question is whether these claims would help Schellenberg to establish Asymmetry. The answer would be yes if there were no plausible evidential, as opposed to logical, reasons to question Asymmetry. But there do seem to be such reasons. Most notably, ultimism's axiological strand seems to make certain patterns of evil we observe unlikely, even if they remain logically possible. This is because perfect goodness makes a serious claim on the world. It constrains not only what happens but also how thinly or thickly we define ultimism's soteriological strand.[21] Here many may want to argue that a guaranteed chance

---

[21] In fact, some might wish to avoid using the term "soteriological" to describe ultimism's connection to humanity since such a term risks conveying the thought that evil

to flourish at some point, or even guaranteed compensation for horrific suffering in the long run, falls short of the mark of perfect goodness.

Put another way, ultimism is a normative thesis.[22] It says that reality at its core is *unsurpassably* great. But then it matters not just that we have a bare chance to flourish at some point; it also matters how people's lives go. Now this evaluative fact might be true but irrelevant if we were talking about a perfectly good divine reality that was somehow causally detached from our world (like some neoplatonists seem to affirm). Schellenberg does not define the ultimate in this way, however, which would only undermine the soteriological dimensions of ultimism. How, then, can he insist that horrendous evil undermines classical theism without reaching a similar conclusion vis-à-vis generic ultimism?

Schellenberg on Evil: The Non-personal Defense

Schellenberg, in at least one place, seems to appreciate the worry that he cannot. He makes the following remarks in a footnote:

> Now it might be thought that claims about evil in particular would be transferable to the more general context, given that a truly ultimate reality, even if nonpersonal, would have to be absolutely perfect. But although evil is *troubling* even in the more general context (and may contribute to doubt about ultimism), *arguments* from evil do not so immediately and naturally suggest themselves there… (2007, pp. 297–8)

So why don't arguments from evil immediately and naturally arise for generic ultimism? As we might expect, Schellenberg invokes the non-personal nature of the ultimate. He states:

> [Ultimism lacks] the specific personal notions and axiological concepts from familiar contexts of behaviour and interaction that seem capable of generating disproofs in the narrower context … [and] if we do not assume a personalist interpretation, we cannot assume that familiar axiological concepts tell the complete and final truth about value, but must rather acknowledge that the latter might be quite beyond us (to do otherwise would be something like taking facts

---

(and the corresponding need for redemption) are natural and unsurprising features of the world under ultimism. I do not mean to imply that Schellenberg intends this meaning.

[22] Here I follow Sharon Street (2012), who refers to theism as a normative thesis.

about planet Earth as representative of the full truth about the universe). (2007, pp. 297–8)

Does such a strategy work? I am not as confident as Schellenberg that it does. Again, Schellenberg's claims about the afterlife are relevant. When it comes to whether there is an afterlife on ultimism, Schellenberg, recall, is very confident that the answer is yes. In fact, Schellenberg does not seem to be at all bothered about how the afterlife should come about. He says, somewhat surprisingly, that the final victory of good over evil, which includes an afterlife, might be "consciously" and "intentionally" brought about or, alternatively, might just be an "undesigned fact" (2009, p. 48).[23]

Now many will likely deny that afterlife, for precisely those who require it, is the kind of thing that would be undesigned (and this despite Schellenberg's claim that many good things can be undesigned). But my point here is slightly different. Whether or not afterlife is a personal, non-personal, quasi-personal, designed or undesigned fact, we can apparently reason about it either way. We can apparently do this, moreover, without worrying too much about whether we are slipping back into the narrow, familiar, personal theistic context.

These claims about afterlife are interesting since, if true, they lower the plausibility of Schellenberg's explanation for why evil poses no serious philosophical threat for ultimism. The reason for this should be clear. If complex goods like afterlife are secure, under ultimism, irrespective of how they come about, this raises the probability that other complex goods would be as well. In particular, it raises the probability that our world would contain less horrific evil than it does, whether as a designed or undesigned fact. In a word, Schellenberg's claims about afterlife, and his apparent openness to conscious and unconscious divine action in that context, seem to be in tension with his claims about the problem of evil.

Three Versions of the Problem of Evil for Ultimism

However, let us set aside the above claims about afterlife. Can we still generate an argument from evil for simple ultimism? I think we can. This argument should not, of course, rest on highly personal or Kantian worries, such as whether it

---

[23] Schellenberg introduces the notion of "undesigned facts" to block what we might call the near theism objection. According to this objection, ultimism really requires that there exists a theistic-like being to intend and ensure that good wins out in the end. I think this move backfires, as I shall now argue.

would be morally permissible for the divine to allow some evil X in order to obtain some greater good Y. Similarly, the argument should not rest on assumptions about what an unsurpassably *loving* being would do or allow, whatever is strictly permissible from a moral point of view. Even with these constraints in mind, however, there is still plenty of room to generate an argument from evil. One option is to go purely axiological, as alluded to earlier. The focus here is not on agents and goodness, but on worlds and goodness. Here it might be argued that if evil can challenge God's goodness, it can also challenge the goodness of true ultimate reality. To better see the worry, consider the following argument, based on recent work from Sharon Street (2012):

> P1. If ultimism of any variety is true, then the world is ultimately unsurpassable in goodness.
> P2. If the world is ultimately unsurpassable in goodness, then everything that happens is either itself ultimately very good, if not optimific, or at least is required to contribute to something that is very good, if not optimific (otherwise we can imagine a reality that is even more ultimate in goodness than this one).
> P3. Some events, like the shootings of small children in an elementary school, are not plausible candidates for being deemed all things considered very good let alone optimific, nor are they likely required to contribute to something very good or optimific.
> C. Therefore, we have at least decent reasons to deny that we are in an ultimistic universe—reasons that could permit at least *some* agnostics to become disbelievers.

I am not claiming that this argument is sound. The question of its soundness goes beyond the scope of this chapter. I am, however, expressing three doubts. First, I am doubtful that Schellenberg's stance about evil and ultimism can be maintained without further engagement with arguments like the one just mentioned. Second, I am doubtful that Schellenberg can resist the above argument, while maintaining that theists cannot. Third, I am doubtful that P3 could be rejected without falling prey to a potentially deep kind of normative or evaluative skepticism. These doubts are intuitive, and while space prevents me from developing them, I think they can be defended.[24]

---

[24] Very briefly, if we deny P1, we deny Anselmian religion. But Schellenberg clearly wants to preserve Anselmian religion and its central claim that the divine is unsurpassable in perfection. If we deny P3, then we are arguably left with a severe form of evaluative or moral skepticism. Skepticism follows from denying P3, since this implies that our most basic

A second challenge from evil for generic ultimism is comparative. Whatever we make of the previous argument, it might be said that naturalism still better explains the seemingly random patterns of suffering we observe than all versions of ultimism, which would be sufficient to raise the argument from evil in its contrastive form.[25] To be sure, other data might better support some versions of ultimism, including theism, over naturalism. So the claim here is not that these religious outlooks are wholly undermined by evil. The claim is rather that evil poses a serious inferential problem for both theism and simple ultimism. Theists will typically acknowledge the problem and will seek to address it. Since Schellenberg rejects all theistic responses to evil (including free will responses, soul making responses, and skeptical theism), a question emerges about how he might seek to answer various arguments from evil. In fact, even if evil poses a *more* severe inferential challenge for theism than for generic ultimism, which may be the case, this is not enough to make ultimism safe from criticism. Arguments from evil might still be severe enough to sometimes justify disbelief in generic ultimism or to seriously lower the plausibility of the view.

Finally, it is important to stress something that could easily be missed by the above discussion. Arguments from evil need not be successful in order for evil to pose an important epistemic challenge for religion (Plantinga, 2000, p. 483; Marsh, 2013, p. 365). In fact, let us suppose that the previous arguments all fail miserably. Still, there is a way for disbelief in ultimism to be epistemically

---

judgments about value—e.g. "the shootings of children is typically very bad for them and typically makes the world a worse place overall"—are radically mistaken. In other words, if there is always a good (personal or impersonal) reason for the horrendous evils we observe, then we are totally in the dark about what moral reasons are. This last claim is made by Sharon Street (2012) in connection to theism: she thinks theists should be moral skeptics. But her claims, if correct, would seem applicable to any version of ultimism; they seem to imply that disbelief in all versions of ultimism is required to resist normative skepticism. This makes me think that P2 would be the best premise for Schellenberg to deny. I suspect, however, that this premise will also be hard to deny. For even if some pointless evil is inevitable, all versions of ultimism can seem to make it likely that: (a) there would not be so much pointless evil; and (b) that certain particular pointless evils, like the school shootings, would not occur. Actually, perfect goodness may require something much stronger than this; as many theistic philosophers of religion have acknowledged, perfect goodness may require that all apparently horrific evils are, in the long run, great benefits in disguise, not just impersonally but also for those who suffer them.

[25] This is because naturalism, unlike ultimism, makes it highly likely that if there are beings like us, they will suffer in seemingly random and often meaningless ways. Naturalism also explains another important fact, which is that some suffering doesn't seem to track what's ultimately good for people but rather more chancy considerations, such as place of birth or genetic traits.

justified, for some, a way that runs more directly than arguments and which concerns irreligious experience. Imagine, for instance, the unfortunate souls that witnessed their loved ones die in the Holocaust. For such persons, their horrifying experience of evil might directly inform them that what is most basic about reality is far from perfect, undermining ultimistic faith. Telling such persons that they need arguments to back up their disbelief ignores the non-argumentative nature of the challenge and ignores developments in religious epistemology that Schellenberg is certainly familiar with.

If that is right, then evil may sometimes pose non-inferential trouble for faith. I mention this because Schellenberg seems to want to claim that disbelief in ultimism is *never* justified (Draper, 2012). If he does want to make this strong epistemic claim,[26] he might wish to consider these (perhaps more challenging) non-inferential considerations in addition to the arguments discussed above.

A Possible Rejoinder and a Final Challenge from the Value of Love

Let us restrict our focus to arguments from evil, though. I have intentionally been brief in my descriptions of the above arguments if only to give a flavor of the kind of challenges I think Schellenberg should engage. But perhaps Schellenberg will retort that all these (brief) arguments obscure an important asymmetry between theism and simple ultimism on the question of goodness. If theism is true, after all, people's ultimate good is clearly going to consist in union with God. But we know, goes the objection, that various evils we observe aren't required to serve this connection (Schellenberg, 2007, pp.252–6).[27] By contrast, if ultimism is true, we are not so sure what people's greatest good might look like and so cannot be sure that evil frustrates or fails to facilitate our greatest good. This might be thought to lend plausibility to Schellenberg's apparent view that anything stronger than doubt in ultimism is philosophically inappropriate.

Although I lack the space to explore a detailed discussion of this objection, or any other objection for that matter, it does not seem plausible to me. After all, if ultimism is a religion, then presumably people's greatest good will involve some sort of contact with the divine (what other candidates would there be?). But we

---

[26] I say "strong" here because I think there are few stances about religion that are rationally required of everyone (Marsh, 2014b). Why not be a pluralist about rationality?

[27] When it comes to theism, Schellenberg states that since "there must be an *infinite number* of ways of growing into wholeness and fulfillment in God ... the idea that the permission of horrific suffering is required for anyone's deepest good in a world including God is therefore implausible in the extreme" (2007, pp.252–3).

have no reason to think that the serious evils people undergo are better served by non-personal divine realities than by personal ones. In fact, if anything, this asymmetry just creates a new axiological problem for ultimism. It is tempting to think that we can just see that nothing lacking the capacity to love or to experience love *could* be unsurpassable in goodness. Suppose that we cannot see this far into axiology, however. Still, a subjective version of the challenge remains. Given our natures, it may be that nothing except a personal and loving relationship could be our greatest good, even if it were objectively speaking maximally valuable. We are persons, after all, and we arguably care more about love and relationships than anything else. Many of us thus might not be capable of valuing, in an ultimate way, something that doesn't have the capacity to love us or to be loved by us. This challenge, though it may well corroborate our earlier cultural worry, also raises a normative question about the coherence of ultimistic soteriology.

To be sure, the value problem just mentioned could be entirely avoided by simply ascribing the property of being unsurpassably loving to the ultimate. But this would make atheistic ultimism look rather theistic and would re-open Kantian worries about evil. For all of these reasons, I think Schellenberg overstates the claim that "with less content comes less vulnerability" (2009, p. 27).[28]

Conclusion

To sum up, although philosophers of religion have long focused on the debate between naturalism and theism, I have examined a third option here: namely, Schellenberg's ultimism. As we saw, such a view faces two distinct challenges. First, CSR creates an important cultural challenge for ultimistic faith. The lesson here was that seeking out an epistemically less vulnerable religion is not the same thing as seeking out a more cognitively natural religion. Second, although sufficient gains in rationality might counterbalance some of these cultural costs, ultimism also faces various versions of the problem of evil—one of the main problems that led Schellenberg to abandon classical theism—and faces an overlooked challenge from the value of love. The lesson here was that defenders of simple ultimism may be overstating the epistemic advantages of generic religion.

---

[28] Needless to say, Schellenberg might have replies to many of these problems, and one cannot expect him to have dealt with every problem in his trilogy, which covers an impressive amount of ground as is. I thus write in order to stimulate further discussion on these matters.

Lastly, lest the reader misunderstand my goals, I have not claimed that ultimism (or theism or naturalism for that matter) is false, nor have I claimed that religious faith can never be rational. My claims have been more modest. Disbelief in ultimism is at least *sometimes* justified and ultimism at any rate faces more epistemic trouble than Schellenberg lets on. Such claims, it should be noted, are compatible with taking Schellenberg's project very seriously and with thinking that he is doing some of the most important work in the philosophy of religion. That said, I also think the problems I have raised here are significant. Unless or until they are answered, we have notably less reason than we previously did for thinking that generic ultimism—the third way—is epistemically all that superior to traditional religion or that it will take off culturally any time soon.[29]

References

Atran, S., 2002. *In Gods We Trust: The Evolutionary Landscape of Religion*. New York: Oxford University Press.

Atran, S. and Norenzayan, A., 2004. Religion's evolutionary landscape: counterintuition, commitment, compassion, communion. *Behavioral and Brain Sciences*, 27, pp. 713–70.

Baron-Cohen, S., 1995. *Mindblindess: An Essay on Autism and Theory of Mind*. Cambridge, MA: MIT Press.

Barrett, J.L., 1999. Theological Correctness: cognitive constraint and the study of religion. *Method and Theory in the Study of Religion*, 11, pp. 325–39.

——. 2004. *Why Would Anyone Believe in God?* Walnut Creek, CA: AltraMira Press.

——. 2007. Cognitive science of religion: what is it and why is it? *Religious Compass*, 1(6), pp. 768–86.

---

[29] An earlier version of this chapter was presented at the University of Oxford and for a symposium on J. L. Schellenberg's trilogy at the 2010 meeting for the Canadian Philosophical Association in Montreal. Thanks to audience members on these occasions for their remarks, including Paul Draper, Steve Wykstra, Helen De Cruz, Lotta Knutsson Bråkenhielm, Omar Sultan Haque, Josh Thurow, Justin Barrett, Roger Trigg, Jack Macintosh, John Thorp, and especially J.L. Schellenberg. Thanks also to John Doris, Jon Marsh, Philip Kitcher, and to departmental members at St Olaf College and Carleton College, for conversations relevant to the ideas presented here. Thanks, above all, to the Cognition, Religion, and Theology project at the University of Oxford for having me on board a highly memorable venture, and to the John Templeton Foundation for supporting that project and by extension this research. The ideas discussed here should not be assumed to reflect the ideas of the John Templeton Foundation or any other institution with which I am affiliated.

Barrett, J.L. and Keil, F.C., 1996. Conceptualizing a nonnatural entity: anthropomorphism in God concepts. *Cognitive Psychology*, 31(3), pp. 219–24.

Barrett, J.L. and VanOrman, B., 1996. The effects of image-use in worship on god concepts. *Journal of Psychology and Christianity*, 15(1), pp. 38–45.

Bering, J.M., 2002. The existential theory of mind. *Review of General Psychology*, 6(1), pp. 3–24.

Bering, J.M. and Bjorklund, D.F., 2004. The natural emergence of after life reasoning as development regularity. *Development Psychology*, 40, pp. 217–33.

Blackburn, S., 2002. An unbeautiful mind. *The New Republic*, 5 August.

Bloom, P., 2004. *Descartes' Baby: How the Science of Child Development Explains What Makes Us Human.* New York: Basic Books.

———. 2007. Religion is natural. *Developmental Science*, 10, pp. 147–51.

Boyer, P., 2001. *Religion Explained: Evolutionary Origins of Religious Thought.* New York: Basic Books.

Chomsky, N., 1965. *Aspects of the Theory of Syntax.* Cambridge, MA: MIT Press.

Cohen, E., 2007. *The Mind Possessed: The Cognition of Spirit Possession in an Afro-Brazilian Religious Tradition.* New York: Oxford University Press.

Dennett, D. 2006. *Breaking the Spell: Religion as a Natural Phenomenon. New York:* Viking Press.

Draper, P., 2012. The will to imagine: a justification of skeptical religion. *Philosophical Review*, 121(2), pp. 291–3.

Evans, E.M., 2000. Beyond scopes: why creationism is here to stay. In: K. Rosengren, C. Johnson, and P. Harris (eds), *Imagining the Impossible: Magical, Scientific and Religious Thinking in Children.* Cambridge: Cambridge University Press, pp. 305–31.

Goetz, S. and Taliaferro, C., 2008. *Naturalism.* Grand Rapids, MI: Eerdmans.

Guthrie, S., 1993. *Faces in the Clouds: A New Theory of Religion.* New York: Oxford University Press.

Hick, J., 2004. *An Interpretation of Religion: Human Responses to the Transcendent*, 2nd edn. New Haven, CT: Yale University Press.

Johnston, M., 2009. *Saving God: Religion after Idolatry.* Princeton, NJ: Princeton University Press.

Kelemen, D., 1999. Why are rocks pointy? Children's preference for teleological explanations of the natural world. *Developmental Psychology*, 35(6), pp. 1440–52.

———. 2004. Are children "intuitive theists"? Reasoning about purpose and design in nature. *Psychological Science*, 15, pp. 295–301.

Keller, J., 2010. The will to imagine: a justification of skeptical religion. *Notre Dame Philosophical Reviews*. Available at: http://ndpr.nd.edu/review.cfm?id=18627.

Kitcher, P., 2012. Challenges for secularism. Nordic Pragmatism Network. Available at: http://www.nordprag.org/papers/Kitcher8.pdf.

Leslie, J., 2007. *Immortality Defended*. Oxford: Blackwell Press.

Lombrozo, T., Kelemen, D. and Zaitchik, D., 2007. Inferring design: evidence of a preference for teleological explanations in patients with Alzheimer's disease. *Psychological Science*, 18(11), pp. 999–1006.

Marsh, J., 2013. Darwin and the problem of natural nonbelief. *The Monist*, 96(3), pp. 349–76.

——. 2014a. Quality of life assessments, cognitive reliability, and procreative responsibility. *Philosophy and Phenomenological Research*. doi: 10.1111/phpr.12114

——. 2014b. Conscientious refusals and reason-giving. *Bioethics*, 28(6), pp. 313–19.

Norenzayan, A., Gervais, W.M. and Trzesniewski, K.H., 2012. Mentalizing deficits constrain belief in a personal God. *PLoS ONE*, 7(5), pp. 1–8.

Pinker, S., 1997. *How the Mind Works*. New York: Norton.

Plantinga, A., 2000. *Warranted Christian Belief*. Oxford: Oxford University Press

Pyysiainen, I., 2003. Buddhism, religion, and the concept of "God". *Numen*, 50(2), pp. 147–71.

Schellenberg, J.L., 2005. *Prolegomena to a Philosophy of Religion*. Ithaca, NY: Cornell University Press.

——. 2007. *Wisdom to Doubt*. Ithaca, NY: Cornell University Press.

——. 2009. *Will to Imagine*. Ithaca, NY: Cornell University Press.

——. 2012. Skepticism as the beginning of religion. In: Ingolf U. Dalferth and Michael Ch. Rodgers (eds), *Skeptical Faith. Claremont Studies in Philosophy of Religion, Conference 2010*. Tubingen: Mohr Siebeck.

Street, S., 2012. The existence of god as a normative question. In: Purdue University, *Knowing in Religion and Morality Conference*. West Lafayette, IN, Fall 2012.

Tremlin, T., 2006. *Minds and Gods: The Cognitive Foundations of Religion*. Oxford: Oxford University Press.

Chapter 9
Cognitive Science of Religion and the Rationality of Classical Theism

T.J. Mawson

Recent discoveries in the Cognitive Science of Religion (CSR) have suggested to some that belief in the God of classical theism is in some sense more natural to our minds than belief in other gods, which in turn is more natural than complete atheism. One might suggest that such evidence supports the claim that, as Augustine might have put it, God has made us for Himself, so our brains are restless unless they find their rest in Him. Another view would be that it supports the hypothesis that our brains have 'made God' for themselves, for they are restless unless they are believing in Him. This chapter investigates the question of whether the findings of the CSR could in principle direct us rationally to favour one of these hypotheses over the other.

In order to 'control for other variables', as it were, for present purposes we would do well to sweep to one side arguments to the effect that there are independent good reasons either to suppose that a God of the Augustinian sort exists or to suppose that He does not. Obviously, if one already had reason in favour of one of these hypotheses over the other, that would need to be weighed in the balance when considering what one had overall reason to believe once the findings of the CSR were thrown into the balance as well, and thus it might affect how these findings would, on balance, best be interpreted. In order to see what weight, if any, these findings themselves add to the balance, we thus would do best to remove from the balance these other factors. That being so, we shall focus in due course on whether those who maintain that it is, for them at least, 'entirely right, rational, reasonable, and proper to believe in God without any evidence or argument at all' (Plantinga, 1983, p. 17) should think of their position as either supported or undermined by the sort of findings that might in principle be revealed by CSR. I shall start with a brief overview of some of the recent findings of CSR, an overview however that 'stretches' these findings a bit further than at least some of its current practitioners would wish. (I hope they and you will forgive me this stretching, as the primary purpose of investigating what, if anything, findings in this field could *in principle* establish with regard to the rationality of classical theism is facilitated by stretching these findings a little bit further than they currently stand in practice.) Then I shall go on to consider their implications for the rationality of classical theism.

Discoveries in CSR seem already to suggest that belief in supernatural agency of some sort is, in some sense, more natural than complete atheism. Stretching things a bit further, one might imagine them showing that belief in the God of classical theism is in turn more natural than belief in other gods. Allow me to expand for a moment or two on such claims, claims that I take to be in themselves purely empirical ones about, roughly speaking, the relative contributions to our propensity to believe that are provided by our natures as opposed to our nurtures. Of course, given that we are naturally nurturing, the division between these two is somewhat artificial, so perhaps we would do best to put it like this: there is increasing evidence that our minds come naturally – that is to say, prior to the effects of any *particular* culture – equipped with, for example, what might be called a 'Hypersensitive Agency Detection Device' (HADD). Now is not the occasion to go into the details of this evidence,[1] but one gets an idea of what the view amounts to and of its plausibility from the following thought experiment.

Imagine yourself going to sleep alone in your house this evening. You've locked the doors and windows; the house is secure; you've had your cocoa; you've set your alarm clock; and you slip easily into what you anticipate will be an uninterrupted night's sleep. In the middle of the night, you suddenly awake, conscious that the cause of your doing so is some unexplained noise elsewhere in the house. What is your first thought?

I hazard that it is something like this: 'There's someone else in the house.' 'I'm being burgled.' And so on. The (true) thought that unexplained noises of the sort that woke you are in most instances caused not by other agents, but by mere events, e.g., a window banging in the wind or somesuch, and thus that something along these lines is probably what has awoken you now can be forced on you by wilful rationalisation on your part. But whatever its relative epistemic virtues, this thought comes less naturally to you than the thought that there's someone else in the house with you. This then is your HADD in action.

What explanation can be found for our minds coming with such an inconvenient device pre-installed in them? Well, we may tell the following evolutionary 'just so' story. In our evolutionary past, such a device was far from

---

[1] A good overview of the field is given by Justin Barrett in his book *Why Would Anyone Believe in God?* (2004).

inconvenient, for supposing that there's an agent present when there's not was, in general, not too dangerous a mistake to make and a less dangerous mistake to make than supposing that there's not when there is. This much may be true even in my own present-day example: the risks attendant upon supposing for a moment or two that there's a burglar in one's house when there's not are slight; the risks of supposing that there's not when there is are high; and perhaps burglaries do happen frequently enough even now to make a HADD one for which the costs are still outweighed by the benefits. But whether or not such is true nowadays, such was certainly true in the past. Nowadays, at least in the sorts of homes we're privileged enough to go to sleep in, it is very unlikely indeed that we'll awake to find ourselves in the company of a dangerous animal or a human being who'd as soon kill us as look at us. The majority of our ancestors were not so fortuitously circumstanced. When your most secure possessions were simply whatever it was you could cling to as you went to sleep, and when animals and other agents were prevented from taking them from you by neither significant contrivance nor significant compunction, having a tendency to err on the side of waking with the belief that some such agent was near when they were not, rather than err on the side of waking with the belief that they were not near when they were, would often have made all the difference between life and death.[2]

Coming to a belief that an agent rather than merely an event is near is in itself of little use of course, even when that belief is arrived at quickly and even when that belief is true. To be of use, one additionally needs to be able to infer something about the likely behaviour of that agent. So, in parallel with the HADD, our remote ancestors could not but have benefited from inclining to attribute desires and beliefs to these agents. Such a 'Theory of Mind', as we might

---

[2] Why then do we not have a hypersensitive *event* detection device? After all, events – earthquakes, forest fires, floods and the like – can be just as dangerous as agents. The answer, it seems to me, must lie in the fact that events were not, on balance, as important as agents in our evolutionary past. Why would this have been? One part of the answer must be that mere events cannot be aiming to take our food or what have you from us; if they threaten such goods, they do so only as a matter of mindless chance. The same is not true of agents. Agents can – and are likely to – want things that we want and thus perform actions to get things we want to keep away from us. In addition to threats to goods and our survival, other agents (of the right species) also provide the chance of reproduction. It is plausible that being especially sensitive to the presence of things that might be out to get you (in contrast to merely mindlessly affecting you) and to things with which one might have fruitful sex was a better type of hypersensitivity for our ancestors to have had than being hypersensitive to events would have been. Thus, we understand evolution's 'choice' in favour of the one rather than the other.

call it, would have facilitated our ancestors in predicting agents' likely behaviours and hence in countering them insofar as it was in their interests to counter them.

Another common feature of the lives of the majority of our ancestors must have been fear in the face of an incomprehensible nature that daily threatened to overwhelm them. Just as there is undoubtedly much plausibility in the psychological thesis that there are no atheists in foxholes, so there is much plausibility in the claim that there are no atheists in storm cellars and the like either. And so there is much plausibility in the claim that there were no atheists in the state of war of all against all and – it must often have seemed – the war of nature against all that characterised the majority of our pre-history. How can we explain this?

The evolutionarily valuable desire to manipulate other agents and one's environment so as to facilitate one's flourishing can avoid apparent frustration even in the known absence of effective means of naturally doing so by supposing itself active in propitiating *supernatural* agencies which have at their direct disposal means of a sort one realises one lacks oneself. We might tell another evolutionary 'just so' story about a 'hypersensitive potency-self-ascription device' if you will. In our evolutionary past, it was better to err on the side of supposing that one could do something about a threat when one could not than to err on the side of supposing that one could not when one could. One can, after all, give in too soon when trying to escape from a threat in a way that one cannot really give in too late. We see this tendency pathetically displayed whenever we witness some lower animal seeking until its last breath to escape from a trap that, from our superior vantage point, we observe sealed its doom the moment it was sprung. Unlike such animals then, we often have the ability to realise that there are no means directly or naturally available to us to help us escape some threat; our desire to do something runs up against knowledge that there is nothing we can do, or at least nothing we can do directly or naturally. With the realisation that it is impossible to help oneself by natural means, one's hypersensitive potency-self-ascription device thus finds another outlet for its energies: the supernatural: 'I realise that I myself do not have the power to make the rain come directly, but I *do* have the power to perform the rain dance, and in doing so I may persuade the rain god to make the rain come.' And so on.

CSR tells us, or at least might tell us, I take it, that belief in the supernatural may be traced back to these or substantially similar springs: a hyperactive tendency to project agency; to think of these agents as minded as we are minded; and to seek to utilise them indirectly so as to bring about improvements in our lives which we realise we cannot bring about directly ourselves. From these or similar springs did our ancestors' belief in the supernatural flow. Towards what sort of supernatural agents would outpourings from these sources have been channelled?

At this stage we might turn to considerations which seem to tell in favour of our minds favouring notions which are what might be called 'minimally counterintuitive', for example, in violating just enough assumptions about the natural world to be interesting, but not so many that we lose a handle on them altogether.[3] Of course, ghosts, tree spirits, voodoo curses and all sorts of things other than the God of classical theism satisfy this requirement. Even if the considerations so far suggest that our minds would find themselves naturally drawn in the direction of believing in things of the supernatural type, why might one say that they would *more* naturally find themselves drawn to God rather than these other supernatural beings?

Since our ancestors became bipedal, perhaps six million years ago, corollary changes in the female pelvic structure have meant that their offspring needed to be born at an earlier stage of their development and thus, if they were to survive, needed more caring parents than did the young of any other species. A newborn gazelle can famously run and jump minutes after birth; there is every reason to suppose that the children of our bipedal hominid ancestors would have been as are our children today – unable to fend for themselves for several years. Belief in what we might think of as morally interested and knowledgeable supernatural agencies would have strengthened the familial ties necessary for our ancestors to survive their first years better than belief in what we might think of as entirely morally disinterested/uninterested and/or ignorant ones; such beliefs would have better encouraged what has been called 'pro-social' behaviour.

If we allow ourselves to consider group selection effects, then we may speculate that, as the extended family units that we may call 'tribes' clashed with one another in our evolutionary past, the tribe which could most effectively persuade its members to sublimate their own individual interests (or, as it might have been useful to portray them, merely *ante-mortem* interests) to those of the group would be able to coordinate a wider range of attacks and thus, when all else was equal, would win out over others. Voltaire has assured us that God is always on the side of the big battalions. Perhaps. But a suggestion of at least equal plausibility is that in our tribal past the most effective battalions usually believed themselves to be on the side of a god, even if not the God. And, of course, for strengthening both familial and tribal ties, the 'bigger' the god, the

---

[3] There is a discussion of the issue of what 'accounts for our commitment to the *reality* of one set of ideas' and not another in Michael J. Murray and Andrew Goldberg (2009, pp. 189ff, esp. 190–92).

better. That being the case, whilst tribally partisan super-beings with powers to reward the righteous beyond the grave would serve the needs we have so far identified to some extent, an unsurpassable and unitary God would serve them even better. Thus, we might expect that, once introduced, God (with a big 'G') would, all other things being equal, 'out-compete' the gods (with a small 'g') as the primary object of devotion.

These observations might seem to suggest a development within the history of humanity along Humean lines, polytheism being the original belief of humanity and belief in an unsurpassable and unitary God evolving out of that. But the considerations to which we have so far adverted started operating so far back in our evolutionary past that they preceded humanity *per se* by several millions of years and thus multiple generations. To the extent that these considerations are cogent, then perhaps there was never a time at which *humanity* as such failed to be naturally drawn at least 'in the direction of' monotheism.

For the reasons sketched, then, the claim that something akin to classical theism is more natural to our minds than any alternative, which in itself – as I say – would stretch the findings of CSR rather further than many of its practitioners would currently wish, would – if it were to be made – need to be combined with a recognition of the fact that nurture can – relatively easily – overwhelm nature at this point. (Only to that extent would it not be disproved by the discovery that the first recoverable steps of humanity's religious journey were largely polytheistic.) But this would be no fatal blow: the claim would not be that no society or individual is able to be polytheist or atheist; rather, it would simply be that in being polytheist, societies and individuals 'run against the grain', as it were, of humanity's natural cognitive structures. And in being entirely atheistic, they run against the grain all the more so.

All this having been said, then, there seems to be great plausibility and perhaps increasing experimental evidence that – however they've got into this state and however providential, fortuitous or disastrous it is for them to be in it – human minds are now naturally inclined towards belief in supernatural agency in general and – to a lesser extent (here I am stretching things a little bit) – towards belief in classical theism in particular. In making any such claims, it must always be stressed that, in combination with our nature, our nurture of course affects the precise content of our religious beliefs and can even eliminate them entirely. The point is simply that the mind does not start as an entirely blank sheet of paper, equally susceptible to being written on by any religious hypothesis whatsoever or by none at all; rather, belief in the supernatural seems to have been heavily 'pencilled in', as it were, by our evolutionary history and – here stretching things a bit – belief in the God of classical theism more lightly pencilled in by it. A belief in God can be written over by other beliefs; it can be erased entirely; but, for good or ill, humans start in this manner with something of a propensity for it.

Allow me to suppose that a view such as that just sketched is correct, at least in broad outline, even if the details may – indeed, almost certainly will – be subject to amendment as CSR develops. Doing so will enable me to concentrate on the philosophical issue of what, if anything, would follow from it were it or anything substantially like it correct. Is CSR for example, giving us reason to believe that, as Augustine might have put it, God has made us for Himself, so our brains are restless unless they find their rest in Him?

A view that would harmonise nicely with this interpretation of the findings has a wide following in the US at the moment, under the banner 'Reformed Epistemology'. Identifying the aforementioned or similar cognitive propensities with the naturally occurring *sensus divinitatis* – as Reformed Epistemologists, following Calvin, usually call it – if combined with a certain type of externalism about knowledge, such as that of the most prominent contemporary Reformed Epistemologist Alvin Plantinga, might even be enough to turn this natural belief in God into a natural knowledge of Him. Although they have been largely silent on the issue of CSR so far,[4] we may expect Reformed Epistemologists to be enthusiastic about these findings and view them as providing empirical support for the suggestion that humans come naturally equipped with the sorts of cognitive structures with which they had always said we came naturally equipped.[5]

Whilst Reformed Epistemologists have as yet not flung themselves into the arms of Cognitive Scientists of Religion, such attempts at joyful embrace, when they come, will be rebuffed by several working in the field – Atran and Boyer, for example – and will seem profoundly inappropriate to some philosophers reflecting on it (Boyer, 2001; Atran, 2002). Perhaps most famously, Dennett, in his book *Breaking the Spell*, argues that the findings of the CSR actually support atheism (Dennett, 2006). These findings, such people suggest, give us reason to suppose that, to invert the Augustinian thought, our brains 'make God' for themselves, for they are restless unless they are believing in Him, or at least unless

---

[4] At the time I first wrote this chapter, this was true. Since then, Kelly James Clark and Justin Barrett have been kind enough to allow me to see 'Reformed Epistemology and the Cognitive Science of Religion', which, at the time of writing, is forthcoming in *Faith and Philosophy*. Also published since my first draft of this chapter has been Jeffrey Schloss and Michael Murray (eds), *The Believing Primate* (2009).

[5] *A fortiori* if CSR moves in the direction I have 'stretched' it.

they are relieved of this restlessness by a proper appreciation of the writings of a 'bright' such as the great Daniel C. Dennett.[6]

One might rather jadedly suppose that the situation in the unfolding debate may safely be predicted to be like this. Those who already believe in God, Reformed Epistemologists say, will believe that the findings of the CSR support their belief. Those who are already atheists, such as Dennett, will believe that its findings support their atheism. However, whilst there is indeed already appearing a rough correlation of this sort, it is by no means perfect: some theists fear that their theism will be undermined by the findings of the CSR and some atheists fear that their atheism will be undermined by its findings.

On a moment's reflection, it is perhaps *un*surprising that some religious people think their religious beliefs threatened by the CSR. After all, in each age some religious people take the scientific developments of their day as the object of such fears. What is perhaps more surprising is that some atheists find their atheism threatened by it. Before I give an example of such a case, I should mention that I have chosen my example as indicative of the fear at its most visceral, not as illustrative of it at its most well-grounded and nuanced. The piece from which I draw comes from a newspaper and, as such, the author, one must assume, was under some time pressure when he composed it. Be that as it may, A.C. Grayling's (2008) stated – even if knee-jerk – reaction in a piece tellingly subtitled 'There's no real evidence to suggest that religion is hardwired – it's just wishful thinking on the part of religious academics' is obviously that *were* the CSR to find what he takes Barrett et al. to think it finds (which is arguably not quite what Barrett et al. do think it finds), *then* theism would be supported. That being so, and because Grayling has decided, in advance of considering CSR, that theism is false, he spends his time in his piece speculating that those working in the field must in general have disingenuous and proselytising motives. It never seems to occur to Grayling to think, as his fellow atheist Dennett thinks, that such findings might actually be interpreted as supportive of atheism. Indeed, the contrast with Dennett could not be starker; it never seems to occur to Dennett that these findings might support theism.

A third view is of course possible and it is one that considerations of the sort mentioned in the previous paragraph must have placed in the forefront of our minds as the most probable. This is the view that the CSR gives us *neither* reason to suppose theism true, *nor* reason to suppose it false and that it cannot, even in principle, give us either of these things. To put the matter in our Augustinian terms: the hypothesis that God has made us for Himself,

---

[6] For a criticism of Dennett, see Taliaferro, 2009.

so our brains are restless until they find their rest in Him, and the hypothesis that we 'make God' for ourselves, for our brains are restless until they find their rest in believing in Him, are empirically equivalent. That being so, Reformed Epistemologists, for example, should not claim that the findings of CSR are supportive of their view, just that they are consistent with it, and similarly so for atheists such as Dennett and Grayling.

This third view is – almost – the view to which I am drawn. Almost, but not quite. In order to expound my view more fully, I wish to introduce some distinctions between the sorts of pathways by which we are led to our beliefs, distinctions between what I shall call 'rationally vindicatory pathways', 'rationally neutral pathways' and 'rationally destabilizing pathways'. In doing so, I draw on the work of my close colleague, Peter Kail (2007). My claim will be that we can have no internally accessible reason, independent of our belief or lack of belief in God, to classify the pathways that CSR eventually settles upon as leading to our religiosity or lack of it as any one of these three pathways. But if we start from our religious beliefs, or lack thereof, we may then have internally accessible reason to classify the pathways. If we are theists, it may well be rational by these standards for us to interpret the findings of the CSR as rationally vindicatory; if agnostics, as rationally neutral; and, if atheists, as rationally destabilising.

It will be easiest to introduce the distinctions between rationally vindicatory, neutral and destabilising pathways by way of some examples.

Let us suppose then that, as far back as I can remember, I have always believed that the Master of my college is a fundamentally honest and trustworthy man. Furthermore, I believe that his judgment on all issues is profoundly nuanced and always correct. In character and judgment, he embodies perfection. I cannot at the moment remember how I first came to this view. Be that as it may, with this belief as foundational, I have naturally interpreted what others see as apparent evidence to the contrary just as evidence that he is much misunderstood by those others (perhaps due to character flaws in themselves) and that his masterplan is more complicated than these others, or indeed myself, can fully appreciate. I am aware of others who have never believed in or recently stopped believing in the Master's perfection; some even doubt that there is a Master (and, I confess, I've never seen or spoken to him directly, only to other college officers who have been dealing with him directly). But, as I have 'defeater defeaters' for what these disbelievers think of as 'defeaters' to my belief in the Master, I do not consider myself irrational in not joining them. This then is the belief in question.

Now I recall how it is I first came to the belief, the pathway, if you will, that led me to it. There are three possible cases that I'd like to consider as illustrative in turn of what I am calling 'rationally vindicatory', 'neutral' and 'destabilising' pathways.

In case one, I realise that I first came to my belief in the Master's perfection as a result of several separate protracted dealings, which I took to be with the Master – albeit mediated by others (his secretary; the Bursar; and so forth) – over complex issues and my sitting down one afternoon to reflect on this wealth of experience, a set of evidence which I took to be best explained by the hypothesis that there was indeed a perfect Master behind it all. I cannot now recall the experiences that I at that stage took as my evidence for the Master's existence and perfection, but I do recall that it was substantial evidence and carefully considered by me at the time. And I recall now that it was as a result of this careful consideration that I came to my confident belief in the existence and superlative virtues of the Master.

Were I to rediscover now that this was the manner in which my belief in the Master had been initially formed in me, I would have discovered that the pathway by which my belief arose was what we might call a 'rationally vindicatory' one, meaning that it is such that the belief would be more likely to have arisen in me had the belief been true than had it been false. The level of rational vindication depends of course on the level of good judgment we suppose my earlier self to have had, but, if we suppose that it is high (as we are free to do; it is our example after all), then it will be true that had the Master not existed or not been as I suppose him to be, it is extremely unlikely that I would have ended up thinking that he existed and was as I think him to be. And I may know these things now. Thus, my now discovering that this is the pathway by which I came to my belief in the Master would increase my rational assurance in that belief. I should believe the belief 'vindicated' by this discovery of its mode of origination in me.

In case two, I come to realise that I first came to my belief in the Master as a result of a bit of Pascal-Wager-style thinking on my part. At one stage, prior to having any beliefs about the Master one way or the other, I ruminated on the fact that *if* I believed the college was under the oversight of a superlative Master, I would feel rather more optimistic about it than if I held any other beliefs on this matter or none at all and, I further realised, that there would be significant benefits and no significant dangers incurred by me were I to have such an optimism, even were such a belief false. So I committed myself at that stage to a project of self-imposed brainwashing, involving such things as listening attentively to those who already believed in the existence and perfection of the Master when they opined on some felicitous happening within the college and actively shunning the company of sceptics. I was successful in my aim in engaging in this in that I was, over time, able to come to the point where I genuinely believed in the existence and superlative virtues of the Master. For a time I then forget that this was the route I'd taken to get to this belief.

Were I to rediscover now that this was the pathway along which I had travelled to get to my belief in the Master, I would have discovered the pathway to be what we might call a 'rationally neutral' one, as I would have discovered that the manner in which I had come to the belief was one that was indifferent concerning the truth of the belief. In finding out that this was the pathway along which I'd travelled, I'd not have found any reason to suppose that the Master did *not* exist or was *not* perfect. Had the Master really existed and been as I suppose him to be, then I'd have believed that he existed and was as I believe him to be via this pathway. But the fact that even had the Master *not* existed and been as I suppose him to be, I'd still have believed that he did and was (if we presume various other easy-to-fill-in things) revealed to me now that the pathway is not a vindicatory one. It is, we might therefore say, 'rationally neutral'; the discovery of it neither supports nor undermines the belief in question.[7]

In case three, I suddenly remember that I first came to my belief in the Master as a result of going along to an event being hosted in the Junior Common Room the previous evening. This was an event where a stage magician provided entertainment by hypnotising people into believing things that were well-known by his audience to be false. As I recall the event now, he asked for volunteers who were prepared to be hypnotised into believing something false; into immediately forgetting that this was the manner in which they had come to believe their particular falsehood; and into only remembering any of this upon awaking the next day. I remember now that I then saw one person getting himself hypnotised into believing that the Earth was flat and another into believing that the moon was made of cheese. It is now the morning after and I thus now recall that it was I who stepped forward next and came away believing in the Master.

This discovery would 'rationally destabilise', as we might put it, my belief in the Master in that it would be my suddenly realising that the pathway by which I had travelled to get to the belief had not been one which favoured true belief (as was the case with the vindicatory pathway); it had not even been one that was indifferent to the truth-value of belief (as was the case with the neutral pathway). Rather, it was one that was actually biased *against* true belief. We can see that my belief in the Master's perfection *should* be undermined by this discovery concerning the nature of the pathway that has led me to it, hence 'rational destabilisation'.

---

[7] Joshua Thurow suggested to me in discussion that this pathway should actually be classified as rationally destabilising, but whilst I might concede that it might (perhaps necessarily) be psychologically destabilising – in learning that the pathway by which one came to the belief had nothing to do with truth, one will incline to lose the belief – I do not agree that it is rationally so; roughly this is because in learning that the pathway had nothing to do with truth, one is not learning that it had something to do with falsity.

Our question then is whether any findings or indeed any potential findings of the CSR do or could give us reason to classify the pathways by which our religious beliefs arise as rationally vindicatory, neutral or destabilising. We shall be assisted in answering this question by considering a fourth case, which is, I shall suggest, most closely analogous to the situation with respect to our religious beliefs.

In the fourth case, I come to believe that my belief in the Master's perfection is a result of my being hypnotised by a mechanism that is, we may suppose, as in the third case. In this case, however, the hypnosis was not carried out by some showman with a bias against instilling true beliefs, but by processes initiated by the Master himself. Further, this Master, having the superlative virtues that he *ex hypothesi* does have, would not have allowed such a process to lead me to significant error about him.

Those who disbelieve in the existence and/or perfection of the Master may agree with me, at least for the sake of argument, about the mechanics of the processes by which I have come to my belief in the Master and about the facts revealed by the cognitive science of this pathway. But, disbelieving as they do in such a Master, they will of course deny that these processes were under his control and thus directed toward truth thereby. Before they could accuse me of being unreasonable in not joining them in categorising the pathway by which we agree I have been led to my belief as destabilising, unreasonable by reference to standards that I myself would endorse, they would need some argument against the existence of the Master and in favour of some falsity-disposed mechanism, an argument to which I had no answer – i.e., one the soundness of which I could not challenge. In the absence of such an 'undefeated defeater' to my belief, I may, in the face of such assertions from them, simply assert back that the situation is rather as follows: 'It is just as I supposed. The Master, being perfect, would have realised how error-prone would have been my own feeble attempts to assess his merits if starting from a blank sheet of paper and left entirely unaided. That being so, through these processes he graciously pencilled-in, as it were, a belief in him. The sciences by which the mechanics of these processes are discovered, in revealing how widespread is the naturalness of such a belief in him (if this is what they do reveal), are revealing that he did the same with my disbelieving colleagues too and thus that they must have corrupted in some way this "imago" in themselves.' If then I do as a matter of fact have 'defeater defeaters' for their defeaters to my belief in the Master, I can – indeed, by reference to all internally accessible reasons, *should* – rest where I am, classifying the pathway as rationally vindicatory.

In the first case we considered, we could assess independently of whether or not we happened to believe in the Master that I would probably not have believed in the Master if he had not existed and been more or less as I suppose him to be (albeit only by assuming various things about my own earlier good judgment); thus, the pathway could be uncontroversially classified as vindicatory. In the second case we considered, we could independently assess that my belief had nothing to do with the facts which would make it true if it were true; thus, uncontroversially neutral. And in the third case, we could independently assess that the mechanism was biased against truth; thus, uncontroversially destabilising. This fourth case differs from any of the first three in this respect: it is one in which we cannot assess and thus classify the pathway independently of our views on the truth-value of the belief to which it has led.

One might wonder whether this does in fact make the pathway neutral. It is tempting to say that the pathway has a 'higher-level' neutrality, by which I mean that it is tempting to say that the reality is that the pathway may – epistemically – be vindicatory, neutral or destabilising, and it is just that we can have no reason to believe that it is one of these rather than another, so over its status as any one of vindicatory, neutral or destabilising we should be neutral. But such a claim, whilst tempting, would be mistaken. We can see this by seeing that to this claim I might respond that I simply *do* have a reason to classify the pathway as vindicatory; the Master himself has told me to do so. If there is such a Master, what better reason could there be? There is, of course, something circular about such a move, but such a circularity besets any attempt to get around hyperbolically sceptical worries of which this, one might say, is just another instance: are perception, memory, etc. in general reliable? And of course this is not to deny – indeed, quite the opposite – that a similar, circular move could be made on the part of those who would wish to classify the pathway as destabilising: Nietzsche, Freud, Marx or whoever could be brought in by them as having told us to classify such pathways thus. As long as Freudians, for example, have 'defeater defeaters' to any anti-Freudian arguments (and they usually take themselves to do so[8]), they may rest as content with continuing to classify the pathway as rationally destabilising as I am with continuing to classify it as rationally vindicatory. So, one cannot show from neutral ground that the pathway should be classified as either vindicatory or destabilising, but that in itself does not entail that the pathway is in fact neutral or that from non-neutral

---

[8] 'Criticisms which stem from some psychological need of those making them don't deserve a rational answer. When people complain that psychoanalysis makes wild and arbitrary assertions about infantile sexuality, this criticism stems from certain psychological needs of these people. Therefore, the criticism that psychoanalysis makes wild and arbitrary assertions about infantile sexuality doesn't deserve a rational answer.' Freud (1933, Lecture XXXIV) quoted by Hodges (1983, p. 230) as exemplary of validity.

ground one should not take its findings as supportive of one's views. Do we have any way out of this impasse? I think not.

An initially promising suggestion is that whatever structures CSR eventually reaches a consensus on as behind people's religiosity, these structures cannot be considered reliably true-belief-inducing when we consider the diversity and mutual incompatibility of the religious beliefs to which they give rise. It's the diversity of the world's religions that gives us reason to suppose that these cognitive structures are not reliable in general across humanity when the resultant objects of belief are supernatural entities. Thus, these pathways are rationally destabilising.[9]

Here, though, there is room for the theist to maintain that these mechanisms simply *are* reliable across a sub-section of humanity, let us call them 'The Elect', the Elect being those – in whose number the believer is of course likely to consider himself or herself to fall – who have been predestined by God to reach the correct views about God and about their status as the Elect. Obviously, *for those souls*, these processes are 100 per cent reliable in informing them with true beliefs; it's just for the others, the non-Elect, that they are unreliable.[10] Consider the following situation, which such a believer may maintain as analogous.

Take a pathway by which you might arrive at the belief that Descartes was born on 31 March 1596 and which would provide for you a paradigm of a rationally vindicatory pathway. Perhaps you're coming to the belief as a result of looking it up separately in 10 of the most recent books on Descartes and finding each in agreement with one another on this as the date (and each citing sources other than one another for their view) would suffice. Perhaps you will think that more is required than this. Be that as it may, it will not affect the essentials of the analogy. Just fill in for yourself that more, if there is a more, as I go on. Assume then that you realise you have got to your belief in this as Descartes' birthday as

---

[9] Clark and Barrett (2010) discuss this in their 'Reformed Epistemology and the Cognitive Science of Religion'.

[10] I make a similar point in T. J. Mawson, 'Mill's argument against religious knowledge' (2009). In the main text of this paper, I brush past a more nuanced alternative, elements of which are explored in my paper on Mill. In brief, the model that would best fit the current findings would have it that God has arranged things so that all people are inclined to develop a confused natural knowledge of Him (this then allows for the diversity in religious beliefs, including polytheism, and the possibility of atheism), and so that a subset – the Elect – come, via more particular revelation, to a fully developed knowledge of Him. It will be recalled that Plantinga separates the operations *sensus divinitatis*, which we may identify with the first part of this process, from that by which the Holy Spirit 'instigates' belief in what he calls 'the Great Truths of the Gospel', which instigation only happens of course when an individual is exposed to the Gospel (and not always then).

a result of going down such a pathway; you realise that the pathway by which you have reached your belief that Descartes was born on 31 March 1596 is a rationally vindicatory one for you.

Now you learn that on Mars there lives a species of aliens who are under the control of a not-entirely-benign dictator, one who has his very-informative telescope trained on the planet Earth and has determined that, for every one human who goes through this process, he will ensure that two of his Martian subjects go through a similar process whereby they look at 10 of the most recent books concerning Descartes, books which are the same in every respect as Earth books *except* that he has doctored the date of Descartes' birth in them; in these Martian editions, it is given 1 April 1596. Thus, the pathway of looking up Descartes' birthday in 10 recent books is – across the solar system and indeed universe we may hypothesise – unreliable in bringing about the true belief that Descartes was born on 31 March 1596. For every one person who gets to it that way, two who travel that way get to the false belief that Descartes was born on 1 April 1596. Would your now discovering this fact about the Martians mean that you should therefore reclassify the pathway by which *you* have come to the belief as a rationally neutral or destabilising one? Surely not. You may just say that it is 'lucky for you' in this respect that you have been born a human rather than a Martian.[11] Similarly, then, the theist may maintain that it is just 'lucky' for him or her that he or she is one of the Elect rather than one of those predestined to come via these processes to significantly false beliefs about the supernatural. And of course in both cases the notion of luck is somewhat ill-used; just as it is plausible to say that we could not have been born Martians and in that sense it cannot be lucky for us that we were not, so the believer may maintain that he or she, being amongst the Elect, could never have been allowed by God to have been given a life in which he or she would have come to substantially false beliefs about that God. He or she may maintain that the Elect are essentially Elect, not accidentally so.

---

[11] As I say in my paper on Mill's argument against religious knowledge (Mawson, 2009): 'There are two levels of luck that need to be distinguished here. The first is the luck present (or not) in a belief-acquiring process pertaining to whether or not that process yields true belief, a less reliable process being more lucky if it's given rise to true beliefs on this occasion than a more reliable one would need to have been. The second is the luck present (or not) in the process by which someone comes to be subject to a process of belief acquisition that gives rise to certain outputs.' Luck of the second sort does not affect one's epistemic credentials. It was perhaps just lucky that I got the university education that I did, being taught in turn by the best undergraduate tutor of the university and the best graduate supervisor. Nevertheless, this education has given me knowledge that is not impugned as such to any extent by any luck in the process by which I was admitted to it.

So, to summarise: the implications of the CSR for the rational acceptability of classical theism all depend on where you are starting from.[12] That may sound like another way of saying that there are no such implications, but it is not. The findings of CSR, if they are in broad outline as I have suggested they are and if they turn out to lie in the direction I have 'stretched' them, may be taken by theists as reason to suppose that they are right – God has made us (or at least some of us) for Himself, so our brains are restless until they find their rest in Him. Its findings may be taken by atheists as reason to suppose that they are right; our brains 'make God' for themselves, for they are restless until they find their rest in believing in Him or in being cured of such restlessness by the writings of Nietzsche, Marx, Freud or perhaps even Dennett. And they may be taken by agnostics to be no reason, one way or the other.

It might be suggested that here I must be speaking merely of 'subjective' reasons, where something is a subjective reason for someone only if it is a reason for them given what they already believe. Well, I do speak of such. But, of course, if the theist is right, then his or her subjective reasons are objective reasons (that's a part of what his or her being right would mean); similarly, if the Freudian, say, is right, then the Freudian's subjective reasons are objective reasons. And so on. 'But which of these, and the multitude of other world-views, *is* right, which one's subjective reasons *really are* objective reasons?' one asks. Good question. All I have shown is that in seeking to answer it, one should not expect to make progress by looking to CSR.[13]

References

Atran, S., 2002. *In Gods We Trust: The Evolutionary Landscape of Religion*. New York: Oxford University Press.

Barrett, J.L., 2004. *Why Would Anyone Believe in God?* Walnut Creek, CA: AltaMira Press.

---

[12] As Peter van Inwagen (2009, p. 134) puts it: 'Any naturalistic explanation of any phenomenon can be incorporated without logical contradiction into a "larger", more comprehensive supernaturalistic explanation of that phenomenon.' He goes on to discuss and endorse the idea that there could nevertheless be things that 'resist ... being incorporated into a larger, more comprehensive supernaturalist account'; I do not follow him there.

[13] I am grateful for the comments of Justin Barrett, Kelly Clark, David Leech and Joshua Thurow on the first draft of this chapter and for the comments and questions raised at the conference at Birmingham University where it was first read out.

Boyer, P., 2001. *Religion Explained: The Evolutionary Origins of Religious Thought*. New York: Basic Books.

Clark, K. and Barrett, J.L., 2010. Reformed epistemology and the cognitive science of religion. *Faith and Philosophy*, 27(2), pp. 174–89.

Dennett, D., 2006. *Breaking the Spell: Religion as a Natural Phenomenon*. New York: Viking.

Freud, S., 1933. *New Introductory Lectures on Psychoanalysis*. London: Hogarth Press.

Grayling, A.C., 2008. Children of God? There's no real evidence to suggest that religion is hardwired – it's just wishful thinking on the part of religious academics. *The Guardian*, 28 November.

Hodges, W., 1983. *Logic*. Harmondsworth: Pelican Books.

Kail, P.J.E., 2007. Understanding Hume's natural history of religion. *Philosophical Quarterly*, 57, pp. 190–211.

Mawson, T.J., 2009. Mill's argument against religious knowledge. *Religious Studies*, 45, pp. 417–34.

Murray, M. and Goldberg, A., 2009. Evolutionary accounts of religion: explaining and explaining away. In: J. Schloss and M.J. Murray (eds), *The Believing Primate: Scientific, Philosophical, and Theological Reflections on the Origin of Religion*. Oxford: Oxford University Press, pp. 179–99.

Plantinga, A., 1983. Reason and belief in God. In: A. Plantinga and N. Wolterstorff (eds), *Faith and Rationality: Reason and Belief in God*. Notre Dame: University of Notre Dame Press, pp. 16–93.

Taliaferro, C., 2009. Explaining religious experience. In: J. Schloss and M.J. Murray (eds), *The Believing Primate: Scientific, Philosophical, and Theological Reflections on the Origin of Religion*. Oxford: Oxford University Press, pp. 200–14.

Van Inwagen, P., 2009. Explaining belief in the supernatural: some thoughts on Paul Bloom's "Religious belief as an evolutionary accident". In: J. Schloss and M.J. Murray (eds), *The Believing Primate: Scientific, Philosophical, and Theological Reflections on the Origin of Religion*. Oxford: Oxford University Press, pp. 128–38.

Chapter 10
Cognitive Science and the Limits of Theology

John Teehan

The application of the methods and findings of the various disciplines that fall under the umbrella term "cognitive science" to religious beliefs and practices constitutes one of the most promising approaches to understanding the religious mind and establishes a new front on the religion/science debates. This is a nascent field and so we must properly temper any conclusions drawn from it. However, as it is making significant claims about the nature of religion, it seems appropriate to begin considering its implications for religious belief. Indeed, the Cognitive Science of Religion (CSR) is already generating interest and controversy across the religious spectrum. It has been touted by some as the final nail in the coffin of religious belief and as decisive evidence of the incompatibility of science and faith; while others, including some of the major figures in the field, argue that there is no conflict at all—that the findings of this field may be integrated into one's belief systems with no theological cost. My thesis is that both sides overstate their positions. I concur that CSR does not entail atheism, nor is it the conclusive case against a religious world-view that some fear/hope it to be. However, I also believe that the implications of this new field for religion are much more challenging than they are often presented to be by theists. Contemporary cognitive science, grounded in an evolutionary perspective, "shakes the foundations" of religious belief in a more profound way than evolutionary theory has done so far.

I want to spend most of my time setting out just what those challenges are, but we do need to have a general sense of what cognitive science claims. Justin Barrett gives us a succinct and workable account. He writes:

> Belief in gods requires no special parts of the brain. Belief in gods requires no special mystical experiences ... Belief in gods requires no coercion or brainwashing ... Rather, belief in gods arises because of the natural functioning of completely

normal mental tools working in common natural and social contexts. (Barrett, 2004, p. 21)

Just what these mental tools are and exactly how we are to conceptualize "mental tools" is open to continuing debate, but there is a growing consensus on the importance of certain tools, or cognitive predispositions, in giving rise to religious beliefs. This religious-cognition tool set is extensive, but here I will mention four in particular:

1. *Agency Detection Device:* humans have a well-attested predisposition to interpret the world in terms of agency.[1] Given the importance, and the potential danger, of undetected agents in our environment, we can understand how evolution would have selected for such a mental tool. In fact, we are hypersensitive to the presence of agents, detecting agency even when there are no intentional agents present. It is argued that the universal human tendency to believe in gods, ghosts, spirits, etc. is grounded in this evolved cognitive predisposition (e.g. Guthrie, 1993; Boyer, 2001; Atran 2002; Barrett, 2004).

2. *Theory of Mind*: not only do we perceive the actions of agents, but we ascribe mental states to those agents (e.g. Boyer, 2001; Atran, 2002; Tremlin, 2006). We perceive agents as acting with intention, having desires, emotions, plans, goals, etc. This also has clear survival value—it is not enough to merely perceive that "something is out there." In order to know how to respond, I need some sense of what that "something" wants, what it might be planning. The mental tools necessary to this task would also be subject to selective pressures.

3. *Common-Sense Dualism*: research suggests that humans have different cognitive systems for dealing with physical bodies and mental events. As a consequence, it is an intuitive move to conceive of bodies without minds, and minds without bodies. As Paul Bloom puts it, "we think of bodies and souls as *distinct*" (Bloom, 2007, p. 149). A naturally dualistic mind that processes bodies and events with different systems supports our predisposition to detect agents at work even if we lack clear physical evidence of their presence, and allows us to ascribe mental states to beings without physical bodies. Bloom argues that this dual system is a result of

---

[1] For examples, see Guthrie, 1993; Kelemen, 1999; 2004a; Boyer, 2001; Atran, 2002; Barrett, 2004; Bulbulia, 2004; Bloom, 2004; 2005; Atran and Norenzayan, 2004; Tremlin, 2006.

the uniquely social environment of the human species and the selection pressure this placed on our cognitive evolution.
4. *Promiscuous Teleology*: this wonderful phrase comes from developmental psychologist Deborah Kelemen (Kelemen, 2004a), whose work indicates that we also naturally interpret the world in teleological terms, i.e. we ascribe purpose and design. Understanding what something *is for* is an important step in understanding how to respond to it, or what to do with it, and this provides an adaptive advantage.

Evolved mental tools such as these predispose the mind to interpret the world in terms that give rise to religious beliefs and practices. Much more needs to be said to flesh out this model and of course there are debates about the relative influence of the various tools that are implicated in the generation of religious beliefs. While these debates are vital for the project of developing a sound CSR, their resolution is not salient to our present discussion. For whatever the ultimate outcome of such debates, the claim that religious beliefs and practices result from the natural functioning of evolved cognitive tools is fundamental to the entire project—and this is the issue at hand: given an evolved/cognitive explanation of religion, what are the implications for religious belief?

It is clear that cognitive science has important implications for both theists and atheists. In terms of the critics of religion, I believe the findings of CSR change the nature of such criticism. Religious belief is not the result of ignorance; it is not the result of particularly irrational or superstitious thinking; it is not the result of intellectual laziness—even if each of these elements is at times involved in religious belief. Religion is not the opiate of the masses (even if it is sometimes used as such); it is not a defense mechanism against death (even if it may serve this function), nor is it a comfort against the terrors of nature (even if can play this role). Religion, from the perspective of cognitive science, is the outgrowth of natural cognitive tools functioning to help us make sense of our world. The cognitive tools that give rise to and sustain religious belief and practice are part of human nature—humans are naturally religious. And this is not an apologetic for religion, it simply follows from the models being developed by cutting-edge research into the workings of the human mind. The dismissive, denigrating attitude sometimes displayed by religion's critics is undermined by the findings of this new field. Nor can the non-religious claim superiority simply by virtue of having seen through the "illusions of faith." These mental tools need not always lead to religious beliefs, but the absence of religious belief does not imply that these evolved tools are no longer functioning. The non-religious are prone to their own forms of unsupported believing.[2]

To conclude that religion is a natural part of the human condition is not to suggest, of course, that religious claims are true, or that a religious interpretation of reality is accurate. While cognitive science does not entail atheism, it can assume an important role in the repertoire of religious criticism. From that perspective, cognitive science shows religion to be a byproduct[3] of mental tools that evolved to promote the reproductive success of our earliest ancestors, and while it may be natural for these tools to give rise to religious beliefs and behaviors, these beliefs and behaviors are, in effect, evolutionary accidents. An evolutionary account of the origins of religion does not merely explain religion, it seems to explain it away. If this is so, then an evolved/cognitive model of religion may be incompatible with many of the central truth-claims of religion (e.g. god beliefs), but of course the question is: is it so? There are many thinkers, some religious, some scientific, some religious and scientific, who reject such a conclusion and argue that the findings of an evolution-based cognitive science do not threaten religious belief; that such findings are either irrelevant to, or compatible with, religion.[4]

One tack in arguing for the compatibility of religion and an evolutionary model of human cognition (i.e., an evolutionary psychology) follows the logic used to argue for the compatibility of religion and evolutionary biology. In the face of the mounting evidence for Darwinian evolution and its perceived

---

[2] See Teehan (2010) for a discussion of how some of these mental tools shape the rhetoric of the "New Atheists."

[3] This is a vibrant debate in the field: is religion a byproduct, the accidental output of cognitive processes that evolved for other purposes (see, e.g., Guthrie, 1993; Boyer, 2001; Atran, 2002; Atran and Norenzayan, 2004; Kelemen, 2004b) or is it an adaptation that played an active role in human evolution (see, e.g., Wilson, 2002; Bulbulia, 2004; Johnson and Kruger, 2004; Sosis and Alcorta, 2004; Alcorta and Sosis, 2005; Bering and Johnson, 2005; Johnson, 2005; Bering, 2006)? Of course, it need not be an either/or issue (see e.g., Bering and Shackelford, 2004; Johnson and Kruger, 2004; Alcorta and Sosis, 2005; Dow, 2006; Teehan, 2010.)

[4] I should comment here on my use of the term "religion" in recognition of the very likely irresolvable debates over the proper denotations of the word. To truly address the issue of the compatibility of cognitive science and religion, we need to be much more specific about just what religious tradition or what particular expression of religious traditions is being considered. The issues being raised in this chapter are those most directly relevant to Judeo-Christian-Islamic religious traditions, and most of the arguments for compatibility are made by and in defense of Christianity. My focus here should not be taken to imply that I believe these issues carry the same weight or have the same implications for other religious traditions.

threat to faith, many theists recognized a deeper connection: evolution is God's plan for creating the diversity of life we find; God works through the laws of evolution, which He designed. The same form of argument can be applied to evolutionary psychology: God used the process of natural selection to guide cognitive evolution to result in minds capable of coming to know Him. Justin Barrett, one of the seminal figures in the field and a self-professed Christian, sets out just such an argument. He writes:

> Even if this natural tendency toward belief in God can be conclusively demonstrated to be the work of evolved capacities, Christians need not be deterred. God may have fine-tuned the cosmos to allow for life and for evolution and then orchestrated mutations and selection to produce the sort of organisms we are... (Barrett, 2004, p. 123)

Kenneth Miller, in response to an earlier version of the evolutionary argument for God, concluded with a similar defense of faith, claiming that "evolutionary forces become just one more tool in the hands of the Almighty" (Miller, 1999, p. 285).

Neither Barrett nor Miller suggests that evolutionary psychology provides an argument *for* belief in God. Each is very careful to point out that such arguments must go beyond science. Their conclusion is simply, but significantly, that evolutionary accounts of religion do not conflict with belief in God, in general, or with Christian belief, in particular.

This is a popular argument that many find persuasive, but just how much can this argument do? On the most basic level it leads to the conclusion that evolutionary psychology does not entail atheism. It is logically possible to accept an evolutionary account of belief in God and accept a theistic account of God. If this is all one means by "compatibility," then the argument suffices. But, of course, that is not typically all one wants; it is not all that Barrett and Miller want: not simply that the existence of God is logically consistent with an evolved psychology, but that the existence of a robust conception of God, the God of the Judeo-Christian-Islamic traditions, is compatible with evolutionary psychology—and it is in this regard, I believe, that evolutionary psychology raises significant challenges for religion, challenges not raised by evolutionary biology.

To argue that the evolution of human cognition was designed to lead to belief in God, understood in a traditional theistic sense, and so belief in such a conception of God is natural is a selective reading of the evidence. The very same evolved mental tools that can give rise to belief in such a God also give rise to belief in numerous supernatural beings: spirits, demons, ghosts, ghouls, witches, as well as a host of other gods. Monotheism has no privileged position. Each of these supernatural beings is as natural an object of belief as is the Christian God—in fact, polytheism, rather than monotheism, seems to be the evolved religious default position.

Interestingly, Barrett anticipated this objection. He asks:

> If God chose this sort of mind for us ... why do the documented conceptual biases only encourage belief in superhuman agents generally and not one true, accurate god concept? Further, if God created humanity to enjoy a loving relationship with Him, why not hardwire into our brains a fully formed belief in God? (Barrett, 2009, p. 97)

While Barrett recognizes this as an objection, it is not one that troubles him. He posits that perhaps God did indeed design our minds to know Him, the one true God, but that due to our fallen nature, our ability to know God is corrupted. He proposes that "the diversity in god concepts we see is a consequence of human error and not divine design" (Barrett, 2009, p. 97; see also 2004). Barrett sees this as an example of how evolutionary thinking and theological thought can be joined together into a more complete explanation of the human condition. We will later turn to a more detailed treatment of this particular theological construct, but for now I will treat it in a more general manner, as a stand-in for a theistic interpretation of the evolution of religious cognition. The question then is: how does a Christian-theological account mesh with an evolved-cognitive account?

Barrett points out that this joining of cognitive science and Christian theology does not constitute evidence for a theistic interpretation of our cognitive evolution, but it does show that such an interpretation is compatible with the findings of cognitive science (Barrett, 2009, pp. 98–9)—and this is true, as far as it goes, but again the discussion must go farther. It is true that one may incorporate an evolved-cognitive account of God within Christian theology, but we must also allow that it would be possible to incorporate an evolved-cognitive approach into any number of theologies. We can imagine that a Hindu religious thinker could also devise a "theologically" valid synthesis of cognitive science and Hinduism that would be quite distinct from, even incompatible with, Barrett's Christian formulation. This is unlikely to bother Barrett as he is consistent in arguing that cognitive science cannot be used to validate any particular religious world-view; that such validation is the province of theology or philosophy, not science. While this is so, it does not follow that cognitive science has nothing to say about the diversity of god-beliefs.

Evolution has designed the human mind so that belief in supernatural beings is a natural outcome, but it does not determine the specific articulation of those god-beliefs. However, it does set a sort of blueprint for such beliefs. The mental tools we have mentioned, as well as numerous others we have not, constitute a cognitive framework for god-beliefs. How those beliefs get fleshed out in detail is a result of the interaction of those mental tools and the particularities of culture, but our evolved psychology does set certain parameters (Atran, 2002). A religion is a cultural expression of these underlying, commonly shared, mental predispositions. This means that it is possible, at least in theory, to develop an account of how different cultural environments give rise to variants in god-concepts. In that case, we do not have to turn to theology to explain religious diversity, we may be able to develop an empirical explanation, grounded in an evolutionary-cognitive account—and such an account may not fit so easily into a theological account.

For example, the Christian theological account of religious diversity privileges monotheism as the true understanding of God, and relegates all others to the status of errors resulting from our corrupted nature. If however, all religions are the result of an interaction between a common evolved religious psychology and the particularities of diverse cultural environments developing in response to particular historical conditions, then no religion has a privileged position. To argue for the superiority of a particular religion is equivalent to arguing for the superiority of a particular species. We may give into the temptation to do so, but such a move is not compatible with an evolutionary account of species. Each species is as fit within its ecological niche as any other. Of course, some species prove more resilient in the struggle for survival; some extend their dominance, some go extinct. These are significant facts about particular species, but they do not allow us to argue that any one is a "chosen" species.[5]

In terms of religion, the challenge of cognitive science is not that it rules out a belief in God, but that it offers an empirical account for the conceptualization of god-beliefs that may in fact conflict with theological accounts. In this it differs from the challenge presented by evolutionary biology. Once evolutionary biology was presented as the method God used to create the world, it had little

---

[5] Of course, there are other grounds upon which to argue for the superiority of a species or a religion, and Barrett is not arguing for the privileged status of Christianity on evolutionary grounds. The point is that a strictly evolutionary understanding of religion results in a perspective that may in fact conflict with a theological perspective. My thanks to Maarten Boudry for pointing out a certain vagueness in my original argument.

to say about theology.[6] Evolutionary psychology, however, reaches further. In making the mind itself the object of evolutionary explanation, it brings belief into the magisterium of science, and with that move sets the grounds for conflict with theology.

To see this in greater detail, let's continue with the issue of religious diversity. At this point we are considering two possible explanations for the diversity of religious beliefs in the world:

> Evolutionary Psychology (EP): the diversity of religious beliefs is the product of varying cultural environments shaping the expression of evolved cognitive predispositions.
> Christian Theology (CT): the diversity of religious beliefs is a product of a fallen world distorting God's message that is then misunderstood by human minds corrupted by sin.

It may be argued that there still is no necessary conflict between the two propositions—that the CT version is simply a theistic interpretation of the same set of empirical facts accepted by the EP version, and that the question of the ultimate meaning of those facts lies outside the realm of science (this is not an uncontested claim in regards to either evolutionary biology or psychology, but for our present purposes, let's accept it). This, however, does not settle the issue of compatibility. It may be reasonable to claim that the EP and CT versions can coexist, that they are not logically inconsistent, but it leaves open a crucial question: why accept one rather than the other? This is the question of the justification of belief—are we justified in accepting either the EP or CT accounts, or in accepting both? If an evolved-cognitive model of religion undermines the justification of religious belief, then the compatibility of the two systems is thrown into question, if not refuted.

For those who wish to argue that EP and CT are compatible, the burden of establishing justification falls on the proponents of CT. We can grant that the justification for believing EP is an open question, but that is a different topic. Our working thesis is, *given* the soundness of EP, is it compatible with CT? For the sake of this argument, the justification of EP must be granted, for if we are not justified in accepting EP, then there is no challenge posed to CT. Of course, it may turn out that we are not justified in accepting EP (although I do not think that is likely), but again, that is a different issue.

---

[6] I would argue that a significant exception concerns the implications of evolution for the problem of evil.

So, the question at hand is: given the soundness of EP, are religious beliefs justifiable? In my opinion, this is the most important front in the ongoing evolution/religion debates. It is far more intellectually legitimate and substantively significant than the more-well known evolution vs. creationism/ID debates (although those debates are far more significant in social and political terms). A recent article by philosopher Michael J. Murray provides a very useful treatment of this issue, and I will use it as a touchstone for my discussion.

In "Scientific explanations of religions and the justification of religious belief," Murray begins by stating quite clearly the conclusion he will argue for: "the mere fact that we have beliefs that spring from mental tools selected for by natural selection is, all by itself, totally irrelevant to the justification of beliefs springing from them" (Murray, 2009, p. 169). The qualification "all by itself" is significant—if there is some reason to "think that religious beliefs are epistemically suspect" (Murray, 2009, p. 169), then there must be something particular about such beliefs that raises that suspicion other than the "mere fact" that they arise from evolved mental tools—and in this, Murray is correct. If evolutionary psychology is correct, then ultimately all of our beliefs arise from the working of evolved mental tools. If all such beliefs are not deemed unjustified (because they are unreliable, *pace* Plantinga, 2000), then there must be something particular about religious beliefs to raise such a claim. Murray sets out four arguments that stem from EP that are proposed to undermine the justification of religious belief, and then sets about refuting each one. I will not here go into each of these arguments. I will say that some are quite compelling, and all are well argued. Instead, I wish to focus on two particular points raised by Murray.[7]

The topic of justification is a complex and contentious one within epistemology. It is not my intention to enter into this topic or into debates on proper theories of justification. Rather, I will work with the terms and definitions Murray uses in his work where he makes a significant argument for an externalist justification of religious belief. According to Murray, the externalist theory of justification holds that for a belief to be justified depends on "whether or not the belief has the right relation to facts in the world" (Murray, 2009, p. 173). For example, consider the following proposition (my example): "I believe that my children are the most wonderful children in the world." Why do I believe that? "I

---

[7] A companion piece to this chapter, written with Andrew Goldberg, further addresses some ostensible shortcomings of evolved/cognitive critiques of belief. See Murray and Goldberg, 2009.

believe that because they bring me such joy and are, in the end, *my* children." This would count as an unjustified belief because there is not the right relationship between the grounds for that belief and facts in the world. That they are my children is materially unrelated to whether they are more wonderful than other children, and the fact that they bring me joy says nothing about their comparative worth. And it should be noted this belief is unjustified even if it is the case that my children happen to be the most wonderful in the world. The truth or falsity of the belief is irrelevant to my holding the belief and so the belief is unjustified. Murray argues that "in cases like this our having the belief is *entirely independent of whether or not the belief is true*. When this is the case, the justification of belief is undermined" (Murray, 2009, p. 174, emphasis in original).

It seems that an analogous argument applies to EP and god-beliefs. EP provides a mechanism by which humans come to believe in gods—it provides the causal mechanism for holding that gods exist, and this causal mechanism is independent of whether or not there actually is a god. Murray concedes this point: "religious belief would, it seems, exist *whether or not there is a supernatural reality*. It seems that the cases are perfectly analogous" (Murray, 2009, pp. 174–5, emphasis in original).

So, it appears that Murray accepts that EP undermines the justification of religious beliefs, and it would, given one further condition—"if and only if the following claim is true: (I) Whether or not there is a God (or other supernatural reality), human minds, honed by such-and-such evolutionary mechanisms, would exist and would hold religious beliefs" (Murray, 2009, p. 175). In other words, EP undermines the justification of god-beliefs *if and only if* the existence of God is not a necessary condition to the production of god-beliefs. Murray, however, rejects this condition:

> I, for example, don't think that there would be a universe if there were no God. I don't think the universe would be fine-tuned for life if there were no God. And I don't think there would be any actual life, believers, human beings, or religion either if there were no God. I might be wrong of course. But let us remember that it is the person arguing against religious belief that bears the burden of defending (I). Good luck to them. (Murray, 2009, p. 175)

Here, Murray's argument fails, and on several points. First, it is not the case that the burden of proof falls on the religious critic. To see why, let's return to my belief about my wonderful children. We can argue that that belief is unjustified if and only if:

(Ia) It is the case that whether or not my children are the most wonderful in the world there are psychological mechanisms that would still lead me to believe they are the most wonderful in the world.

I might reject this condition, along the lines that Murray used to reject (I), by arguing: "I do not think that I would believe my children were the most wonderful in the world unless they were in fact the most wonderful in the world. I do not think I would receive such joy unless they were the most wonderful children in the world. I might be wrong, but the burden of proof does not lie with me."

Of course the burden lies with me. There are good psychological explanations for why I might believe my children are the most wonderful in the world without it being so. The question is, rather, what grounds do I have for rejecting (Ia).

The same condition holds with Murray's rebuttal. There are good EP explanations for how humans came to have minds and how those minds come to believe in God, and these explanations do not require that there actually be a god. All Murray has done is to *assert* that he does not accept (I), but he has not provided reasons to believe (I) is not true. Now, there might be arguments that can be brought in to defend the position that we could not believe in a God unless there actually were a god, but those arguments need to be made by the believer, not the skeptic, who has already provided a justification for accepting (I) (i.e., a naturalistic evolutionary account of human cognitive origins); and if the ultimate goal is to argue for the compatibility of EP and CT, then those reasons cannot be defeater arguments for EP (for the reasons stated above).

A deeper problem with Murray's refutation of (I) is that his arguments for rejecting (I) can themselves be explained by an evolved-cognitive approach. We need to ask why it is that Murray believes there can be no life or humans without a God? Cognitive science provides an explanation. One of the cognitive predispositions that gives rise to god-beliefs is the tendency to see the world in teleological terms. As Kelemen has argued, this is a cognitive default position. It is not simply a response to external stimuli, it is an active perceptual strategy to find patterns and purposes in our environment. These evolved mental tools work beneath the level of reflective thought and so are experienced as intuitively right. When such intuitions are integrated into emotionally powerful, widely shared beliefs, such as the belief in God, it makes for a compelling intellectual framework, one resistant to merely rational objections. So, Murray's belief that there must be a God in order to have minds designed to believe in God *can itself be explained* as the product of our evolved mental tools—an explanation that does not require that there actually be a god. Murray's refutation faces the same suspicion of being unjustified.

This is part of the deep threat of cognitive science in regards to religion: it provides an explanation for the origin, ubiquity and persistence of belief in God that does not require that any such being exist, but, even more challenging, it also provides an explanation for why people would continue to interpret the world in theistic terms, even when there is no external justification for such a belief, or in the face of evidence to the contrary. An evolutionary/cognitive analysis provides a debunking argument for religious belief.[8]

There is another aspect of justification that comes into play here: that of the reliability of the cognitive mechanisms that produce a particular belief. According to certain epistemologies, we may be justified in holding a belief if that belief is the product of the proper working of cognitive mechanisms that are reliably truth-tracking. For example, take the belief that one has when, for example, teaching a class, i.e., that there is a room filled with students. I can be justified in holding this belief if it is the result of cognitive processes which, when working under the appropriate conditions, reliably result in true belief. Therefore, I could justify my belief that there are people in the room by demonstrating that: (a) the belief is based on visual information processed by the optical-neural systems of my brain; and (b) that those systems are constructed to provide reliable information in response to visual stimuli—in other words, that the optical neural systems are truth-tracking. To fully justify this belief, I would also have to claim that I am not presently under the influence of any hallucinogenic/intoxicating agents that might interfere with the proper functioning of these systems (these systems are not designed to provide reliable information when you are drunk).

It is also important to keep in mind the qualification that truth-tracking systems provide "reliable" information, not infallible information. Since these cognitive systems are the product of evolution, they are subject to the same design limitations of any evolved organ or structure—that is, they are not designed to work optimally, but to be as effective as they can be given the constraints and costs of developing the system. The fact that we sometimes experience visual errors does not refute the claim that we are generally justified in believing our eyes (see Fales, 2002; Griffiths and Wilkins, in press).

Perhaps this offers a different strategy for justifying religious beliefs. Can Murray's belief in the existence of God as a necessary condition for cognitive

---

[8] See Kahane (2011) and Griffiths and Wilkins (in press) for valuable discussions of evolutionary debunking arguments and religion.

evolution be justified in this way? I believe it cannot and this is because of the way in which cognitive tools that lead to religious beliefs differ from cognitive tools that lead to visual beliefs. There is no biologically plausible explanation for the visual beliefs generated by the normal functioning of our visual-neural system that does not necessitate there be objects in the environment that at least roughly approximate those beliefs; there are, however, biologically plausible explanations for god-beliefs that do not require there actually be anything even roughly approximating a divine being (Fales, 2002; Ramsey, 2002; Griffiths and Wilkins, in press). When our hypersensitive agency detection device detects the presence of an agent that is not actually there, it is not malfunctioning. As Guthrie has made clear, agents do not always make their presence apparent—some of the most dangerous agents are those that are hidden, or working from a distance—and so over-interpreting stimuli in terms of agency is a valuable strategy, one that is open to selection pressures (Guthrie, 1993).[9] According to the byproduct model, god-beliefs are the results of false-positives generated by cognitive mechanisms working as designed. In other words, these mental tools are not truth-tracking in regards to religious beliefs.

Curiously, Murray takes the fact that the evolved cognitive mechanisms for religious belief are not truth-tracking, and so are unreliable, to defend the justification of religious beliefs (Murray, 2009, pp. 176–8). It is argued, most famously by Alvin Plantinga (2002), that natural selection hones in on beliefs that have adaptive value, not truth value, and therefore beliefs that arise via evolved mechanisms are unreliable. It is possible that a belief be false and yet still be adaptive. Murray suggests the belief in other minds is a good candidate. Whether or not others have minds, believing that they do allows me to understand their behavior in a way that will contribute to successful action in the world, i.e., it is adaptive, even if it turns out to be false. Belief in God may be in a similar category. There are cognitive scientists who argue that religious beliefs are adaptations, or can assume an adaptive function, that promote social cohesion and so contribute to inclusive fitness, whether on an individual or a group level (e.g., Wilson, 2002; Bulbulia, 2004; Johnson and Kruger, 2004; Alcorta and Sosis, 2005; Bering and Johnson, 2005; Johnson, 2005; Bering, 2006). If this is so, it is so whether or not there is a God. Therefore, religious beliefs can also be false and still adaptive. While we might take this to undermine the justification of religious belief, the ostensible unreliability of evolution in producing truth-

---

[9] In comparison we can say that a visual system that is not more discriminating in terms of false-positives and false-negatives is much less likely to prove adaptive. Therefore, selection pressures will favor visual systems that are more reliable in terms of truth-tracking; see Fales, 2002; Kahane, 2011; Griffiths and Wilkins, in press.

tracking cognitive tools is a challenge to all beliefs and so, it is claimed, does not result in any particular damage to the justification of religious beliefs. In fact, Plantinga argues that the categorical unreliability of beliefs produced via evolved cognitive mechanisms is itself an argument in favor of a theistic worldview in that a non-natural explanation is then required to secure the reliability of our belief-forming mechanisms (Plantinga, 2002).

Barrett and Church take a similar line of argument in a recent paper (Barrett and Church, 2013). They argue that classifying religious beliefs as false-positive results of overly sensitive mental tools raises a serious problem unique to atheism:

> Even though we occasionally wrongly detect a monster under the bed, our agency-detection faculties might nevertheless still be generally aimed in the right direction (at truth) and extremely reliable. In the case of distinctly religious beliefs, however, it is difficult to see how the atheist could see them as somehow aimed in the right direction or in any way indicative of a more general and reliable cognitive faculty. (Barrett and Church, 2013, p. 318)

What Barrett and Church seem to be suggesting is that if religious beliefs, a species-wide, ubiquitous category of beliefs, are false, then this casts doubt on our belief formation tools in general and raises the specter of a potentially crippling skepticism; a skepticism only to be avoided by granting the general soundness of religious belief. Rather than undermining the justification of religious beliefs, cognitive science may in fact undermine religious non-belief, and conversely provide indirect support for a religious world-view.

However, this conclusion seems grounded in confusion about the relationship between our cognitive tools and religious beliefs. Consider the claim that "for the atheist, the cognitive faculties that naturally produce distinctly religious belief are not aimed at truth, they are presumably aimed at falsehoods" (Barrett and Church, 2013, p. 318). But why would that be the case? The idea of the false positives argument is that the mental tools that "naturally produce distinctly religious belief" *are* aimed at truth, but under certain conditions misfire and, e.g., detect agents that are not actually present, or interpret coincidence as purpose, or infer intention where there is none—and these misfires are consistent with a generally reliable cognitive system. The problem that Barrett and Church identify might arise if there were distinct mental tools for producing religious beliefs, but as Barrett himself has consistently emphasized, there are no such special religious-belief-formation tools.

Instead, the confusion turns on the notion that our mental tools are *aimed* at "distinctly religious beliefs" and since such beliefs, for the atheist, are false, these mental tools are aimed at falsehood rather than truth. But these mental tools are not aimed at distinctly religious beliefs, or at beliefs of any distinct content; they are aimed at beliefs that helped our ancestors successfully navigate the physical and social worlds they inhabited in their struggle for survival and reproduction—and sometimes their aim is off target. This is certainly a reason for caution in regards to our beliefs, but is it a cause to doubt the general reliability of our evolved cognitive faculties?

This a complex matter, deserving and receiving a much more detailed response than is appropriate at this time,[10] but as already discussed in terms of the visual system, natural selection is not insensitive to the truth value of beliefs in any systemic way. False beliefs are often maladaptive and so are subject to the pruning work of natural selection. There are no grounds for a general skepticism about natural epistemology. The claim that there can be false-yet-adaptive beliefs is correct, but this does not leave us in a position of epistemic relativism—we have a method for evaluating beliefs. Let us once more return to my wonderful children.

The belief that my children are the most wonderful in the world may also be seen as a false-yet-adaptive belief. It might be argued that a deeply felt bias towards one's own children is an evolutionary adaptation that promotes the intensive, long-term investment of resources that raising human children requires. This deeply felt bias, or some variant of it, will not be unique to me, but will be widely shared. This evolutionary/cognitive explanation should be a cause for suspicion as to the reliability of my belief. If I am concerned with the truth-value of that belief, I must go beyond my subjective reasoning and seek out objective verification of my claim. I need to gather evidence and determine if the evidence supports my conclusion. I suspect that the evidence of such research would show that my children are indeed wonderful, just not uniquely or superlatively so. This then, the scientific method, allows us to evaluate our beliefs to determine if those beliefs are supported by the evidence. Given the innate human propensity toward biased thinking, such a method is a necessary corrective toward unreliable believing.

So while Murray's initial assertion that the evolutionary origin of our religious beliefs *in itself* does not make them any less justified than other beliefs is correct, an evolutionary understanding of belief formation does suggest that the justification of such a belief is undermined to the extent that a belief cannot be empirically verified. Now, this does not argue that belief in God as the author of our cognitive evolution is false, nor does it argue that this belief cannot be

---

[10] See Beilby (2002) for a collection of essays addressing just this issue, along with a reply by Plantinga.

justified, but it does shift the burden of justification to the believer, and it raises the specter that any justification that invokes religious concepts may itself be explained away on evolutionary-cognitive grounds.

There is one further challenge that flows from cognitive science that I would like to raise. Even if we were to grant, for the sake of argument, that, contrary to what I have just said, evolution has resulted in cognitive tools that lead to reliable god-beliefs, there would still be a significant problem for a Christian theology, one mentioned earlier: that of religious diversity.[11] Even if our cognitive tools were truth-tracking in terms of religious belief, the true beliefs they track do not seem to be the truths of Christianity.[12] Barrett, however, believes Christian theology can meet this challenge:

> One possible answer is that a perfectly adequate concept of God does come as part of our biological heritage but that living in a sinful, fallen world this concept grows corrupt as we grow ... The diversity in god concepts we see is a consequence of human error not divine design. (Barrett, 2009, p. 97)

This is not an idiosyncratic belief on Barrett's part, but is consistent with a long tradition of Christian thinking on epistemology. It is in fact a central tenet of Reformed Epistemology. This school of thought sees itself in the tradition of Protestant thinking going back to the Reformation, particularly to the works of John Calvin. I should state that I am not claiming that Barrett embraces or is a proponent of Reformed Epistemology—I have no knowledge of this one way or the other. However, his position is in concert with that school of thought, and I believe it will be instructive to spend some time looking at this position, as it plays a role in the current debates.

One of the central thinkers in this tradition is philosopher Alvin Plantinga. Working with the theology of John Calvin and Thomas Aquinas, Plantinga

---

[11] One of the evolutionary arguments against religious belief that Murray raises and refutes is the claim that the fact that our mental tools result in diverse and incompatible religious claims constitutes evidence that these tools are not truth-tracking. Murray provides what I believe to be a compelling refutation of this particular argument from religious diversity, but it is important to be clear that this is not the argument I am making here concerning religious diversity. My claim is not that religious diversity means that the mental tools for religious belief are not truth-tracking, but that if we were to grant that they are truth-tracking, the truth they track does not seem to be the truth of Christian theology.

[12] See Marsh (2013) for an extended and valuable treatment of just this challenge, which he calls "natural non-belief." Natural non-belief does not imply that atheism is natural; rather, it recognizes that polytheism is the cognitive default position, and consequently the naturalness of lack of belief in the high god-concept of monotheism.

proposes that humans come equipped with a *sensus divinitatis* (the term comes from Calvin). This is, he says, "a disposition or a set of dispositions to form theistic beliefs in various circumstances, in response to the sorts of conditions or stimuli that trigger the working of this sense" (Plantinga, 2000, p. 173). This is a significant definition as it could very well stand as a description of religious cognition as revealed by cognitive science, and it therefore lends support to Barrett's contention that cognitive science and Christian theology can be made compatible. Indeed, Plantinga uses the *sensus divinitatis* to provide justification for Christian belief (although for reasons we need not concern ourselves with here, he prefers the term "warrant"). This faculty is, he claims, designed to be truth-conducive in producing certain types of beliefs (i.e., theistic beliefs) when triggered by certain stimuli (typically the grandeur of nature, or the sense of our own moral and physical vulnerability). But of course, he must also account for the wide diversity of beliefs, the incompatibility of many religious beliefs, and the fact of unbelief, and this is explained as Barrett has suggested: these are the consequences of our sinful, fallen nature—a fall which had, says Plantinga, "ruinous cognitive consequences" (Plantinga, 2000, p. 205).

However, this move by itself does not solve the problem. Plantinga wants to argue that the *sensus divinitatis* provides justification for theistic beliefs, but how can a deeply corrupted cognitive mechanism produce reliable beliefs?

The answer is that our corrupted cognitive tools are supplemented by what Plantinga refers to as the "internal instigation of the Holy Spirit." The work of the Holy Spirit, which is a "cognitive matter," allows us to "see the truth" of the Christian world-view (Plantinga, 2000, p. 206). So, God *has* endowed us with a set of reliable cognitive tools that lead to the truth of Christianity. These tools, unfortunately, have been corrupted by the virus of original sin, but God has provided a supplemental cognitive program—i.e., the Holy Spirit—that can correct the malfunction.

There are two objections we can make to this position—one logical, the other stemming from cognitive science, both raising the question of justification. From the perspective of cognitive science, we can see that the move to bring in the Holy Spirit to solve the problem of justification is one that is itself open to an evolutionary/cognitive analysis. Cognitive science allows us to argue that belief in the Holy Spirit is, like belief in other supernatural entities, the product of cognitive mechanisms that are not truth-tracking in the religious domain. We then have a debunking argument for that belief, and this leaves theologians in the unenviable, perhaps impossible, position of having to devise a justification for belief in the Holy Spirit that itself is not open to an evolutionary/cognitive debunking argument.

Cognitive science aside, we also must question how the belief that the "internal instigation of the Holy Spirit is truth conducive" can be logically justified. Since that belief in the Holy Spirit is itself the product of cognitive mechanisms, which, on the terms of this theory, are corrupted and thus unreliable, we have no grounds to accept the truth of that belief. The argument is ultimately circular and thus self-refuting. This problem is in fact more damaging than any challenge brought by cognitive science, for if the initial premises of the argument are true and we are working with a corrupted, and thus unreliable, *sensus divinitatis*, then no theological speculation can be justified—even the belief in a *sensus divinitatis*. This would be, to play with Plantinga's language, a defeater argument for theology.

In conclusion, it is correct to say that an evolutionary/cognitive account of religious belief does not entail atheism, but it is not correct to say that it does not challenge theism. That challenge goes beyond simply not providing support for theism, it challenges the justification for believing in religious propositions and shifts the burden of proof to the theist. I do not claim that this challenge cannot be met, but to do so requires a deeper engagement with the implications of an evolutionary/cognitive account of belief, one that recognizes that such challenges exist.

Now, none of this argues that there may not be other modes of epistemic justification available to believers. For example, John Bishop discusses (although he ultimately rejects) the possibility of justifying theistic belief through an isolationist epistemology in which the grounds for evaluating a belief are internal to the belief system in question (Bishop, 2007, pp. 79–86). From an isolationist perspective, justified religious beliefs are those that are consistent with the beliefs and grounds of belief employed by that belief tradition. Some form of such an epistemic move may be implicit in the faith of many a theist. Religious beliefs may just make sense to a person, and more significantly allow a person to make sense of their lives and the world they live in. In this domain, theology may speak just as rightfully as science or logic, and it is within this domain that arguments for the compatibility of a biological understanding of religion and a faith-based understanding may be most compelling. An individual's claim that a religious belief works for him/her in this way is not one that is subject to evolutionary/cognitive debunking arguments (although it may be open to pragmatic criticism, or as Bishop argues, moral criticism).[13] However, to move from that domain

---

[13] Although Bishop makes a strong case for the moral inadequacy of isolationist justification this does not lead to a moral critique of faith. Indeed, his ultimate goal is to justify a Jamesian fideism, and he does so in a very compelling manner. In fact, this may be one of the more promising strategies for finding common ground between cognitive science and faith.

of personal faith to faith as externally justified—a move centrally important to many believers, whether professional theologians or not—is made much more difficult, if not impossible, by the evolutionary/cognitive study of religion.[14]

References

Alcorta, C. and Sosis, R., 2005. Ritual, emotion, and sacred symbols: the evolution of religion as an adaptive complex. *Human Nature*, 16(4), pp. 323–59.

Atran, S., 2002. *In Gods We Trust: The Evolutionary Landscape of Religion*. New York: Oxford University Press.

Atran, S. and Norenzayan, A., 2004. Religion's evolutionary landscape: counterintuition, commitment, compassion, communion. *Behavioral and Brain Sciences*, 27, pp. 713–30.

Barrett, J.L., 2004. *Why Would Anyone Believe in God?* Walnut Creek, CA: AltaMira Press.

——. 2009. Cognitive science, religion, and theology. In: J. Schloss and M.J. Murray (eds), *The Believing Primate: Scientific, Philosophical, and Theological Reflections on the Origin of Religion*. Oxford: Oxford University Press, pp. 76–99.

Barrett, J.L. and Church, I., 2013. Should CSR give atheists epistemic assurance? On beer-goggles, BFFs, and skepticism regarding religious beliefs. *The Monist*, 96(3), pp. 311–24.

Beilby, J., 2002. *Naturalism Defeated? Essays on Plantinga's Evolutionary Argument Against Naturalism*. Ithaca, NY: Cornell University Press.

Bering, J., 2006. The folk psychology of souls. *Behavioral and Brain Sciences*, 29, pp. 453–62.

Bering, J. and Johnson, D., 2005. "O Lord … you perceive my thoughts from afar": recursiveness and the evolution of supernatural agency. *Journal of Cognition and Culture*, 5(1–2), pp. 118–42.

Bering, J. and Shackelford, T., 2004. Supernatural agents may have provided adaptive social information. *Behavioral and Brain Sciences*, 27(6), pp. 732–3.

Bishop, J., 2007. *Believing by Faith: An Essay in the Epistemology and Ethics of Religious Belief*. Oxford: Oxford University Press.

---

[14] This chapter is based on presentations made at the conference *Darwin in the 21st Century: Nature, Humanity and God*, Notre Dame University, 2009, and at the Annual Meeting of the Society for the Scientific Study of Religion, 2010. My thanks to Maarten Boudry, Paul Griffiths, John Wilkins and F. LeRon Shults for comments.

Bloom, P., 2004. *Descartes' Baby: How the Science of Child Development Explains What Makes Us Human*. New York: Basic Books.
——. 2005. Is God an accident? *Atlantic Monthly*, December, pp. 105–12.
——. 2007. Religion is natural. *Developmental Science*, 10(1), pp. 147–51.
Boyer, P., 2001. *Religion Explained: The Evolutionary Origins of Religious Thought*. New York: Basic Books.
Bulbulia, J., 2004. The cognitive and evolutionary psychology of religion. *Biology and Philosophy*, 19, pp. 655–86.
Dow, J., 2006. The evolution of religion: three anthropological approaches. *Method and Theory in the Study of Religion*, 18, pp. 67–91.
Fales, E., 2002. Darwin's doubt, Calvin's Calvary. In: J. Beilby (ed.), *Naturalism Defeated? Essays on Plantinga's Evolutionary Argument Against Naturalism*. Ithaca, NY: Cornell University Press, pp. 43–58.
Griffiths, P.E. and Wilkins, J.S., in press. When do evolutionary explanations of belief debunk belief? In: P. Sloan (ed.), *Darwin in the 21st Century: Nature, Humanity, and God*. Notre Dame, IN: Notre Dame University Press.
Guthrie, S., 1993. *Faces in the Clouds: A New Theory of Religion*. Oxford: Oxford University Press.
Johnson, D., 2005. God's punishment and public goods: a test of the supernatural punishment hypothesis in 186 world cultures. *Human Nature*, 16(4), pp. 410–46.
Johnson, D. and Kruger, O., 2004. The good of wrath: supernatural punishment and the evolution of cooperation. *Political Theology*, 5(2), pp. 159–76.
Kahane, G., 2011. Evolutionary debunking arguments. *Nous*, 45(1), pp. 103–25.
Kelemen, D., 1999. Beliefs about purpose: on the origin of teleological thought. In: M. Corballis and S. Lea (eds), *The Descent of Mind: Psychological Perspectives on Hominid Evolution*. Oxford: Oxford University Press, pp. 278–94.
——. 2004a. Are children "intuitive theists"? Reasoning about purpose and design in nature. *Psychological Science*, 15(5), pp. 295–301.
——. 2004b. Counterintuition, existential anxiety, and religion as a by-product of the designing mind. *Behavioral and Brain Sciences*, 27(6), pp. 739–40.
Marsh, J., 2013. Darwin and the problem of natural nonbelief. *The Monist*, 96(3), pp. 349–76.
Miller, K., 1999. *Finding Darwin's God: A Scientist's Search for the Common Ground between God and Evolution*. New York: Cliff Street Books/HarperCollins.

Murray, M. J., 2009. Scientific explanations of religion and the justification of religious belief. In: J. Schloss and M. J. Murray (eds), *The Believing Primate: Scientific, Philosophical, and Theological Reflections on the Origin of Religion*. Oxford: Oxford University Press.

Murray, M.J. and Goldberg, A., 2009. Evolutionary accounts of religion: explaining and explaining away. In: J. Schloss and M.J. Murray (eds), *The Believing Primate: Scientific, Philosophical, and Theological Reflections on the Origin of Religion*. New York: Oxford University Press, pp. 44–75.

Plantinga, A., 2000. *Warranted Christian Belief*. Oxford: Oxford University Press

——. 2002. The evolutionary argument against naturalism. In: J. Beilby (ed.), *Naturalism Defeated? Essays on Plantinga's Evolutionary Argument Against Naturalism*. Ithaca, NY: Cornell University Press, pp. 1–12.

Ramsey, W., 2002. Naturalism defended. In: J. Beilby (ed.), *Naturalism Defeated? Essays on Plantinga's Evolutionary Argument Against Naturalism*. Ithaca, NY: Cornell University Press, pp. 15–29.

Sosis, R. and Alcorta, C., 2004. Is religion adaptive? *Behavioral and Brain Sciences*, 27(6), pp. 749–50.

Teehan, J., 2010. *In the Name of God: The Evolutionary Origins of Religious Ethics and Violence*. Oxford: Wiley-Blackwell.

Tremlin, T., 2006. *Minds and Gods: The Cognitive Foundations of Religion*. New York: Oxford University Press.

Wilson, D.S., 2002. *Darwin's Cathedral: Evolution, Religion, and the Nature of Society*. Chicago: Chicago University Press.

Chapter 11

Some Reflections on Cognitive Science, Doubt, and Religious Belief

Joshua C. Thurow

Introduction

Religious belief and behavior raises the following two questions:

(Q1) Does God, or any other being or state that is integral to various religious traditions, exist?
(Q2) Why do humans have religious beliefs and engage in religious behavior?

One can pursue either of these questions independently of the other. Historically, philosophers have expended much effort discussing (Q1), but have spent comparatively little time on (Q2) (David Hume being a notable exception). Conceptually, the questions concern separate subject matter and answers to one question don't have any obvious entailments to answers to the other question. Scholars in the human and social sciences have worked at answering (Q2), while staying largely neutral about (Q1).

Although these questions are conceptually distinct and have been pursued via distinct enterprises, there is an interesting connection between them. How one answers (Q2) can affect how reasonable individuals can be in accepting a particular answer to (Q1). Consider an analogous pair of questions:

(Q1a) Do aliens from other planets exist?
(Q2a) Why do people believe that aliens from other planets exist?

Suppose that we have a community of people who believe that aliens exist from reading the National Enquirer, a periodical known for fabricating stories. We thus have an answer to (Q2a), and this answer has clear implications for how rational the people in this community of alien-believers are in accepting their answer to (Q1a): once they learn that their beliefs arise from such a patently unreliable source, they would be unjustified, or irrational, in continuing to hold their belief in aliens. In principle, then, answers to (Q2) could affect how rational or epistemically justified people are in accepting a particular answer to (Q1). The genealogy of a belief can impact its epistemic status. But this leaves us with some questions: in what kinds of ways can genealogy affect epistemic status, and is belief in God or any other religious belief rendered doubtful by what we know about their genealogy?

The burgeoning field of cognitive science has given these questions an added urgency. Cognitive scientists, anthropologists, and evolutionary biologists have used the insights in their respective disciplines to construct novel, testable, and naturalistic theories of why humans are disposed to have religious beliefs and engage in religious behavior. These theories in what has come to be known as the Cognitive Science of Religion (CSR) have been described in some detail elsewhere in this volume, so here a description of some of their general features will suffice. Some of these theories say that religious beliefs are byproducts of adaptive cognitive mechanisms that, when used in environments typical of our human ancestors, tend to produce belief in some sort of invisible agent (such as ghosts, ancestor spirits, or gods; e.g., Boyer, 2001; Atran, 2002; Barrett, 2004). Other theories say that religious belief and behavior is adaptive because it helped humans solve various problems of cooperation that, once solved, led to the survival and spread of humans (e.g., Wilson, 2002; 2005; Sosis, 2006). Others say that religious beliefs and behavior are exaptations—they arose as byproducts but were later selected-for (e.g., Bering, 2006; Bulbulia, 2009). These theories are all naturalistic—that is, the explanations they offer do not at any point appeal to the existence of any supernatural entity. The theories assume only the laws of nature and facts and hypotheses about humans and their environment. One might begin to wonder: do these genealogies of religious belief in some way cast doubt on belief in God? Might belief in God be shown to be unjustified, either somewhat analogous to how the genealogy of belief in aliens in the example above shows belief in aliens (for that community of people) to be unjustified, or in some other way? Some would say "yes," including evolutionary psychologist Jesse Bering, who states that his account of why humans are disposed to have religious beliefs shows that God is an illusion—that God is "a sort of scratch on our psychological lenses rather than the enigmatic figure out there in the heavenly world" (Bering, 2011, p. 38).

My aim in this chapter is to carefully distinguish the various ways in which an answer to Q2 might affect the rationality of believing in God. A literature has sprouted around this exact issue, but it has heretofore focused almost exclusively on one way in which a genealogy for p can affect the rationality of believing p—namely, by the genealogy functioning within a debunking argument. However, there are other ways a genealogy can affect the rationality of a belief. I suggest that we should be interested in whether genealogies more broadly *cast doubt* on religious beliefs rather than on the more specific issue of whether genealogies debunk religious beliefs. Debunking is one way of casting doubt, but not the only way.[1]

The plan of the chapter is as follows. First, I discuss the notion of casting doubt and distinguish several different ways that a proposition may cast doubt on another proposition. I then discuss in greater detail two ways that theories in CSR might cast doubt on belief in God: via a debunking argument and by undermining reasons for believing that God exists—in particular, religious experience. My main goal is: (i) to argue that CSR does not cast doubt on theistic belief in a few of the primary ways that propositions can cast doubt on other propositions, including via a debunking argument; and (ii) to suggest that one plausible way in which CSR might cast doubt on theistic belief is by undermining various traditional theistic reasons, and to illustrate how this might work with one example of a traditional theistic reason—religious experience.

Casting Doubt[2]

We need to clarify what notion we are interested in when we say that proposition X casts doubt on proposition Y. To cast doubt could mean either: (i) to create or cause doubt; or (ii) to give good grounds for doubt. The first sense plainly isn't of much interest for our purposes because we are interested in how, rationally, we ought to modify our beliefs in the light of genealogies of religious beliefs. A proposition could in fact cause us to doubt our religious beliefs without actually giving us good grounds to doubt; e.g., seeing some Christians do bad things might cause one to doubt Christianity even though such behavior isn't good grounds for doubt. The second sense is more apt to our concerns.

The notion of doubt must be clarified as well. There are two relevant locutions: "to doubt p" and "p is now more (or less) doubtful than it was." Doubting p could mean either: (i) regarding p as less than certain; (ii) suspending judgment

---

[1] This chapter is a sort of companion paper to Thurow (2014), which is engaged in the same project, but focuses on other ways of casting doubt.

[2] Much of this section overlaps with section 2 of Thurow (2014).

about p; or (iii) disbelieving p. The latter phrase can be interpreted as implying that one now has a lower degree of confidence in p than in the past. We are interested in whether CSR gives good grounds for doubting religious beliefs. Nearly all of these senses of doubt fit with our interests, the exception being the first sense, "regarding p as less than certain." It wouldn't be terribly interesting if CSR gave good grounds for regarding religious beliefs as less than certain. After all, Descartes showed us long ago that nearly all of our beliefs are less than certain, and it wouldn't be too surprising or interesting if we found yet another reason to regard belief in God as less than certain. In addition, probably most religious believers don't treat belief in God as certain.[3] With these clarifications in mind, we can now offer the following definition of "casting doubt":

(CD_{def}) Proposition X (belief in which is justified) casts doubt on proposition Y =$_{def}$ X gives good grounds for either (i) decreasing one's degree of belief that Y relative to the degree of belief that would be justified by one's other grounds for and against Y, in the absence of X, (ii) suspending judgment about Y, or (iii) disbelieving Y.

It is important that belief in X be justified, unjustified beliefs don't have the power to cast doubt on our beliefs. "I am in the Matrix" doesn't affect the degree of justification of any of my beliefs about the external world because I have no reason to believe that I am in the Matrix. "I might be in a Matrix for all I know" might affect the degree of justification of my external world beliefs, as my belief in it is justified.

There are at least five interesting ways that a proposition can cast doubt on another in sense CD_{def}:

CD1. X entails that Y is false.
CD2. X entails that belief in Y is formed in an irrational way.
CD3. X is evidence against Y.
CD4. X removes/undermines what was once regarded as a source of evidence/good grounds for Y.
CD5. X contributes to explaining various phenomena on the hypothesis that Y is false at least almost as well as the hypothesis that Y is true explains the phenomena.

---

[3] Sosis and Kiper (2014) argue that religious adherents commonly doubt their beliefs.

If CD1 were true, then as long as the background evidence for Y wasn't higher than the background evidence for X, X would give good grounds for disbelieving Y. In CD2, by "irrational way" I mean any kind of belief-forming process that isn't reliable at getting the truth. If CD2 were true, then X would cast doubt on Y because justified belief that X would give one good grounds for thinking that one's belief that Y was formed in a way that is not likely to get the truth, and one ought to suspend judgment about propositions, belief in which was formed in this way. If CD3 or CD4 were true, X would cast doubt on Y because belief that Y would be justified to a lower degree than it was prior to knowing X. However, this would not entail that Y is unjustified or false; Y might still be quite reasonable. Whether belief that Y is justified would depend, in the case of CD3, upon how strong the evidence X is against Y and what other sources of justification one had. In the case of CD4, whether belief that Y is justified would depend on how many grounds were undermined, the extent to which they were undermined, and how strong the remaining non-undermined grounds support Y.

The way in which CD5 casts doubt is a little more complicated than the others. The rough idea is this. The more empirical facts that can be explained, and the better those facts can be explained, without appeal to the truth of Y, the less empirical reason there is to believe Y. Occam's razor grounds this principle, because the more facts that can be explained, and the better they can be explained, without appealing to the truth of Y, the less Y is needed to explain things, and thus the more it appears to be superfluous and empirically unmotivated to believe that Y is true.[4] Assume, then, that CD5 is true for two propositions X and Y, and that belief that X is justified. How much doubt is cast on Y? The answer depends upon many factors. First, even if there are no empirical facts that Y is needed to explain, and all empirical facts are explained as well or better without Y, as with assuming Y, there may still be excellent *a priori* reasons for believing that Y. The above principle only governs empirical

---

[4] Peter van Inwagen (2005) discusses an argument like the one I give for a principle like this (without the restriction to empirical evidence. Van Inwagen seems to endorse the principle, but denies that theism is not needed to explain anything (in the essay, strictly, he says that the naturalist hasn't given good reasons to think that theism is not needed). However, later in the essay he asserts that an assumption of this kind of principle is that belief in God is an explanatory hypothesis. He then goes on to argue that belief in God is not an explanatory hypothesis. Perhaps he thinks that the falsity of this assumption (as he sees it), undermines the principle. But I think this is incorrect. Even if belief in God is not an explanatory hypothesis, God is taken to be the kind of being that is supposed to explain things, and if one found out that God is not needed to explain things, this could, via the principle I have discussed, affect the justifiability of believing that He exists. I discuss this issue in further detail in Thurow, 2014.

evidence, not *a priori* evidence. Second, if either: (i) there are some facts that Y is needed to explain; or (ii) Y provides at least a slightly better explanation of some facts, then even if X increases the amount that can be explained without assuming Y, there may still be some, or even quite a bit of, reason to believe Y, and so belief in Y may be justified to a lower degree than before (that is, prior to knowing X), but still to a high degree. But if there are no *a priori* reasons for believing that Y, and there are no empirical facts that Y is needed to explain, and the empirical facts are explained at least as well, or better without Y than assuming Y, then suspending judgment about or disbelieving Y may be justified.[5]

The aliens example in section 1 is an example of CD2 and CD4-type casting of doubt. X = "the people believed in aliens on the basis of the National Enquirer, which is an unreliable source." Once the people in the community come to be justified in believing X, then one of their sources of evidence is removed (i.e., the National Enquirer), and their belief is shown to have been formed in an irrational way, via an unreliable process.

It is pretty clear that CSR does not cast doubt on belief in God in way CD1, for the CSR theories merely provide a genealogy of religious belief. Any genealogy of religious belief is consistent with the existence of God, as long as the genealogy doesn't have the form "belief in God arose via process P and God does not exist." But none of the genealogies have this form; they do not include the second conjunct. They're concerned simply to describe the process P. This point is widely accepted, even by scholars who think that CSR does in some way cast doubt on belief in God (Bloom, 2009, p. 125; Bering, 2011, p. 195).

Most of the literature has so far focused on whether CSR undermines belief in God by showing that belief in God is formed in an unreliable way. These arguments, which have come to be known as debunking arguments, cast doubt in way CD2 if they are successful. Although debunking arguments are very interesting—indeed, I shall discuss them below—they are not the only way that CSR might cast doubt on belief in God. For a full picture of the epistemic implications of CSR for belief in God, we need to also examine whether CSR casts doubt in ways CD3, CD4, and CD5. After discussing debunking

---

[5] Whether suspending judgment or disbelieving is justified in these circumstances is controversial. The issue is closely connected to the issue of whether disbelief or suspension of judgment is justified for p in the absence of evidence for p. Michael Tooley (Plantinga and Tooley, 2008, pp. 87–93) argues that, in the case of theism, disbelief is justified, while Peter van Inwagen (2005) argues that disbelief would not be justified in these circumstances. I suspend judgment on this issue for the purposes of this chapter. Also, those familiar with the notion of a defeater will note that X provides an overriding defeater in ways CD1 and CD3 and X provides an undercutting defeater in ways CD2, CD4, and CD5.

arguments, I shall then turn to consider whether CSR casts doubt in way CD4 by undermining the evidential force of religious experience.[6]

Debunking Arguments

In the aliens example discussed above, the communities' belief in aliens is undermined because it was shown to have arisen through an unreliable process—a process that does not reliably deliver true beliefs about the subject matter in question. Once one realizes that a belief that one holds has arisen through an unreliable process, one should suspend judgment regarding that belief, for one will then realize that one's belief is not likely to be true, given how one formed the belief. It is epistemically irrational to believe a proposition that one recognizes as being unlikely to be true from one's epistemic perspective. Thus, belief in aliens (for this community) is rendered irrational or unjustified; it is debunked by awareness of its genealogy.

Several scholars have argued that belief in God is debunked in a similar way.[7] Their argument can be developed as follows. We noted earlier that all of the CSR explanations that have been developed are naturalistic—they explain theistic belief solely by natural processes and the properties (real or hypothesized) of humans and their environment. These processes look unreliable, for humans would still believe in a god of some kind, via these processes, even if there were no gods. These processes are not sensitive to the existence of gods. This sort of sensitivity is ordinarily a good mark of unreliability. For instance, in the aliens example, the people in the community would believe in aliens even if there were no aliens. Consider another example: we learn that Joe tends to perceive orange things as red. He sees a new object and believes it to be red. We know that he would perceive it as red even if it weren't red and were orange instead. Joe's ability to distinguish red from orange is unreliable. Since the way that humans form belief in God is unreliable, given the CSR theories (we grant that we are justified in believing one of these theories, for the sake of argument), humans should suspend judgment regarding the existence of God.

This argument can be refined in various ways (see Thurow, 2013), but ultimately, even after various refinements, it fails. It fails because many people

---

[6] In Thurow (2014) I argue that CSR decreases the degree of justification for belief in God a small degree via way CD5.

[7] See, e.g. Bloom, 2009; Kahane, 2011; Wilkins and Griffiths, 2012; Leben, 2014. Others have discussed, though not endorsed, the argument: Barrett, 2007; Murray, 2009; van Inwagen, 2009; Leech and Visala, 2011.

believe in God at least partly on the basis of traditional kinds of reasons that have been offered for believing that God exists—religious experience, the appearance of design, the existence of something rather than nothing, experiences of miraculous events or testimony of such events. The CSR theories say nothing about whether any of these reasons are good reasons. If they are good reasons, and one believes in God at least partly because of such reasons, then one is justified in believing that God exists. Furthermore, one is justified even after learning about the CSR theories because those theories do not undermine the evidential force of any of these reasons.

To illustrate my point, consider John Wilkins and Paul Griffiths' (2012) recent discussion of evolutionary debunking arguments. Wilkins and Griffiths argue that the various evolutionary theories in CSR debunk religious belief because these processes do not track the truth. They argue that in order to avoid this evolutionary debunking argument, there must be a "Milvian Bridge" linking belief in God to evolutionary success "in such a way that selection will favour organisms which have true beliefs" (2012, p. 134). Since there is no such bridge, religious beliefs stand debunked, and religious belief is unjustified. However, Wilkins and Griffiths also argue that science is not debunked by a similar evolutionary argument because there is an indirect Milvian bridge connecting scientific beliefs to truth: evolution has selected for accurate commonsense beliefs, such as belief in the presence of various physical objects, and science is the process of using these beliefs systematically to weed out incorrect beliefs and build a more accurate system of beliefs. Since the results of science are checked by common sense through observation judgments—and common sense is generally reliable—the results of science are generally reliable as well. In other words, science is a reliable byproduct of a system of accurate beliefs (or belief-forming processes) that were selected for, and so there is a Milvian bridge of sorts linking science to the selection of accurate beliefs.

If the traditional theistic reasons are in fact good reasons, then there will be an indirect Milvian bridge linking theistic belief to the selection of accurate theistic beliefs. For in recognizing the traditional theistic reasons as good reasons, humans will be using general abilities to recognize and assess evidence, which are generally reliable and were surely selected for because they are reliable. At any rate, if they were not selected for because they are reliable, the evolutionary debunking argument will show that it is irrational to use our evidence-assessing abilities, which would lead to a deep-cutting skepticism.[8] Note that this reply

---

[8] See Plantinga's many essays (e.g. 2002a; 2002b; 2011) defending the evolutionary argument against naturalism.

stays neutral on the psychology of our general abilities to recognize and assess evidence—this ability could be a central skill that operates in a roughly subject-independent way or it could amount to a constellation of relatively modularized domain-specific skills. So, whether or not there is a Milvian bridge for theistic belief depends upon whether the traditional theistic reasons are good reasons. If they are, there is a Milvian bridge, and theistic belief avoids the evolutionary debunking argument.

In effect, then, the debunking argument can succeed only if CSR undermines the evidential force of traditional kinds of reasons and arguments; that is, the debunking argument can succeed only if CSR casts doubt in way CD4. This important point should lead us to focus more on whether CSR casts doubt in way CD4; so far the literature on the epistemic implications of CSR has barely touched on way CD4.

My argument assumes that:

(A1) CSR theories do not undermine traditional kinds of reasons that people have for believing that God exists.

There are a couple of different ways that (A1) could turn out to be false. First, CSR could provide unique reasons for doubting several of the traditional kinds of theistic reasons. We would need to march through the traditional reasons one by one, checking whether CSR casts doubt on each, in order to assess this possibility. I have begun this task in other work (Thurow, 2014), where I argued that CSR undermines C.S. Lewis' Argument from Desire, but that it does not undermine the cosmological or design arguments. I will continue this task in the concluding section of this chapter by outlining what it would take for CSR to undermine religious experience. Second, CSR could otherwise provide some global reason for doubting our ability to properly assess the traditional theistic reasons. There are two different lines of argument for such a global reason to doubt.

First, it seems plausible that if one is disposed to believe that p, then one will also be disposed to accept arguments for p (and reject arguments against p). Psychologists have uncovered a variety of evidence that humans have just such a disposition, which is often called the confirmation bias. Each of the CSR theories sets humans up with a disposition toward belief in God, which the confirmation bias transforms into a disposition to accept putative reasons supporting the existence of God. Furthermore, this cascade of dispositions would be present whether or not God exists, and indeed whether or not the traditional theistic reasons are in fact good reasons. Once we recognize we have such a disposition, we have grounds for doubting that we accurately assess the traditional theistic reasons. So, if any of the CSR theories are true (and we have good reason to believe it), then we have grounds for doubting that we accurately assess the traditional theistic reasons. We would then not be justified in believing in God on the basis of such reasons. Thus, (A1) is false, and my attempt to evade the debunking argument fails.

There is something right about this line of argument, but ultimately I believe that it fails to challenge (A1). No doubt the confirmation bias together with a CSR disposition to believe that God exists would give humans a disposition to accept putative reasons for believing that God exists, but it is far from clear that this disposition would be strong enough to undermine our ability to assess the traditional theistic reasons. First, if it was strong enough, then it seems that we would have good grounds for doubting our ability to assess *any* argument or reason regarding *any* issue where we are disposed toward accepting one position or another. This way lies deep skepticism. Even worse, self-defeat looms. Are we disposed to regard religious belief as justified or unjustified? If we are disposed one way or another, then given the confirmation bias, we have reason to doubt our ability to assess *this very argument under consideration* (that is, the argument in the previous paragraph).

Second, plainly there are cases where one is disposed to accept p, and reasons offered for p, and yet one adequately evaluates the evidence and believes appropriately. To illustrate this, consider the following two cases.[9] Case 1: A father loves his son deeply. His son is accused of raping a girl. There is some evidence for this, but the father firmly believes his son is innocent simply because he loves him. In this case, the father is disposed to believe his son is innocent because of his love for him, and this disposition interferes with his ability to see the evidence. As a result, he is unjustified in his conviction that his son is innocent. Case 2: same father. The father loves his son just as deeply, but now there is substantial evidence that the son is innocent, which the father is aware of, and so the father believes that the son is innocent on the basis of this evidence. In this case, although the father is disposed to think that his son is innocent simply because of the love he has for his son, the father's belief is still justified. He is aware of the evidence and evaluates it competently. It is true that if he didn't have such strong evidence, he would believe his son was innocent anyway, but that kind of disposition does not undermine his justified belief in case 2 where he has the evidence of innocence in front of him and he recognizes it as evidence for innocence. So, whether our judgment of the evidence regarding p is

---

[9] This example and some of the phrasing in this paragraph are taken from Thurow (2013) and Thurow (2014).

affected in an epistemically significant way by a disposition to believe/disbelieve p depends upon the evidence we have, how strong it is, and on our abilities to evaluate the evidence. Some theists may well rationally evaluate the traditional theistic reasons, and those reasons may well be good reasons, even if humans have a disposition to believe in gods by virtue of a mechanism described by one of the CSR theories.

We now turn to a second global reason to be skeptical of our ability to assess the traditional theistic reasons. Derek Leben notes that many people hold religious beliefs at least partially on the basis of traditional theistic reasons. Leben argues, however, that one's religious beliefs remain debunked by the debunking argument if there is reason to think that the traditional religious reasons are in fact rationalizations, where "rationalizing can be described as a process of ad hoc reasoning about a belief that is already held, usually appealing to information currently available to the rationalizer" (Leben, 2014, p. 343). Are there grounds for thinking that the traditional religious reasons are in fact simply rationalizations? One clear sign that a putative reason is a rationalization is if the putative reason is, upon reflection, quite poor. Although some think that the traditional reasons are very poor, their quality is very much in dispute. Some arguments based on the traditional reasons are clearly poor, but the reasons themselves may make religious belief reasonable even though it is difficult to come up with a convincing argument on the basis of those reasons. Analogously, it is difficult to give an argument for the existence of the external world based on our experiences, although it seems clear that our experiences somehow make belief in an external world rational. So, it is hasty to assume that the traditional reasons are clearly bad, and thus infer on these grounds that the traditional reasons are rationalizations.

Leben presents a different test for determining whether a putative reason R is a rationalization. If an unreliable psychological mechanism M is a better predictor of S's belief B than is R, then it is more likely that M causes B and R is a rationalization than it is that R causes B.[10] Leben (2014, p. 346) then argues that "agent-detection devices can predict a large range of religious beliefs," while "none of the standard arguments for the existence of God are convincing or influential enough to be the source of more than a handful of actual religious beliefs," and theists "tend to reject the same type of historical argument" that they often state in support of their own beliefs. So (generalizing a bit), the CSR theories can

---

[10] Leben does not explicitly state this principle; it is my best interpretation of what best fits with how he describes the test. The principle described is true in Bayesian confirmation theory provided that the P(M caused B and R is a rationalization) and P(R caused B) on other evidence is about equal.

predict religious beliefs well, whereas the traditional theistic reasons are too weak to predict religious beliefs and are not consistently accepted by theists.

The CSR theories aren't nearly as good predictors of religious belief as Leben thinks. No CSR theory predicts that humans will believe in Christianity, Islam, Judaism, or any other particular set of actual religious doctrines. The CSR theories predict that religious beliefs will be widespread and that they will tend to have a certain kind of content: they will concern invisible agents who are concerned about human affairs. Predicting an abstract feature of people's actual religious beliefs is a far cry from predicting actual religious beliefs. CSR theorists readily acknowledge that historical circumstances shape how the general disposition to believe in invisible agents is transformed into a living and breathing religious tradition. And those historical circumstances typically include accounts of events, experiences, and reasons that determine the content of the religious doctrines. Religious experiences, miracles, and the appearance of design in the world all play a role in shaping particular religious traditions. So, the CSR theories do not predict what people believe in (e.g., Christianity); the CSR theories together with accounts of religious experiences (e.g., Paul's experience on the road to Damascus), historical events (such as Jesus' life, miracles, death, and resurrection), and perhaps others traditional reasons, all of which are preserved in collective memory by an institution (the Church), come much closer to predicting people's belief in Christianity. But, then, the traditional theistic reasons play a role in explaining belief, and if those reasons are good, then Christians who are sufficiently well-informed about their tradition may well be justified in their beliefs (and obviously a similar argument can be given for other theistic traditions).

It is true that religious believers in one tradition who accept a historical argument for their own beliefs tend to reject historical arguments offered by the members of other traditions for the beliefs of those other traditions. But this is not a good reason for thinking that historical arguments don't play a role in explaining people's religious beliefs. We all believe lots of things on the basis of testimony, but sometimes rightly reject testimonial arguments. Indeed, we often reject some testimonial claims on the basis of other things we think we know from testimony. There's nothing inconsistent about this—often it is perfectly rational—and certainly the fact that we do this doesn't at all suggest that our beliefs are rarely explained by the testimony of others. So, the fact that religious believers are resistant to historical arguments given by traditions other than their own doesn't imply that they are irrational in being resistant, or that they don't themselves rely on historical arguments for their own religious beliefs.

To review: I have argued that the debunking argument fails because (A1) CSR theories do not undermine traditional kinds of reasons that people have for believing that God exists and people who believe on the basis of such reasons, or who are sufficiently well-informed members of religious traditions that have been shaped by such reasons, may well be justified in their beliefs if those reasons in fact are good. Furthermore, we have not seen any good global reason for rejecting (A1). However, as I mentioned earlier, CSR could provide reasons for rejecting various individual theistic reasons. For my money, this is where we need to look to see if CSR casts any significant doubt on theistic belief. I conclude by briefly outlining how one might investigate whether CSR undermines one of the most central of the traditional theistic reasons: religious experience.

Way CD4 and Religious Experience

So far I have argued that CSR does not cast doubt on theistic belief in way CD1 and that it does not cast doubt in way CD2 unless it provides some local reasons for doubting a variety of traditional theistic reasons. Doing so would cast doubt in way CD4. So, we need to focus on CD4 in our investigation of whether and to what extent CSR casts doubt on theistic belief. Elsewhere, I have argued that CSR undermines C.S. Lewis' Argument from Desire, but that it does not undermine the cosmological or design arguments (Thurow, 2014). So, CSR can and does cast doubt on theistic belief in way CD4. In this section I will show how the evidential force of religious experience could be undermined by findings and theories in CSR. My aim is to illustrate how CSR could undermine religious experience, not to argue whether and to what extent it does; I believe the science of religious experience is far too young to make any useful judgments on this matter, and in any case it would take much more space than I have here to fully discuss the work that has been done.

There has been recent work investigating which features of the brain produce religious experiences and how they do so.[11] One might wonder: if this science continues to develop and produces purely natural explanations of why people have many kinds of religious experiences, would such explanations undermine the evidential force, such as it is, of many peoples' religious experiences? This question has received some treatment in the literature on religious experience, and most philosophers have argued that findings about how religious experiences are produced can undermine the evidential force of religious experience. Since CSR

---

[11] See, e.g., McNamara, 2009 and references therein.

is broadly concerned with identifying features of the mind that lead humans to find belief in gods and other supernatural agents plausible, the causes of religious experience fall within its ambit. Work in CSR on religious experience may thus be relevant to evaluating the evidential force of religious experience. Jerome Gellman (2001), a defender of the evidential force of religious experience, addresses this issue extensively and argues persuasively that the evidential force of religious experiences would be largely undermined if we had evidence that:

(a) There is a set of naturalistic circumstances C, such that most (perhaps all) subjects who perceive God are in some C-circumstance.

(b) Being in a C-circumstance gives reason to expect or suspect those subjects would have had God perceptions, even if their perceptions were illusory, or being in a C-circumstance gives reason to expect or suspect those subjects had illusory God-perceptions.

(c) There is no set C1 of naturalistic circumstances such that: most subjects who perceive God are in some C1-circumstance and being in a C1-circumstance counts significantly in favor of the subjects having had veridical experiences of God and:

(d) A person's being in C does not give reason to expect or suspect the person's perceptions would be veridical, if God existed. (Gellman, 2001, p. 60)

In short, Gellman is saying that religious experience would have little to no evidential force if most religious experiences happen in naturalistic circumstances that would lead people to have these experiences whether or not God exists, and no extra details about those circumstances give reason to think that these experiences are veridical, and there aren't good grounds for thinking that if God were to exist, then people would experience him in these circumstances. Consider a hypothetical example. Suppose most religious experiences are caused by seizures. People would then have these religious experiences whether or not God exists because people would have seizures whether or not God exists. Suppose no additional details about such experiences give reason to think that the experiences are veridical: for example, we don't find a correlation between having religious experience-inducing seizures and praying or asking God for some sort of guidance. There is no reason to think that God would appear to everyone who has a seizure, or that what people experience in a seizure would be accurate about

God, even if God existed. Gellman is saying that in my hypothetical example, religious experiences would have little to no evidential force.

Why exactly would religious experience have little to no evidential force in the conditions described by Gellman? Suppose (b), (c), and (d) were satisfied for a particular religious experience. Then, we would have reason to think that this experience was produced by natural circumstances that would have held whether or not God existed (and, given (d), we would not have special reason to think that God overdetermined or set those circumstances up in this particular case), and that experiences produced in this way are not reliable, or do not track the truth, in the right kind of way. When we have reason to believe that our experiences aren't reliably produced or don't track the truth, then we are not justified in relying on them, despite what their content may *prima facie* indicate. Both internalists and externalists about justification allow this kind of defeat (although they will quibble about whether to call the lack of proper connection between experience and the facts a lack of reliability, truth-tracking, or proper fit between the content of experience and reality). If (b)–(d) are satisfied when condition (a) is satisfied, then almost no religious experiences will have any evidential force. Of course, partial undermining could also occur if there were fewer religious experiences for which conditions (b), (c), and (d) applied.

Although it is quite possible that the evidential force of a wide range of religious experiences could be undermined if (b), (c), and (d) are satisfied for a wide range of religious experiences, it is not clear that this would be very likely, since (d) could very easily fail to be satisfied by many religious experiences even if there were good naturalistic explanations for those experiences. For example, suppose scientists find a good naturalistic explanation of why some people feel God's presence in various aspects of everyday life and why it seems to them as though God is speaking to them in prayer. If God exists, then God might well be expected to build into humans some natural way of sensing his presence and feeling as if he is listening. It isn't clear that we should expect God to directly intervene in the physical causal processes in these everyday sorts of religious experiences. As long as the natural process that explains these experiences in the circumstances in which they arise isn't too odd to expect God to use, (d) will not be satisfied.

So, if (d) is a genuine criterion, then it seems unlikely that the evidential force of a wide range of religious experiences would be undermined by future scientific endeavors. But there is some reason to doubt whether (d) is a genuine criterion. Suppose (a), (b), and (c) are satisfied. Then, we would know that humans would have nearly all the religious experiences they in fact have whether or not God exists. Such experiences don't seem sensitive to God's existence.

If our grounds aren't sensitive to the object of our belief, then we shouldn't trust our grounds. So, the evidential force of religious experiences would be undermined. But now what if we learn that (d) fails to be satisfied—if God exists, he might very well be expected to use these grounds to reveal himself. So what? How can we tell which it is—whether the grounds genuinely reveal God or whether they don't? Both options are equally likely simply on the data of the religious experience, given that we know we'd have the experience whether or not God exists, and given that our independent evidence about God's existence is neutral. But, then, the experiences don't evidentially distinguish between the existence and non-existence of God. If a piece of evidence doesn't distinguish between A and not-A, then we should suspend judgment regarding A on the basis of the piece of evidence.[12]

Certainly more needs to be said regarding (d), but suppose what I've just argued is correct. There is a different, more plausible, criterion that can take the place of (d):

> (d*) Given that a person S has independent reason for thinking that God exists, S's being in C does not give reason to expect or suspect the person's perceptions would be veridical, if God existed.

For if S has independent reason for thinking that God exists (via the cosmological argument or design argument or some other non-debunked set of religious experiences), then one would have reason for thinking that the religious experiences for which we have naturalistic explanations that don't satisfy (d*) are actually designed by God to reveal Himself in a naturalistic way. The evidential force of those experiences would then not be undermined. This illustrates once again, and in another way, my main point in this section: that we need to first evaluate how plausible the traditional theistic reasons are before we are able to evaluate whether belief in God is undermined by CSR. If some of the traditional theistic reasons are good, then a wider range of religious experience will likely escape potential debunking by future scientific discovery than if the traditional theistic reasons are not good.

Gellman goes on to consider a variety of naturalistic explanations of religious experiences and argues that none of these satisfies all four of these conditions. For reasons given earlier, I don't have the space here to fully evaluate whether he

---

[12] This is a version of the debunking argument, now applied to the evidential force of experiences rather than beliefs. I discuss a similar sort of debunking argument for beliefs in more detail in Thurow (2013).

is correct. Instead, I simply observe that: 1) it seems clear that empirical findings about the way religious experiences are produced, including those produced by CSR, can in principle undermine the evidential force of religious experience (whether (d) or (d*) is a genuine criterion for when religious experience is undermined); 2) it is controversial whether and to what extent the evidential force of religious experience is undermined in this way (Gellman is on one side of this issue, while Evan Fales (1996a; 1996b; 2004), e.g., is on the other); and 3) the extent to which religious experience is undermined depends upon the evidential force of various other traditional theistic reasons.

Conclusion

CSR has developed fascinating genealogies of theistic belief, which have the potential to cast doubt on religious belief. I have argued that CSR does not: (i) entail that God does not exist; or (ii) undermine, via a genealogical debunking argument, the justification of theistic belief. Even after becoming aware of the CSR theories, theists who believe partially on the basis of the traditional theistic reasons may still be fully rational if the reasons are good. However, CSR may cast doubt on theistic belief by undermining the evidential force of some of these traditional theistic reasons, including religious experience. It takes a case-by-case investigation to determine which of the traditional theistic reasons are undermined, and whether some of the reasons are undermined depends upon the strength of the other reasons. Genealogies of theistic belief, like those developed by CSR, are not nuclear weapons that wipe out the justification of religious belief; if they were, then, like real nuclear weapons, they would take out a whole lot more than the immediate target. However, these genealogies may, more surgically, eliminate or weaken some of the traditional grounds for theistic belief. It takes work and good old philosophy—via an assessment of the evidential force of the traditional theistic reasons—to figure out the extent to which such surgical strikes are effective.

References

Atran, S., 2002. *In Gods We Trust: The Evolutionary Landscape of Religion*. New York: Oxford University Press.

Barrett, J.L., 2004. *Why Would Anyone Believe in God?* Walnut Creek, CA: AltaMira Press.

——. 2007. Is the spell really broken? Bio-psychological explanations of religion and theistic belief. *Theology and Science*, 5(1), pp. 57–72.
Bering, J.M., 2006. The cognitive psychology of belief in the supernatural. *American Scientist*, 94, pp. 142–9.
——. 2011. *The God Instinct: The Psychology of Souls, Destiny, and the Meaning of Life*. London: Nicholas Brealey Publishing.
Bloom, P., 2009. Religious belief as an evolutionary accident. In: J. Schloss and M.J. Murray (eds), *The Believing Primate: Scientific, Philosophical, and Theological Reflections on the Origin of Religion*. Oxford: Oxford University Press, pp. 118–27.
Boyer, P., 2001. *Religion Explained: The Evolutionary Origins of Religious Thought*. London: Vintage.
Bulbulia, J., 2009. Religiosity as mental time-travel: cognitive adaptations for religious behavior. In: J. Schloss and M.J. Murray (eds), *The Believing Primate: Scientific, Philosophical, and Theological Reflections on the Origin of Religion*. Oxford: Oxford University Press, pp. 44–75.
Fales, E., 1996a. Scientific explanations of mystical experience, part I: the case of St. Theresa. *Religious Studies*, 32, pp.143–63.
——. 1996b. Scientific explanations of mystical experience, part II: the challenge to theism. *Religious Studies*, 32, pp. 297–313.
——. 2004. Do mystics see God? In: M.L. Peterson and R.J. Vanarragon (eds), *Contemporary Debates in the Philosophy of Religion*. Oxford: Blackwell, pp. 145–57.
Gellman, J., 2001. *Mystical Experience of God*. Aldershot: Ashgate.
Kahane, G., 2011. Evolutionary debunking arguments. *Nous*, 45, pp. 103–25.
Leben, D., 2014. When psychology undermines beliefs. *Philosophical Psychology* 27.3, pp. 328-50.
Leech, D. and Visala, A., 2011. The cognitive science of religion: a modified theist response. *Religious Studies*, 47(3), pp. 301–16.
McNamara, P., 2009. *The Neuroscience of Religious Experience*. Cambridge: Cambridge University Press.
Murray, M.J., 2009. Scientific explanations of religion and the justification of religious belief. In: J. Schloss and M.J. Murray (eds), *The Believing Primate: Scientific, Philosophical, and Theological Reflections on the Origin of Religion*. Oxford: Oxford University Press, pp. 168–78.
Plantinga, A., 2002a. Introduction: the evolutionary argument against naturalism. In: J. Beilby (ed.), *Naturalism Defeated? Essays on Plantinga's Evolutionary Argument Against Naturalism*. Ithaca, NY: Cornell University Press, pp. 1–12.

———. 2002b. Reply to Beilby's cohorts. In: J. Beilby (ed.), *Naturalism Defeated? Essays on Plantinga's Evolutionary Argument Against Naturalism*. Ithaca, NY: Cornell University Press, pp. 204–75.

———. 2011. *Where the Conflict Really Lies: Science, Religion, and Naturalism*. Oxford: Oxford University Press.

Plantinga, A. and Tooley, M., 2008. *Knowledge of God*. Oxford: Blackwell.

Sosis, R., 2006. Religious behaviors, badges, and bans: signaling theory and the evolution of religion. In: P. McNamara (ed.), *Where God and Science Meet, Vol. 1*. Westport, CT: Praeger, pp. 61–86.

Sosis, R. and Kiper, J., 2014. Religion is more than belief: what evolutionary theories of religion tell us about religious commitments. In: M. Bergmann and P. Kain (eds), *Challenges to Religious and Moral Belief*. Oxford: Oxford University Press, pp. 256–76.

Thurow, J.C., 2013. Does cognitive science show belief in God to be irrational? The epistemic consequences of the cognitive science of religion. *International Journal for the Philosophy of Religion*, 74, pp. 77–98.

———. 2014. Does the scientific study of religion cast doubt on theistic belief? In: M. Bergmann and P. Kain (eds), *Challenges to Religious and Moral Belief*. Oxford: Oxford University Press, pp. 277–94.

Van Inwagen, P., 2005. Is God an unnecessary hypothesis? In: A. Dole and A. Chignell (eds), *God and the Ethics of Belief*. Cambridge: Cambridge University Press, pp. 131–49.

———. 2009. Explaining belief in the supernatural: some thoughts on Paul Bloom's "Religious belief as an evolutionary accident." In: J. Schloss and M.J. Murray (eds), *The Believing Primate: Scientific, Philosophical, and Theological Reflections on the Origin of Religion*. Oxford: Oxford University Press, pp. 128–38.

Wilkins, J. and Griffiths, P., 2012. Evolutionary debunking arguments in three domains: fact, value, and religion. In: G. Dawes and J. Maclaurin (eds), *A New Science of Religion*. New York: Routledge, pp. 133–46.

Wilson, D.S., 2002. *Darwin's Cathedral: Evolution, Religion, and the Nature of Society*. Chicago: University of Chicago Press.

———. 2005. Testing major evolutionary hypotheses about religion with a random sample. *Human Nature*, 16(4), pp. 419–46.

Chapter 12
Human Nature and Religious Freedom

Roger Trigg

Can Sociology Explain Religion?

Is religion 'natural'? Is a predisposition, at least, to religious belief written in some way into human nature? This question impinges on the venerable arguments about how far any characteristics can be 'innate' and about the respective contributions of genes and environment. Our growing understanding of the importance of the human genome in influencing human character and behaviour should not blind us to the fact that very few qualities are entirely dependent on our genes and heredity alone. Eye colour or skin colour may be examples, but for the most part human development comes from a subtle interplay between genes and environment. Even the migration of birds has to be triggered by external factors.

Just because of the undoubted influence of external circumstances on human behaviour, not to mention that of animals, it is easy to think that in the human case social differences and social influences provide a full explanation of why we act as we do. This tendency is reinforced when such actions vary considerably in character according to time and place. It would seem reasonable to assume that the human genotype is not going to explain differences between human societies, if it is assumed to be fairly constant. In fact, this has been a working assumption of sociology for the last 50 years, albeit one that is now being increasingly challenged. Sociologists, in perhaps an example of academic imperialism, have wanted to claim that social explanations are sufficient to explain humanity, in all its multi-faceted variety.

This attitude lingers on, even in the face of new scientific research which appears to cast doubt on it. David Martin, for instance, a renowned sociologist of religion whose work began in the 1960s, still betrays the assumptions of that generation. Explicitly dealing with new research in the Cognitive Science of Religion (CSR), he continues to assert the priority of the social as a source of explanation. At first sight, he may appear to have right on his side, as religions come in many shapes and sizes, and it might appear that one form of explanation is not going to fit them all. How could a single explanation explain difference? Do we not need to turn to social differences for that? If religion is grounded in human nature, is not a uniform human nature going to produce a uniform religion? It could provide a single explanation to fit every case, but it would have to be put at such a level of generality as to be virtually useless as a form of explanation, and it could certainly only hope to explain underlying similarities and not the real and important differences.

Martin argues this, pointing out that, say, an evolutionary constant could not 'account for the variable presence and absence of religion' (2011, p. 217). He further argues: 'Christians used to take comfort from universal traces of what they thought were natural apprehensions of the divine, however distorted, but religion is not a natural given of that sort.' He stresses that it is passed on by 'socialization from parent to child'. His view, which he emphasises, is that 'religion varies in its form and intensity, and in its absence and presence, under specifiable historical and social conditions'. He says baldly that 'the conclusion has to be that "religion" is a cultural product' (Martin, 2011, p. 217).

Martin draws empirical conclusions from this, in particular in connection with secularisation theory. Although he has independent reasons for questioning the latter, he does not believe that it can be criticised because of 'the 'natural' resilience of religion or on grounds of an 'instinct for religion'' (Martin, 2011, p. 217). One might question the use of the term 'instinct' in this context, but the thrust of his argument is clear. Since the 1960s, many sociologists have predicted the progressive demise of religious influence in the face of a process of secularisation, fuelled by an ever-increasing respect for scientific rationality, which, allegedly, has no room for religion. The plight of religion in Western Europe may seem to bear this out, but the resurgence and persistence of religion elsewhere seems in emphatic contradiction to the thesis. Might one explanation be that secularisation, involving the banishment of religion to the private sphere, and perhaps its elimination, goes against the grain of human nature and is therefore unlikely to succeed for any significant period? Martin denies this and looks for other social explanations:

> While supporters of a strong secularization theory are waiting for the predicted disappearance of religion in the USA and Poland, cognitive scientists, supposing they know anything at all about the empirical evidence, are waiting for its predicted reappearance in the former DDR, Estonia and the Czech Republic. (Martin, 2011, p. 217)

He comments that thus far 'the secularization theorists have the empirical advantage'. He would make much of say, the religious differences between the Czech Republic and neighbouring Slovakia, suggesting that only social and historical reasons can explain the difference. Their common humanity clearly cannot.

One problem with words like 'secularisation', of which (like 'globalisation') sociologists are very fond, is that they suggest remorseless and mechanistic processes in society, which humans are unaware of and are unable to control. They appear to give the means to social scientists to make empirical predictions, as Martin has suggested. Yet this is to let sociology overreach itself. The 'reification' of such processes, making it appear that they have a life of their own, is a dangerous mistake. It may make sociology appear more scientific, but it can undercut the basic truth about all human societies: they are human and reflect the desires, needs and interests of humans. We are not set in any already-constructed social world, which exists apart from humans. It is true that we are each individually born and inducted into a society produced by previous generations. It is also true that the cumulative effect of countless individual actions can produce social contexts which are unintended and are even harmful to human interests. Nevertheless, at root they were produced by humans and can be controlled by humans. The social world is not like the physical world acting as an external, and sometimes unalterable, constraint on us all. Because the social world is human in origin, its nature is bound to reflect what humans are like.

No one doubts that sociology can identify trends, and significant tendencies, in human behaviour. It can show, for instance, whether there is a correlation between 'the degree of scientific advance' and 'a reduced profile of religious influence' (Martin, 2011, p. 125). It can certainly try to explain cultural (and religious) differences. It seems less able to account for the apparent universality of dispositions to religious belief in the first place. The absence of religion of any kind in a society for more than a short time would seem very remarkable. It certainly does not seem typical of human experience through time. Anthropologists, for example, can be confident that even if they find no archaeological traces of religious practices in a given place, it is still unlikely that the people concerned had no religion.

The issue in question here is not the truth of religion. The fact that there are so many different religions, with claims that are not only diverse but often contradictory, shows that they cannot all be completely true (see Trigg, 2014). All of them could be false. That is not the issue, which is simply the fact of universality. Martin, like many, believes that the presence or absence of religion is due to social, not biological factors. The differences between religions seem to be in such need of explanation – that the mere fact, if it is one, of the religiosity of human beings seems to be taken for granted. Yet it should be very remarkable that in diverse places and times, human beings have constructed communal systems of belief and ritual which have been passed on through the generations. It is remarkable not just that recognisably similar patterns of reactions to the world appear to arise independently in many different kinds of societies, but also that these appear to be so easily transmitted from one generation to another. The human mind seems deeply receptive to certain ways of looking at the world.

The Threat of Relativism

A concentration on cultural diversity, let alone specifically religious diversity, leads quickly to a concentration on the environmental influences on human beings which can be many and various. It will then be hardly surprising that human behaviour, as demonstrated in cultural practices, will also be many and various. Inputs determine outputs, and any intervening connection between the two, can be ignored as irrelevant to any explanation. This was typically the programme of behaviourists, who thought of the link between inputs and outputs of behaviour as belonging to an inaccessible 'black box', the contents of which were irrelevant for their studies, if they existed at all.

This type of reasoning inevitably leads to a downgrading of the idea of 'human nature'. What, or who, we are is determined by our environment or, more specifically, our society, and our actions are the product of that. The idea of a shared common humanity quickly drops out as irrelevant. Yet if everything is socially constructed, including our own identities and characters, our needs and interests, there are important consequences. We are imprisoned within the different worlds that are socially constructed. By definition, one world will not be related to another. There will be no common reality in which we are all placed, because our beliefs about that reality will already have been determined by the society which has produced us. There will, it will be assumed, be no common reaction to our different environments. Our shared humanity is not, by definition, a resource.

This brings us to a relativism that is all too common nowadays, which sees people as sealed in separate social compartments, each with their own separate conceptual schemes and ways of thought. The philosophical consequences are massive. Without the concept of an objective reality in which we are placed, we also lose the idea of common shared reactions to particular features in it. We do not all live in the same world and there is no common human nature that we can all share. There will be no way in which mutual understanding between people of different cultures and religions is even theoretically possible. There is no common ground. There is no way, in principle, in which bridges can be built between people, who, it is agreed, are sealed in mutually exclusive, socially constructed worlds. When difference and diversity is stressed, there comes a point at which there is no commonality left. All basis for mutual comprehension is removed. Indeed, the possibility of translation between the languages of different worlds is removed. Even if we could understand what the languages conveyed, there is little chance that we could find the people using the motivations and interests of those using them. By definition, as the creatures of a different socially constructed world, their beliefs and practices would be beyond our understanding.

This is all a *reduction ad absurdum* of the relativist position, but its main features often recur in a variety of philosophical positions. The minute that translation and mutual understanding becomes difficult between 'forms of life' (as in the later Wittgenstein), or incommensurability between paradigms is taken for granted (as in the work of Thomas Kuhn in the history and philosophy of science),[1] we are losing our grip on the idea of an objective reality to which all cultures have equal access. We equally have lost the idea of a common human nature in which all share, so that our reactions to that same world will take broadly similar forms and be recognisable across cultures.

In more recent years, a radical overthrow of the idea of a common rationality linking and underpinning different traditions has led to the repudiation of many of the principles of the Enlightenment. So-called 'post-modernism' takes the same route as earlier forms of relativism and inevitably locks concepts into particular traditions linked to time and place. This perspective has the result, in particular, of making the whole concept of human rights problematic. If our humanity is constituted by our local tradition, that in effect means there is no such thing as a common human nature. Each culture has to set its own standards, and the idea of appealing to an abstract humanity that is left with no content is pointless. This is the danger of 'multi-culturalism' and references to 'pluralism'. Both offer little more than the banal observation that there is great diversity in the human worlds. We do not all agree. That is a sociological observation, however, that can then be built up into a dangerous philosophical principle that there is no underlying communality behind the apparent diversity. The diversity is all there is. Then, words like 'multi-culturalism' develop into a full-fledged

---

[1] See my *Reason and Commitment* (Trigg, 1973) for an attack on all such forms of relativism.

relativism, according to which there are no external benchmarks beyond those posited by particular cultures.

Ideas referring to humanity, like 'human rights', inevitably come to be seen as the mere posturing by particular cultures, using schemes of thought peculiar to themselves which can have no general application. That is precisely the criticism levelled by some against what are seen as specifically 'Western' attitudes that can have no general application to all humans. The idea of 'humans' becomes virtually an empty concept, or at least a contested one. As one writer, Bhikhu Parekh (2008 p.226), points out: 'Universal declarations of rights are sometimes perceived as being instruments of Western domination and arouse hostility because, among other things, they entitle the West to demand that all societies should organize themselves in certain ways.'

Parekh further makes the point that 'since human beings lead organized lives and their nature has been profoundly shaped by layers of social influences, we have no access to it in its raw form and cannot easily separate what is natural from what is social' (2008, p. 209). That may be a difficulty, but again it can be transformed into a philosophical principle, so that what is social, in all its variety, becomes primary, and the 'natural' recedes into becoming a 'something we know not what', which can be easily forgotten and which plays no role in our understanding.

Yet that must be wrong, since, as we have already seen, all communication between different languages, cultures, theories, conceptual schemes or whatever, depends on access to some commonality shared by all. It is ironic that Parekh upholds respect for difference and plurality and denies that anyone has access to any 'transcendental or Archimedean standpoint' (2008, p. 226). Yet he immediately goes on to advocate an 'intercultural dialogue', which 'enables each cultural community to look at its beliefs and practices from the standpoints of others' (2008, p. 226). The crunch question is what has to be the case for such dialogue to take place. If we are all locked into distinct and separate communities, it will be impossible. If, on the other hand, we all bring a common human nature, with shared interests, desires and common human reactions, other beliefs and practices, however apparently alien, will still be intelligible to us.

It is in this context of an encroaching relativism that threatens our understanding of others as human beings, much like ourselves, that modern scientific work becomes of great importance. It shows us not just how 'we' as citizens of particular time and place are constituted, it also tells us how 'we' as human beings are likely to react to the world. It informs us how humans naturally think and what their basic tendencies, dispositions and desires are. The practice of science itself aspires to universality. It tells us not just what is true in London, Beijing or Washington DC, but what is everywhere the case. In the case of research into human beings, it aspires to tell us how humans are liable to think and act, not just how the Americans or the Chinese do. Indeed, all relativism leads to the death of science, since science then becomes reduced to the cultural expression of one society in one place. Hence, the pejorative term 'Western science' can be used. The very same scepticism which undermines any possibility of referring to human rights also renders science impotent and reduces human rationality to a series of local prejudices.

Being Human

The cognitive science of religion claims to be truly scientific and to be based on empirical evidence gained through proper scientific method, particularly in the fields of psychology and anthropology. It conducts cross-cultural research and its findings are intended to apply across cultures. The conclusions to be drawn from it are also going to concern human beings as such, and not just the members of particular society. The assumption must be that we can identify a similar cluster of typical, and similar, human reactions to their environment that can be called 'religious' in different social contexts across time. There is a content to being human, and the inclination to take up definite patterns of belief, practices and rituals is central to the human condition.

To take one example of research in the area, it is fascinating to see how children naturally develop a 'theory of mind'. At first young children of about three find it difficult to realise that their mother does not know everything and may not even know what they themselves know.[2] Typically between the ages of three and about four, they can come to understand that different people have different perspectives, and those may be limited. If you put an apple beneath one of two or three dishes while a child's mother is watching, and move it to under another one when she has left the room, a child of three will assume she will know where the apple now is when she comes back. Mummy, it is assumed, knows everything. Children of four or so will know different and will understand that she cannot know what has happened if she did not see it happen. So far so good, but an interesting facet of this is that if children are questioned about God and are asked if God knows where the apple is, they often, even at the age of four, find no difficulty in assuming that He will know. 'God knows everything' one will say, while another child said simply 'God is God'.[3]

---

[2]   See, for example, Barrett, Richert and Driesenga, 2001.

[3]   These are the remarks of my own twin grandchildren when I tried this experiment on them at the ages of three and then four. Their reactions bore out the scientific studies reported.

This tale of 'false belief tasks' can be replicated in many similar experiments, but an immediate response is that it shows something about the child's upbringing. After all, it will be said, a child will clearly have been taught about who 'God' is so as to be able to use the concept in the first place. The sociologist will claim that so-called 'natural' reactions are clearly culturally conditioned in a strong way. Yet it is significant that similar studies can be conducted in very different cultures with similar results. Nicola Knight (2008), who worked with us on our Oxford project, found that children in different cultures with different understandings about non-natural entities were still easily able to develop nuanced distinctions of their ability to know. As he says, 'they do not appear to use humans as a basis to reason about God' (2008, p. 242). They were also able to distinguish between humans and the classical Maya divinities.

The issue is not that children can have a ready-packaged concept of the Christian God without any teaching. Ideas that our thinking can be 'hard-wired' in that way so that they are totally detached from environmental influences are wide of the mark. An analogy is in fact the learning of language. No child is born 'hard-wired' to speak English. The language a child learns depends on the language spoken regularly in the child's hearing. Yet the opposite conclusion would be equally mistaken: that language learning is only subject to environmental influences and has nothing to do with capabilities that are part of human nature. If that were not the case, there would have been much more success in getting the higher apes to communicate linguistically. Propensities and capabilities go to constitute what it is to be human. Mentally, we are inclined to notice some things rather than others. The human mind is already tilted towards finding some things salient and others not.

We find it easier to think in some ways than others and we are naturally able to grasp some concepts more easily than others. CSR charts these dispositions and tendencies. The experiments that show how easily children can attribute 'super-knowledge' to non-natural entities, and indeed find it easy to refer to 'God' as knowing everything, show us something of how children's minds develop. Many, including philosophers, have assumed that all our reasoning about agents proceeds by analogy with our experience of humans. We have to think anthropomorphically. Yet these experiments suggest that thinking about God and other spiritual agents can easily part company with beliefs about human capabilities. We start with certain natural assumptions about knowledge and soon find that humans do not measure up. Children do, though, find it obvious that God and other agents still can meet our initial expectations.

The issue is what humans find easy to conceive, the stories they can grasp best and remember, even the religious doctrines that resonate best with our conceptual scheme. CSR shows not only why individuals may find it easy to hold on to certain beliefs, but also why certain conceptual patterns are so readily grasped and transmitted. One issue is always not just why people are religious, but why religions, both beliefs and practices, can be passed on through the generations. There must be something in the human mind that inclines it to think in religious turns and be able to grasp them when communicated. As we have seen, this must also be true on a cross-cultural basis. We are not all locked up in our own particular cultures, but the way in which we all share the same form of basic cognitive architecture means that humans can easily understand each other across what might appear unbridgeable chasms of time and space. Human minds work the same way simply because they are human.

We can all easily grasp the idea of someone knowing everything, just as other ideas that go to build up characteristic religious attitudes are also easily grasped, understood and communicated. CSR shows how we can all understand the idea of non-physical agency, the idea of mind existing apart from body, and life after death. We are 'intuitive dualists' (Bloom, 2004), just as we indulge in 'promiscuous teleology' (Kelemen and Rosset, 2009), being prone to see purpose rather than mere mechanical explanation in events around us. CSR shows how different biases and dispositions in the way we think go to build up what can be seen as characteristically religious pictures of the world in which we set.

Three charges will immediately be laid at this picture. Why should we be guided by what are admitted to be infantile understandings? Even if they are 'natural', what does that prove, since not all our natural tendencies are good? Third, even if we do have unthinking beliefs growing out of what we have termed human cognitive architecture, this does nothing to show that they are reliable, let alone true. All these objections invite us to ignore the fact that we all, as humans, have certain natural reactions and immediately go on to criticise them as guides to action. Yet this is to miss an important point. The issue should not be whether such reactions are true, and certainly the fact that we naturally have them proves little of their worth. There are many normal human reactions (such as disgust at the sight of blood) that it may be important for some to overcome, particularly if, say, they wish to practise surgery. They may be useful in some contexts and even have developed for evolutionary reasons, but that does not mean that they are always good guides to action.

In any case, it is clear from the mere existence of differing religions that basic human reactions, including inclinations to conceive of non-natural agents, underdetermine the kind of religion we might adopt. There seem to be desires and tendencies built into human nature which can be manifested in very many different ways. We may be biased at a fundamental level to populate reality with more entities than we can see and touch. We may want to see events as basically having a purpose. We may think that this life is not all there is. None of this, however, leads firmly in the direction of one religion rather than another. Indeed, it may not even point very firmly to any idea of monotheism. There seems a lot of space left to be filled by a variety of different types of religion, all answering the basic slant in human cognition.

One theological response from a Christian point of view might be that this demonstrates the necessity for special revelation, because we know very little about the nature of ultimate reality. Yet it might also prepare the ground for it. A human mind totally devoid of preconceptions, the archetypal 'blank slate', would be unlikely to be able to recognise a divine revelation as such. Only those with, as it were, minds prepared because they find certain things salient might be able to recognise revelation for what it is, assuming it were genuine.

This last point illustrates a general truth about the character of the inchoate quasi-religious reactions to the world, which CSR exposes. Such ideas need considerable elaboration by what, at the extreme, becomes a body of doctrine passed through the generations. They also invite more rational reflection on their nature. Theology is one such mode of reflection and atheism, indeed, is another. The former gives some rational grounding and validation for our impulses, whereas the latter suggests that they are characteristically unreliable. Both involve the exercise of reason and both have to take for granted the fact of our initial reactions. In other words, religion, of a rather unformed kind, is our default option. We are not natural atheists, with theologians coming along to impose some alien pattern of thought on us. We do not even interpret the world in a neutral way. Our uninformed reactions to the world are much less sceptical and are inclined to entertain minds apart from bodies, post-mortem survival, disembodied agency and so on. Our minds, as we are so often told by cognitive scientists of religion, find it easy to grasp what is 'minimally counter-intuitive'. Something out of the ordinary grabs our attention quite naturally, as long as it is not too much removed from our experience. For this reason, as Justin Barrett says, 'belief in gods is common precisely because such beliefs resonate with and receive support from a large number of mental tools' (2004, p. 21).

Our natural reactions to the world arise out of what Barrett calls our 'mental tools'. We have to make sense of the potentially bewildering array of data flung at us so that we each can conduct our lives in the environment presented to us. Therefore, there are different levels of mental activity. First we have natural reactions which occur without any process of conscious reasoning. These are typically human traits and are not constructed by specific cultures. We can hear a rustling in the trees and immediately assume an agent – perhaps an animal or maybe a spirit – has caused it. This experience can then be explained in different cultures by different sets of doctrines and beliefs, explaining perhaps what the nature of the spirit might be. We can have the illusion of total diversity, but the cognitive architecture supporting them all in their variety is ultimately the same.

Yet above all of this, we still have the capacity as humans to indulge in rational reflection and have 'meta'-beliefs: beliefs about our beliefs. That is where science and philosophical and religious systems themselves come in. Even CSR itself is an attempt to explain rationally the universality of similar systems of belief in the supernatural. Rational reflection on the nature, and possible reliability, of beliefs that come naturally to us is itself a normal human activity.

Desires and Freedom

Human beings can think rationally about what might be true. If this is denied, the physical sciences themselves are undermined as a rational activity, and CSR itself loses any pretension to be taken seriously, along with all science. Part of the raw material of the rational reflection has to be our own nature as human beings, our own capabilities and potentialities. Yet this brings us back to the question of our 'raw' religious reactions to the world. They are both there, as part of our nature, and they also invite rational reflection on how significant they are, or whether they are indeed infantile reactions which we should grow out of.

It is almost part of received wisdom in some quarters that 'faith' is a purely subjective matter, impervious to reason and even probably irrational. The consequence of this stance is that it is assumed that faith can offer no contribution to public life, let alone provide any reasons for the grounding of law. To take one example, the words of one English judge, Lord Justice Laws, are regarded as sufficiently important as to be quoted as authority in other cases:

> In the eye of everyone save the believer, religious faith is necessarily subjective, being unconstrained by any kind or proof or evidence. It lies only in the heart of the believer who is alone bound by it.[4]

This is itself a highly contentious statement in the philosophy of religion that demands public debate. Many would see a much more robust connection between faith and reason, and would not wish to restrict the idea of reason to

---

[4] *R (Eunice Johns and Owen Johns) and Derby City Council* [2011] EWHC 375 (Admin), para. 55.

excessively narrow ideas of what constitutes proof or evidence. They would not, for example, see them as defined by physical science. Yet the contrast between private faith and public reason, between subjective reaction and objective truth, is all too often made. It suggests that faith is not only impervious to reason, and to be contrasted with it, but that it is actually irrational, and maybe even divisive and dangerous. Indeed, if it were not susceptible to rational challenge, this might be so.

Yet one implication of making faith subjective in this way is that it appears idiosyncratic and perhaps even a minority concern. As such, freedom perhaps lies in making the choice to have or not have 'faith', whatever that might be. It becomes a marginal matter, which can be safely ignored in the conduct of business in the public sphere. Reason is public and faith is private. Religion, in all its diversity, can then be made irrelevant by definition to our common concerns.

Some may wish to retort that religion, as such, is a human good and ought to be encouraged. An immediate response will be that this is certainly not true of all religion. There can be pathologies of religion, whereby religious impulses can be warped and twisted so that practices (such as mass suicide) can be encouraged which are certainly not conducive by any standard to the common good or to human flourishing. Yet this very fact can make it more vital that all religions are susceptible to public examination and rational discussion in the public here, otherwise they will be left to fester without being confronted.

What grounds might there be for suggesting that religion has anything to do with human flourishing or can be called a human good? How, anyway, are human goods to be determined? Clearly, this must go back to issues concerning human nature, and our basic desires, and the needs that arise from them. Other things being equal, thwarting them must be deleterious. Depriving people of food and drink cannot help them to flourish. Needs and wants are not easily split from our basic nature. They constitute it. What it is for humans to flourish can only be understood by paying attention to our common character as human beings, and the drives and impulses that define humanity. If that is so, the fact that human cognition so consistently leads humans to see the world from a religious point of view has to be significant.

Religious viewpoints, however diverse, spring from the same human cognitive roots. Despite what David Martin and others have maintained, the absence of religion in a society is far more an occasion for surprise than its presence. We do not start from a position of cognitive neutrality, waiting to soak up whatever our environment produces. That is not to say that any particular religion, or religion in general, can necessarily be justified from an intellectual point of view. That is a separate argument. The important fact is that religion is there at the heart of human life. Anyone who assumes it can easily be ignored as a basic force in human society is deeply mistaken. They will be going against the grain of human nature. In one sense, it is irrelevant how religious impulses evolved, although it would be reasonable to suppose that their continued persistence through time does give an evolutionary advantage.

All this is to say that the characteristic impulses to religion – its building blocks – may be channelled in different directions. It is the function of human rationality to engage with the question how 'good' particular religions are and whether they really do add to human flourishing. Certainly there would seem to be something wrong (even from a theological point of view) with a religious practice, such as a literal human sacrifice on the altar of some religion, that unquestionably increased the sum of human suffering. Even the theologies giving rise to such practices must be suspect. Arguments about the contribution religions make to human good and harm are part of the stuff of controversy of modern public life. They cannot be shirked by pretending that 'faith' is a personal and private matter of no public concern. On the other hand, it is clear that not all manifestations of all religions in public are conducive to the common good.

Such controversies are inevitable and right. Yet a more fundamental issue remains. While the blanket term 'religion' covers a multitude of different beliefs and practices, all of which are the fruit of basic human responses to the world, we must not become so obsessed with arguing about this or that manifestation of religion, and the benefits and harms that might ensue, that we forget a basic truth. If humans typically want something, then, all other things being equal, it is good that they can have it. People immediately seize on the implied conditions, but the assumption must be that their desires should not be thwarted without very good reason. In other words, the default position should be that they can be free to try to get what they want. Without desires, and without the freedom to implement them, human beings are paralysed. Reason can modify desires, control them and even restrain them, but if we do not have any, we are undoubtedly going to cease to be agents.

The cognitive science of religion demonstrates that many typical human responses, both desires and initial beliefs, are cross-cultural and develop naturally in children. We cannot pretend that they are not there, or that they do not, at a pre-reflective level, lead us to react to our environment in particular ways. These are conducive to characteristic religious beliefs, such as belief in supernatural agency, or non-physical entities. Those who wish to restrain such impulses are making a judgment, which may or may not be justified, about a basic element in our common nature. Whether, though, it ought to be indulged or controlled must be the subject of informed public debate. Issues of individual freedom then inevitably arise. Is the state, or any other authority, to tell me that some of my most basic desires are misplaced? Might this not be, in a free society, a decision that is properly left to the individual, perhaps after rational discussion with others? Fundamentally, the issue is one of individual liberty. If I want a drink or some food, that is a reason for my having it. Other people should not deny me it, without very good reasons that must themselves be susceptible to public examination.

Religious impulses are not the chance creation of particular kinds of societies, present in some and absent in others. They are not the chance choice of a few individuals. The cognitive science of religion is making the bold empirical claim that they are the starting point for everyone. All find it easy to latch on to religious concepts. They are an integral part of the very way we have come to think. What constitutes human flourishing can only be decided with reference to human nature. That in turn makes reference to our wants and needs inevitable. The freedom to be what we wish to be must be fundamental to free society. Reason may not be the slave of the passions, as David Hume maintained, but our basic human reactions certainly give us the raw material with which to fashion our lives. Empirical science in general, and cognitive science in particular, can give us an enlarged understanding of what that material is. It underlies all societies. Some go with the grain of human nature. Others go against it, probably at a cost, and probably not for a long period.

Human well-being and fulfilment are intrinsically linked to our ingrained nature. Human rights in general acknowledge the fact that humanity is not at root socially constructed. Similarly, the particular right to religious freedom answers the universal fact that we seek some larger spiritual reality and impute purpose to even apparently random events. Even a rational atheism is a considered attempt to deal with an issue that would not arise unless there was an inbuilt bias to believe in the opposite. The right to religious freedom (both to believe and to manifest that belief) is a recognition of the fact that we all, as human beings, have to come to terms with our nature, and decide whether to follow and fulfil it, or to control and restrain it. After all, such freedom includes the freedom to deny all purported religious truth as well as to assert it. What the right to religious freedom does recognise is that this is a fundamental issue for humanity that is not likely to disappear whatever the apostles of secularisation might believe.

References

Barrett, J.L., 2004. *Why Would Anyone Believe in God?* Walnut Creek, CA: AltaMira Press.

Barrett, J.L., Richert, R.A. and Driesenga, A., 2001. God's beliefs versus mother's: the development of natural and non-natural agent concepts. *Child Development*, 71(1), pp. 50–65.

Bloom, P., 2004. *Descartes' Baby: How the Science of Child Development Explains What Makes Us Human.* New York: Basic Books.

Kelemen, D. and Rosset, E., 2009. The human function compunction: teleological explanation in adults. *Cognition*, 111, pp. 138–43.

Knight, N., 2008. Yukatek Maya children's attributions of belief to natural and non-natural entities. *Journal of Cognition and Culture*, 8, pp. 235–43.

Martin, D., 2011. *The Future of Christianity: Reflections on Violence and Democracy, Religion and Secularization.* Farnham: Ashgate.

Parekh, B., 2008. *A New Politics of Identity: Political Principles for an Interdependent World.* Basingstoke: Palgrave Macmillan.

Trigg, R., 1973. *Reason and Commitment.* Cambridge: Cambridge University Press.

———. 2014. *Religious Diversity: Philosophical and Political Dimensions*, Cambridge: Cambridge University Press

Index

accessibility bias 6
adaptation 38, 181; *see also* evolution by natural selection
    vs. by-product, religion as 4, 170, 179
agency 2, 11, 75, 77, 85
    attribution of 17–18, 20–22, 27
    non-physical 217–18
    supernatural 131, 150, 154, 221
agency detection; *see* hypersensitive agency detection device (HADD)
Agency System, Core 39–40, 48–52
agents 5, 8–9, 21, 39–40, 70, 91, 100–101, 105, 109, 121, 151–2, 168, 216, 221
    as causes of order and purpose 8, 27–8; *see also* teleological reasoning
    dead 58
    gods as counterintuitive 19, 41–6, 49, 135–6, 153
    mentalistic 132
    in religious rituals 58
    superhuman or supernatural 7, 22–3, 37–8, 40, 47, 113–15, 118, 131, 133–4, 136, 172, 190, 200, 202, 216–17
ancestors 7, 76, 91, 96–7, 151–3, 170, 181, 190
animals 19, 44, 46, 82, 100, 102, 109, 133, 135, 152, 209
    agency detection and 9, 21, 38, 151, 218
    as body and soul or mind 37, 40, 42, 47, 49–50
    gods and possible relationships between 135
    human vs. nonhuman 47, 50
    intuitive knowledge about 27, 40–42, 45, 47–8
    theory of mind (ToM) in nonhuman 52

anthropology 3, 9, 21, 37, 60, 215; *see also* evolution by natural selection
anthropomorphism 77, 82–3, 136
    and agency detection 132
    of supernatural agents 21, 134, 216
anti-teleological 78–9, 81–2, 84–8; *see also* teleofunctional reasoning; teleological arguments; teleological beliefs; teleology
arguments from design; *see* teleological arguments
Aristotle 46–7, 77–9, 81
Atran, Scott 3, 19–21, 23–4, 60–62, 113, 131, 135, 155, 168, 173, 190
artifacts 60, 135
atheism 1, 10–12, 149–50, 155–6, 162, 167, 170–71, 180, 182, 184, 218, 222; *see also* theism
attention 5, 20, 114, 131, 218
autism 133

babies; *see* infants
Bacon, Francis 78–9
Barrett, Justin 2–3, 5, 7–8, 18, 20–22, 27, 34, 37–8, 40–44, 46–8, 50, 72, 75–6, 89, 113–14, 120, 128, 131–2, 134–5, 146, 140, 150, 155–6, 162, 164, 167–8, 171–3, 180, 182–3, 190, 195, 215, 218
beliefs 5, 8, 18, 25–6, 30–31, 41, 43, 47, 49, 60, 76, 78, 84, 86–8, 91–5, 101, 104–6, 115–23, 131–2, 143–4, 146, 162–3, 212–17, 219, 221; *see also* non-reflective beliefs; reflective beliefs
    afterlife 5, 7, 58, 134
    definition of 75

false; *see* theory of mind (ToM)
  formation of 18, 27, 44, 76, 151, 180, 193–4
  justification of 33, 174–6, 178, 180, 184, 190, 192–6, 198, 201
  religious 1, 4, 6–10, 19, 28, 30–33, 69, 89, 91, 98, 114, 116, 131, 133, 156–7, 160, 162, 167–70, 174–6, 178–84, 189–92, 196, 199–200, 205, 209, 211, 221–2; *see also* cognitive science of religion (CSR); religion
  in supernatural 4–5, 7–9, 22, 37–8, 40, 44, 70, 81, 85, 109–10, 113–14, 117–18, 120–21, 123, 131, 134, 149–50, 152–60, 162–3, 167, 170–73, 176–9, 181–4, 190–97, 202, 204, 218; *see also* God; gods
  theistic 2, 113, 116–18, 122, 133, 154, 183, 191, 195–7, 201, 205; *see also* theism
  truth of 116, 120–21, 161, 181–2, 184
Bering, Jesse 4, 7–8, 113, 137–8, 170, 179, 190, 194
blank slate 5, 9, 154, 160, 218
Bloom, Paul 7, 37, 39–40, 42–5, 48–50, 113, 131, 133, 168, 194–5, 217
Boyer, Pascal 2–3, 5, 7, 17–19, 21, 27–9, 37, 40–48, 50, 52, 55–62, 113, 131, 135, 155, 168, 170, 190
Brahman 134
brain 26, 59, 61–2, 66, 70, 95, 97, 113, 118–19, 149, 155, 157–8, 164, 167, 172, 178, 201; *see also* nature-nurture; mind-body problem
brain-mind distinction 59, 61–2, 95, 97; *see also* mind-body problem
Brazil 2
Buddhism 135–6

Calvin, John 9, 155, 182–3
Carnap, Rudolf 91, 103, 105–8
causal relevance 31, 64
children 153, 176–7, 181; *see also* infants
  folk knowledge and 42, 47–8, 52

  intuitive dualism in 37, 39–40, 42, 44, 49–50
  language acquisition 216
  natural cognitive abilities of 3, 11, 18
  naturalness of belief in gods in 133, 215–16
  perception of agents in 27, 42
  religious ideas in, acquisition of 7, 10, 210, 216
  teleological reasoning in 83
  theory of mind (ToM) in 47–8, 133, 215–16
chimpanzees 39
Christianity 79, 81, 170–74, 182–3, 191, 200, 210, 216, 218
Churchland, Patricia 92–3
Cicero 81
cognition 39, 42, 59, 93, 98–103, 105–6, 133; *see also* cognitive science; cognitive science of religion (CSR)
  and religion 33–4, 40, 51, 72, 131, 168, 170–72, 183, 218, 220
cognitive load 135
cognitive mechanisms 19, 22, 26, 37–8, 58–9, 65, 70, 116, 169, 178–83, 190
cognitive ontology 99–110
cognitive processes 10, 56, 72, 94, 98–9, 103, 109–10, 117, 131, 136, 168, 178
cognitive psychology 3, 43, 61
cognitive science 59, 61, 116, 118, 160, 167, 177, 182–4, 210; *see also* cognition; cognitive science of religion
  and theology 127, 129, 133, 172
cognitive science of religion (CSR) 4–6, 11, 18, 21–8, 30–31, 33–4, 55–9, 61–3, 71–2, 75–6, 86, 88–9, 91, 94, 103, 106, 109, 114, 131–3, 135–6, 145, 160, 162, 185, 209, 215, 218, 221–2; *see also* cognitive science
  and anthropology 2, 60
  as an application of cognitive science to religion 2–5, 9, 17, 169–70, 178

and counterintuitiveness 19
and evolutionary studies of religion (ESR) 4, 8
and god concepts 7, 24, 37, 149–50, 152, 191, 199, 216–17, 219
and natural theology 10
and reformed epistemology 155–7, 162
on *sensus divinitatis* 19, 155, 162, 183–4
theology, as a contribution to 12, 134, 154, 164, 218
and truth of religious beliefs 1, 9, 113–14, 116–23, 128, 155, 167, 169, 173, 190, 192, 194–202, 204–5
cognitive stimuli 29
cognitive structure 5, 8, 12, 40, 42, 52–3, 70, 95–7, 103, 154–5, 162, 180, 217, 219
Cohen, Emma 2, 7, 72, 134
color perception 51, 94
communication 58, 214; *see also* linguistics
computation 98, 107
concepts 11, 17, 20–22, 37–49, 53, 58, 66, 71, 94, 99, 103–4, 107, 114–16, 131–3, 140, 172–3, 213, 216; *see also* cognition; cognitive science; gods
religious 1, 7, 55, 57, 134–6, 182, 222
consciousness 81, 130
contact principle 18, 39
cooperation 23–4, 190
coordination, social 17, 23–5, 34
core knowledge 39, 50–52
counterintuitiveness 10, 19, 21, 44–5, 49, 52–3
minimal 20, 37, 40–43, 48, 114, 135, 153
as a property of gods 46, 48
and religious teaching 19
and theological correctness 2
cosmological arguments 197, 201, 204
creationism 133, 175; *see also* teleological arguments
criterion of knowledge 30–31
culture 2–7, 11–12, 22–3, 25, 29, 37, 40–41, 46, 55–62, 70, 72, 81, 83, 87–8, 95, 97–8, 108, 128, 130–38, 145–6, 150, 173–4, 210–19, 221;

see also anthropology; environment; nature-nurture
and religion 3, 56, 59, 61, 65, 132–3, 135–6, 213

Darwin, Charles 78–9, 85
Darwinism 62, 81, 87–8, 170
Dawkins, Richard 28–9, 113
defeaters of religious belief 9, 157, 160–61
defection 23–4
demons 47, 171
Dennett, Daniel 103–6, 113, 132, 155–7, 164
developmental psychology 3, 37–9, 50, 52–3, 72, 169
dissonance, cognitive 24, 40, 43–5, 49
divine; *see* God; gods; religion
doctrines 9, 87, 109, 200, 216, 218–19
dualism 37, 39–40, 42–3, 47, 49–50, 52, 62, 66, 72, 92, 97, 133, 138, 168, 217
dual systems theory 44; *see also* two systems approach

emotion 21, 23, 44, 97, 168, 177
Enlightenment 213
environment 2, 4–6, 9, 11, 56, 60–61, 64–5, 76, 94, 96, 104, 115, 121, 132, 135, 152, 168–9, 173–4, 177, 179, 190, 195, 209, 212, 215–16, 218, 220–21; *see also* culture; nature-nurture
epistemology 6, 25, 28–34, 53, 81, 92, 108–10, 114, 117, 120, 122–3, 144, 175, 178, 181, 184; *see also* reformed epistemology
Evans, Margaret 7, 133
evolution by natural selection 4, 78–9, 81, 85, 87, 94, 171, 175, 179, 181
evolutionary psychology 2–4, 38, 62, 91, 96–7, 103, 114–16, 170–71, 174–5, 190
evolutionary studies of religion (ESR) 1–4, 8, 185
experiences, religious 1, 6, 58, 70, 113, 131, 144, 167, 191, 195–7, 200–205; *see also* ritual

explanation 4, 52, 92–3, 100, 114, 141, 150, 194, 212, 217
  religious 12, 33, 164, 172
  in science 2, 77–81, 83–5, 101, 133, 164, 172
  scientific, of religion 3, 7, 9–11, 21–2, 24, 27–8, 31–2, 39–41, 49, 56–72, 115, 139, 169, 173–5, 177–81, 190, 195, 201, 203–4, 209–11
explicit beliefs 5–6, 134; *see also* reflective beliefs
eye-gaze 97

faith and reason 219–21
false belief 52, 119–21, 123, 216; *see also* theory of mind (ToM)
false positives 22, 38, 115, 120, 121, 132, 179–80
fitness 4, 94, 101, 103, 106–9, 138
  inclusive 179
folk biology 5, 47, 50–52
folk mechanics; *see* naïve physics
folk psychology; *see* theory of mind (ToM)
folk theories 48, 52
free will 143
Freud, Sigmund 161, 164

ghosts 7–8, 20, 37–9, 45–7, 131, 135, 153, 168, 171, 190
ghouls 71
God; *see also* gods
  belief in, arguments against, 113–14, 117–23, 190–99, 201, 205
  belief in, as evolutionary by-product 113
  cosmological arguments for the existence of 204
  as counterintuitive 19–20, 41, 46, 153
  creator 1, 31, 181, 183
  and divine action 133
  fitness advantages of belief in 153–4
  inferential potential of 31–2
  naturalness of belief in 9–10, 37, 69–70, 128, 131, 149–50, 155–7, 162–4, 171–3, 176–9, 182–3, 189–90, 197–9, 202–4
  as person 127–8
  teleological arguments for the existence of 77
  teleological reasoning and belief in 177
  and theological correctness 174, 215–16
  and ultimism 129, 144; *see also* ultimism
gods; *see also* God
  belief in, as evolutionary by-product 4
  cognitive explanation of 5, 7–8, 58, 106, 170
  creator 7
  cross-cultural recurrence of concepts of 5, 7
  and divine actions 152
  fitness advantages of belief in 108–9, 153–4
  inferential potential of 21–4
  interaction with the world and people 80, 82
  as literary formality 84–5
  naturalness of belief in 37, 88, 113, 149–50, 167–8, 172–3, 176–9, 182, 190, 199, 202, 218
  as persons 91, 110; *see also* intuitive ontologies
  revelations of 84
  teleological reasoning and belief in 177
  and ultimism 129; *see also* ultimism
group selection 153, 179; *see also* selection
Guthrie, Stewart 3, 7, 37–40, 76–8, 81–5, 89, 131–2, 168, 170, 179

habituation 95
hard-to-fake commitments 19
hard-wired 86–7, 156, 172, 216; *see also* nature-nurture
heuristic 98
Hinduism 172
Holy Spirit 162, 183–4
hypersensitive agency detection device (HADD) 8, 22, 27–8, 38, 75–6, 78, 82, 85–9, 115, 120–23, 132, 150–51, 168, 179

infants; *see* children
inferential potential 21–2, 48
information; *see* cognition; cognitive processes; cognitive science
innate 27, 131, 181, 209; *see also* nature-nurture
instinct 75, 88, 210
intentionality 5, 8, 21, 30, 44, 62, 67, 89, 91–2, 100–107, 109–10, 115, 127, 132, 138, 141, 144, 168, 175, 180
intuitive beliefs; *see* non-reflective beliefs
intuitive dualism 37, 39–40, 43, 49, 72, 133, 138, 168
  in afterlife beliefs 134, 138
  in spirit possession 134
intuitive knowledge 43; *see also* non-reflective beliefs
intuitive ontologies 48–9, 52; *see also* ontological categories
irrationality in religion 116, 169
Islam 170–71, 200

Jesus Christ 20, 200
Johnson, Dominic 3, 23, 170, 179
Judaism 170–71, 200
judgments 5, 11, 26, 44, 117, 133, 143, 157–8, 161, 191–6, 198, 201, 204, 221

Kahneman, Daniel 5–6, 43–4, 98
Kant, Immanuel 53, 99, 141, 145
Kelemen, Deborah 7–8, 83, 131, 133, 168–70, 177, 217
Krishna 134
Kuhn, Thomas 213

language 4–5, 11, 27, 37, 43, 45, 51–2, 79, 92–3, 105–8, 184, 213–14, 216
learning 43, 52, 95, 124, 159, 196, 216
Lewis, C.S. 197, 201
linguistics 91, 105–8, 131, 216; *see also* language
Lucretius 79–85, 88

mathematics 29

maturational naturalness 11
McCauley, Robert
  on explanatory pluralism 57, 70–71
  on maturational naturalness 11
  on religious ritual 7
  on science and religion 3, 10, 12
memes 137
memory 3, 26–7, 41, 44, 161, 200
mental tools 5–6, 20–21, 26, 33, 113, 115, 120, 132, 134, 136, 168–71, 173, 175, 177, 179–83, 218
methodological naturalism 34
mind 28–9, 44, 61, 71, 77, 80, 95, 104, 130, 136, 167, 171–4, 176–9; *see also* blank slate; brain; cognitive science; mind-body problem
  modules of the 91, 95–9, 103, 105–6, 109
  natural cognition in the 3–6, 9, 11, 20, 27, 39, 48, 51, 55, 75, 89, 113, 128, 131, 149–50, 153–4, 169, 202, 212, 216–8
  philosophy of 17
mind as computer; *see* computation
mind-body dualism; *see* intuitive dualism
mind-body problem 2, 7, 11, 32, 40, 47, 50, 59, 62, 217
minimal counterintuitiveness; *see* counterintuitiveness; minimally counterintuitive concepts (MCI)
minimally counterintuitive concept (MCI) 20, 114–15, 120, 135–6; *see also* counterintuitiveness
miracles 136, 200
modularity 38, 51, 91, 95, 97–110, 132, 197
monotheism 9, 113–14, 154, 172–3, 182, 218; *see also* atheism; polytheism; theism
moral intuitions 2
morality 5, 18, 22
  development of 1
  and religion 7, 23, 25, 34, 131, 142–3, 183–4
  supernatural punishment and 8, 153

mystical experiences 113, 167

naïve physics 20, 47, 51–2, 99, 104, 107–8
natural cognition; *see* cognition; cognitive science; cognitive science of religion
naturalism 32, 62–3, 78, 100, 202
    broad 65–7
    evolutionary argument against 196
    explanations of religion and 4, 10, 31, 56, 60, 62, 177, 190, 193, 195, 203–4
    and metaphysics 57
    methodological 34
    ontological 61
    philosophical 61
    vs. theism 127, 129, 131, 137, 143, 145–6
natural religion 145, 169–70, 209; *see also* religion
    vs. atheism 10, 149–50, 218
    and cultural scaffolding 11
    and language 11
natural selection; *see* evolution by natural selection; selection
natural theology; *see* theology
nature-nurture 150, 154
nervous system 104
non-reflective beliefs; *see also* reflective beliefs
    and counterintuitiveness 20
    and intuitions 75–6
    and reflective beliefs 6, 75
nontheism; *see* atheism
Norenzayan, Ara 5, 8, 19–21, 133, 135, 168, 170
norms 116–17, 128, 136, 138, 140, 142–3, 145
    moral 34
    social 23

omnipotence 21
ontological categories; *see also* non-reflective beliefs
    Animal 40–42, 46–8, 52
    and counterintuitiveness 19

    Living Things 47
    Mind 47–8
    Person 40–41, 47
    Plant 40–41, 47
    Objects 40–42, 46–8
Oxford University 37, 72, 216

perception 21, 26, 29–31, 44, 51, 81, 94–5, 99, 102, 161, 202, 204
philosophy
    and belief 26
    and dualism 37, 92, 97
    history of 52–3, 75–9, 82–4, 86–7, 89
    and intuition 18, 25, 37, 43
    materialist 47
    of mind 17
    and psychology 103
    of religion 17, 128, 146, 172, 205, 219
    of science 29, 213
physicalism 28, 59–61, 66, 92, 138
Plantinga, Alvin 122, 127, 143, 149, 155, 162, 175, 179–84, 194, 196
Plato 77, 80, 140
polytheism 9, 154, 162, 172, 182
practices, religious; *see* experiences, religious; ritual
prayer 7, 203
predestination 162–3
promiscuous teleology 83, 85, 133, 169, 217; *see also* teleology
psychology 26, 47–8, 58–9, 62, 71, 81, 197, 215; *see also* cognitive psychology; cognitive science; developmental psychology; evolutionary psychology
    orthodox 95–7
    and philosophy 37, 43
punishment
    cooperation and 24
    supernatural 24, 137
Pyysiäinen, Ilkka 57, 135–6

quantum
    mechanics 32, 51, 104
    particle 99

physics 110
question begging 117
Quine, Willard van Orman 91, 103, 105–6, 108–10

realism 92, 105, 109–10
reasoning 5, 10, 43–4, 51, 88, 95, 98, 116–17, 133, 139, 181, 199, 212, 216, 218
reflective beliefs; *see also* non-reflective beliefs
   and agency detection 87–8
   and non-reflective beliefs 6, 20, 27, 75–6
reformed epistemology 155–7, 162, 182; *see also* epistemology
Reid, Thomas 6
religion; *see also* atheism; beliefs; cognitive science of religion (CSR); experiences, religious; God; gods; mystical experiences; natural religion; non-reflective beliefs; prayer; reflective beliefs; revelation; ritual; teaching, religious; theism; theology
   challenges for 143
   and culture 61, 65, 132
   definition of 6–7, 19
   hermeneutical approaches to 59
   in human society 23, 25
   naturalism and explanations of 4, 10, 31, 56, 60, 62, 177, 190, 193, 195, 203–4
   in public life 10
   traditional 127, 136–7, 146
Religion Explained 17, 55–6
representations 23, 26, 40, 45, 48–51, 56, 57–8, 60–61, 65, 91, 93, 97–104, 107, 110, 134
   agency 39, 91, 101, 131
   counterintuitive 10, 135
reproduction 40, 81, 96, 151, 181
revelation 9, 84, 162, 218
reward, supernatural 24, 154
Richert, Rebekah 215

ritual; *see also* experiences, religious
   religious 4, 7, 19, 24–5, 27, 58, 131, 212, 215

sacrifice 19, 24, 80, 221
St. Paul 79, 200
St. Thomas Aquinas 77–8, 182
science
   behavioural 71
   death of 215
   history of 33
   ideal 62
   image of 104
   modern 56, 113
   natural 60, 62–3, 70
   physical 60, 64–6, 71, 219–20
   practice of 214
   reliability of 196
   social 66, 68, 70
   and the study of religion 4
   and theology 11, 113, 174
   as a tool 108
   Western 215
scripturalism 7
selection 4, 58, 196
   artificial 85
   group 153, 179
   natural 78–9, 81, 85, 87, 94, 171, 179, 181
   pressures 169, 179
self-propelled 21
Sellars, Wilfrid 103, 105, 110
sensus divinitatis 9, 155, 183–4
simulation 133
snakes, fear of 12
society 9, 23, 25, 34, 56, 62, 66, 81, 85, 154, 209, 211–12, 214, 220–22; *see also* culture
Sosis, Richard 3, 24, 170, 179, 190, 192
soul 2, 39, 44, 46, 80, 138, 143–4, 162; *see also* spirit
   and body 7, 37, 40–42, 49, 168
Sperber, Dan 3, 6, 62–3
spirit 7, 53, 219; *see also* soul; vitalism
spirit possession 2, 134

spirits 21, 37, 46–7, 91, 106, 109–10, 153, 168, 171, 190
spiritualists 2
supernatural; *see also* counterintuitiveness
    agents or beings 19, 21–3, 30, 37–8, 40–41, 47, 82, 113–14, 118, 131, 133–4, 136, 150, 152–4, 162, 171–3, 183, 190, 202, 221
    beliefs 31–2, 40, 163–4, 219
    concepts 39–40, 43–4, 46–8
    as counterintuitive 20
    instruments 22
    punishment 24, 137
    reality 176
    views 44
superstition 33, 169
survival 3, 27–8, 33–4, 78, 96, 115, 151, 168, 173, 181, 190, 218
Swinburne, Richard 92–3, 97, 100–101

tabula rasa; *see* blank slate
tacit knowledge; *see* intuitive knowledge
teaching, religious 2, 216
teleofunctional reasoning 7
teleological arguments; *see* creationism
teleological beliefs 76, 78–82, 110, 177
teleology 78, 133; *see also* promiscuous teleology
    intuitive 72
testimony 27, 29, 114, 120–23, 196, 200
theism 91, 113, 117, 127–30, 136–7, 140–41, 143–6, 149–50, 153–4, 156, 164, 184, 193–4; *see also* atheism; monotheism; polytheism
theologians 4, 9, 12, 129, 134, 183, 185, 218
theological correctness 2, 12
    vs. theological incorrectness 2, 133–4
theology
    Aristotle and 77

    cognitive science and 172, 183
    defeater argument for 184
    evolutionary psychology and 174
    and human flourishing 221
    Lucretius and 81
    vs. natural religion 12
    negative 128
    and reflective beliefs 218
    and religious diversity 173, 182
    science and 11
theory of mind (ToM) 168
    and autism 133
    children and 215
    and Core Agency 48
    existential 137–8
    and folk psychology 5, 20, 47, 51–2, 72, 104, 107
    and gods 120, 133
    in humans 151, 133
    intuitive ontology, as part of
    as mental tool 115, 132–3
    as module 97
thinking; *see* cognition; cognitive science; computation; memory; reasoning
Trinity 29
two systems approach 5–6, 98, 103; *see also* dual systems theory

ultimism 128–30, 136–46

van Fraassen, Bas 67
Virgil 79, 83
Vishnu 134
vitalism 52

Whitehouse, Harvey 3, 7
Wilson, David Sloan 94, 96, 109, 113, 170, 179, 190

Zombie 46

CPSIA information can be obtained
at www.ICGtesting.com
Printed in the USA
BVHW041318050320
574123BV00010B/141